Liberty, Equality, and Plurality

An AMINTAPHIL *Volume*

Liberty, Equality, and Plurality

Edited by
Larry May, Christine Sistare, and Jonathan Schonsheck

University Press of Kansas

Published by the University Press of Kansas (Lawrence, Kansas 66049), which was organized by the Kansas Board of Regents and is operated and funded by Emporia State University, Fort Hays State University, Kansas State University, Pittsburg State University, the University of Kansas, and Wichita State University.

Library of Congress Cataloging-in-Publication Data

Liberty, equality, and plurality / edited by Larry May, Christine
Sistare, and Jonathan Schonsheck.
p. cm.
Includes bibliographical references and index.
ISBN 0-7006-0847-8 (alk. paper)
1. Liberty. 2. Equality. 3. Pluralism (Social sciences)
I. May, Larry. II. Sistare, C. T. (Christine T.), 1951–
III. Schonsheck, Jonathan.
JC585.L426 1997
323.44—dc21 97-3124

British Library Cataloguing in Publication Data is available.

Printed in the United States of America

10 9 8 7 6 5 4 3 2 1

The paper used in this publication meets the minimum requirements of the American National Standard for Permanence of Paper for Printed Library Materials Z39.48-1984.

CONTENTS

INTRODUCTION

The appellate courts of the United States have recently heard arguments debating the legitimacy of hate speech codes on college campuses. On one side, defenders of codes argue that the codes are needed to maintain equality, which can easily be disrupted by racist and sexist epithets hurled at minority members of college communities. On the other side, opponents of the codes argue that it is an affront to freedom of speech for universities to stifle speakers because of the content of what they say. As the chapters in this volume indicate, this is just the most recent incarnation of conflict, or seeming conflict, between appeals to liberty and appeals to equality.

What, precisely, is the relationship between liberty and equality? This issue—or more accurately, the wide array of issues raised by this seemingly simple question—has proved to be among the most fecund and the most recalcitrant issues in social and legal philosophy.

Consider the clarion call of the French Revolution: "Liberté! Égalité! Fraternité!" Set aside the complications of fraternity. Can we pursue, simultaneously, liberty and equality? At the level of political sloganeering, of a call to arms, we suppose so. But when it comes time to create public policy or enact laws, matters are much more murky. Both "liberty" and "equality" are extraordinarily complex and variegated "concepts" (to use the broadest possible term); different thinkers mean *quite* different things by each. Once each is specified, we find a panoply of possible relationships. Some sorts of liberty and some sorts of equality seem perfectly compatible; in fact, it is common to talk of equality of liberty. Indeed, some sorts of liberty presuppose some specifications of equality—and conversely. But other specifications of liberty do seem incompatible with equality; for example, it seems that in the case of hate speech codes, we must choose equality or liberty.

In a pluralistic society, much of our time is taken up with public debates about how to resolve potential conflicts between liberty and equality. When there is no common agreement about a short list of goods in terms of which disputes are to be settled, the debates become even more intense. Democratic institutions allow for structured debate, which ultimately is time-bound—at the end a vote is taken and the majority decides how much liberty or equality, and which types of each, should be reflected in public policies and laws. Consensus on the truth of the matter is abandoned in favor of compromises that garner the most votes. And the compromises shift, often from one election to another.

There is a tendency to think of modern "democracy" as a single tradition—originating in John Locke's *Second Treatise of Government*, relied upon heavily by Thomas Jefferson in writing the Declaration of Independence, further developed in the Federalist Papers, and gaining eloquence in John Stuart Mill's *On Liberty*. But there is a second tradition, fully entitled to call itself "democratic," with quite different roots and a quite different development: the one that originated with Jean-Jacques Rousseau. While Lockean democracy was developing in England and the United States, Rousseauean democracy was evolving on the Continent. And although these two great traditions have much in common, they can be distinguished as having differing sources and impulses.

The essence of Lockean democracy is an impulse toward liberty; there is a strong propensity, when a conflict arises between liberty and other ideals, to choose liberty. This preference for liberty or freedom is often embodied in the language of rights. It is central in Locke's famous argument about property acquisition, beginning with one's right to one's labor: "Every man has a property in his own person; this nobody has a right to but himself."[1] Additionally, people have a right to barter goods that they have rightly acquired; the institution of money is based on consent; and "it is plain that men have agreed to a disproportionate and unequal possession of the earth."[2]

The essence of Rousseauean democracy is an impulse toward equality; there is a strong propensity when a conflict arises between equality and other ideals to choose equality. Rousseau contends that civil society has as its chief goal to create a "moral and collective body" that will guarantee equality by making sure that "no one has an interest in making it burdensome for the others."[3] In regard to property, we find Rousseau arguing that "laws are always useful to those who have possessions and harmful to those who have nothing. Whence it follows that the social state is advantageous to men only insofar as they all have something and none of them has too much."[4]

George Sabine, historian of social, political, and legal thought, comments on these separate democratic traditions:

> That the program of democracy might harbor incompatible purposes is of course no new idea. From its very beginning the theory of democracy linked together the two ideals of liberty and equality, and quite early it became apparent that these two would not unite as easily as the democrats of Thomas Jefferson's generation had hoped. . . . Thus in the accusations of its enemies, both conservative and radical, the democratic argument seemed caught in a dilemma: the more liberty the less equality, and the more equality the less liberty.[5]

The conflict between liberty and equality is embodied in the modern conceptions of democracy. Rousseauean democracy has evolved into communism and communitarianism; Lockean democracy has evolved into liberalism and libertarianism.

But even here things are not as simple as they appear, for within both liberalism and communitarianism conflicts remain about liberty and equality. Within the Lockean tradition, we find a battle with some theorists supporting unimpeachable liberties. Robert Nozick, for one, proclaims: "Individuals have rights, and there are things no person or group may do to them (without violating their rights)."[6] Others within the Lockean tradition try to carve out an important place for equality, or at least equal liberty, as when John Rawls supports a "tendency to equality."[7] Within the Rousseauean tradition, one finds communitarians who put great weight on certain individual liberties, as does Michael Sandel when he remarks, "If I cannot be the owner at least I can be the guardian of" possessions.[8] But others within the Rousseauean tradition remain steadfast in arguing for the primacy of equality, as in the communistic writings of Kai Nielsen, where a "right to an equal share" is the fundamental principle.[9]

There is significant diversity in conceptions of liberty and significant diversity in conceptions of equality. Some conceptions of liberty are compatible with some conceptions of equality; some conceptions of liberty are incompatible with some conceptions of equality. Indeed, the chapters in this volume are a testament to the diversity of perspectives on the relationships between liberty and equality. But the question arises: Why have philosophers ventured into this quagmire? The facile answer is that this is the sort of thing philosophers do. The serious answer is this: liberty and equality will be essential elements of a fully defensible conception of *justice*. And developing a fully defensible conception of justice, designing the perfectly just society (a society as just as the human condition permits) has clearly been the central aim of social and legal philosophy since Plato's *Republic*.

It is safe to say that those of us in the Western tradition have a prereflective impulse in favor of "equality." But this impulse wants specification. Minimally, we consider all persons equal before the moral law, and we consider all citizens equal before the civil law. At this point there is a schism in the Western tradition. Some subscribe to the principle of equality of material wealth, or at least minimization of economic inequality. According to this view, justice requires establishing institutions that reduce the disparity in material holdings—and thus reduce the disparities in power and opportunity that are created by disparities in wealth. Some others subscribe to equality before the moral and civil law but reject the redistribution of wealth, power, and opportunity. Indeed, they view redistribution as "takings," which are themselves serious violations of justice.

It also is safe to say that those of us in the Western, liberal tradition have a prereflective impulse in favor of liberty. But this impulse also wants specification: What is, and what is not, included in this liberty? Once this rather large question is answered, there are questions about the best laws and institutions to secure and preserve this liberty, as well as about the limits of the law. In addition, there are specific questions about what should be done in a deeply pluralistic society with little agreement about the common good. These three issues—of conceptualization; of institutional and legal structure; and of practical application to multicultural cases—organize the three parts of this volume.

The chapters in Part I represent a significant portion of the broad spectrum of theoretical views that philosophers have taken on the compatibility or incompatibility of liberty and equality. We have included the works of various liberals (James Sterba, David Phillips, Alistair Macleod, Steven Lee), as well as of a libertarian (Jan Narveson) and of a communitarian (Patricia Werhane). The libertarian view that liberty and equality are incompatible and that we must choose liberty over equality is our point of departure. Liberal responses to this position all assert that there is either a narrow or wide overlap between liberty and equality, and indeed that liberty without some forms of equality makes no practical sense. The communitarian response points out that the self is ultimately "community-based," and that arguments for liberty that presuppose an abstract disembodied self are misguided.

Part II takes up the goals of the law in both limiting and preserving liberty. Its chapters deal with civil laws that promote equality through apparent intrusions on economic liberty (Kenneth Henley) and with civil laws that restrict freedom of speech to protect privacy (Wade Robison). In addition, the use of the law to circumscribe individual medical choices (Natalie Dandekar, Robert Moffat) and the use of the law to deal with those whose exercise of liberty causes harm (Deirdre Golash) are examined. In all these cases, the central question is what role the law should play in limiting the liberty of some so as to secure greater equality for all. Each author confronts the use of the law to balance liberties and opportunities.

Part III considers cases that arise out of the clash of cultures in a deeply pluralistic society. It begins with a look at the concept of tolerance in multicultural settings (Emily Gill). Two chapters reflect on whether hate speech should be legally sanctioned or sanctioned in some other way (Diana Meyers, Joan McGregor); and two whether Christian Scientists should be legally required to allow medical scientists to care for their sick children (Richard De George, Kenneth Kipnis). It closes with a comparative look at economic equality in Japan and the United States (Richard Parker). In multicultural settings, securing equality is fraught with perils undreamt of in more homogenous societies.

All of these chapters came about as a result of a call for papers for the 1994 meeting of AMINTAPHIL, the American section of the International Society for Law and Social Philosophy. After extensive discussions at a meeting at the College of Charleston, where these papers and others were examined at great length, a volume was constructed by the Publications Committee of AMINTAPHIL. Although AMINTAPHIL has published six previous volumes (most recently *Kindred Matters*, Cornell University Press, 1993), this volume represents our first publication venture with the University Press of Kansas. We are grateful for the help that Rex Martin and Fred Woodward have provided in making this venture a successful one. Nancy Scott and Rebecca Knight Giusti took great care in producing this volume, and Angela Bolte did a fine job constructing the index. We are also grateful for help received from many members of AMINTAPHIL whose papers do not appear as chapters in this volume. Here, as in all good interdisciplinary scholarly organizations, equality of respect breeds productive collaboration, which, in turn, inspires the best efforts by individuals exercising their freedom of speech.

Notes

1. John Locke, *The Second Treatise of Government* (1690; reprint, Indianapolis: Bobbs-Merrill, 1952), 17.

2. Ibid., 29.

3. Jean-Jacques Rousseau, *On the Social Contract* (1762), trans. and ed. Donald Cress (Indianapolis: Hackett, 1987), 24.

4. Ibid., 29.

5. George H. Sabine, "The Two Democratic Traditions," *Philosophical Review* 61 (October 1950): 451–52.

6. Robert Nozick, *Anarchy, State, and Utopia* (New York: Basic Books, 1974), ix.

7. John Rawls, *A Theory of Justice* (Cambridge: Harvard University Press, 1970), 100–108.

8. Michael Sandel, *Liberalism and the Limits of Justice* (Cambridge: Cambridge University Press, 1982), 144. Also see Larry May's discussion of the role of rights in communitarian theory in *Sharing Responsibility* (Chicago: University of Chicago Press, 1992), chap. 9, sec. 4.

9. Kai Nielsen, *Equality and Liberty: A Defense of Radical Egalitarianism* (Totowa, N.J.: Rowman & Allanheld, 1985), 55.

Part I

The (In)Compatibility of Liberty and Equality

More than a few issues separate egalitarians from liberals from libertarians, but they center on disagreements about liberty and equality: whether liberty and equality conflict (and if so, which ought to take precedence); whether one can be derived from the other (and if so, which from which); whether some citizens may morally be coerced in order to enhance the standing of other citizens (and if so, is it liberty or equality that must be sacrificed, and which is it that is thereby enhanced). The chapters in this section are the most general and most abstract of the volume; they take up these rarified issues. All are addressed to the question: Were we to survey the moral topography of the just society, what would we record about liberty and equality?

We begin with Jan Narveson's forceful articulation of a libertarian, "incompatibilist" conception of liberty, a version of so-called negative liberty: "A principle calling for liberty in some domain enjoins us all to refrain from interfering with those who wish to act in the domain in question: within the area over which he is to have liberty nobody may intervene to prevent him from doing whatever he chooses to do." The person with liberty has a negative right; this right imposes a negative duty on others not to interfere with that person's doing those things. Among the things we have the liberty to do is to acquire property and to keep it.

If the citizens of some society were to subscribe to this conception of liberty, then each would consider it a demand of justice that each not interfere with (specified) actions of the others. Nothing *more* than this noninterference is required of anyone, however. Thus, one can satisfy one's obligations to others by remaining quiescent or even by being unconscious.

According to Narveson, liberty so conceived is inconsistent with *every* principle of equality. This is so because any institution that redistributes material wealth necessarily interferes—*forcibly* interferes—in the domains of those from whom wealth is taken. Of course, the wealthy are perfectly free to *give* money to the poor; at issue is whether such a transfer is a demand of justice (Narveson believes that it is not), making it permissible for the state to use force to ensure it (Narveson believes that it is not).

If we believe that justice demands redistribution, then the state will exercise force in taking resources from the rich and distributing them to the poor. Narveson asks: What can be said to the wealthy by way of justifying this state activity? For Narveson, the question is rhetorical; he believes that there is no satisfactory answer. At the end of this introduction, Narveson's question will be posed literally: What do the other philosophers believe *should* be said to the wealthy, to those from whom material resources are taken?

Now it is clear how some people would be attracted to the conception of liberty championed by Narveson: those whose starting position and abilities (natural and developed) constitute marketable skills in their respective economies. It is equally clear that those lacking the natural and social contingencies that would enable them to advance their interests in the marketplace will be reluctant to subscribe to this conception of liberty—especially if it has the consequences for redistribution that Narveson claims that it has.

But *does* it have those consequences? James P. Sterba argues that it does *not;* indeed, he argues that the "dispute" between liberty and equality "can be resolved, for all practical purposes, by proceeding from premises that libertarians endorse to a conclusion that socialists endorse." Sterba begins by adopting a libertarian conception of liberty as negative liberty, a conception not unlike Narveson's. He then sketches the typical conflict between the rich and the poor and claims that "the liberty of the poor is at stake in such conflict situations. What is at stake is the liberty of the poor not to be interfered with in taking from the surplus possessions of the rich what is necessary to satisfy their basic needs." According to Sterba, then, the "real" dispute is not between liberty and equality but between the negative liberty of the rich and the negative liberty of the poor. Whose liberty ought to prevail? Sterba invokes, in a novel way, a fundamental moral principle: "ought" implies "can." Strictly speaking, the poor "can" relinquish their right not to be interfered with in taking from the surplus possessions of the rich: the poor can starve. But, says Sterba, it would be unreasonable for the rich to ask them to do this or to require them to do it. On the contrary, it is *not* unreasonable to ask the rich to not interfere with the poor's taking from the surplus possessions of the rich, nor to compel them to not interfere with that taking. The rights of the poor ought to prevail. But then we must ask, how is this right to be respected? By what mechanism will the rich satisfy their moral obligation to not interfere with the poor's taking from their surplus possessions? Sterba argues that the most efficient way for the rich to safely satisfy their moral obligation to not interfere is to take action: to establish institutions that, in an orderly fashion, take from the rich and redistribute to the poor. Although the rich libertarians continue to deny that there is a positive welfare right, they will find it in their interests to establish institutions that function *as if* there were positive welfare rights.

How much should be taken from the surplus possessions of the rich, so that they can be assured of the moral rectitude of their keeping the rest—that is, that retaining their remaining possessions does *not* in fact violate the rights of the poor to not be interfered with while taking from the rich? As the chapter concludes, Sterba endorses this right for people distant in geography (citizens of other nations) and time (people of future generations). Carried to this extreme, so much would be taken from the "rich" as to compel drastic changes in their standard of living. If Sterba is correct, respecting the negative liberty rights of the poor will require redistributions that result nearly in equality.

In the introduction to this volume we stated that there is a prerational impulse in favor of liberty, but that the impulse needs significant investigation and specification. In the chapters by David Phillips and Steven Lee, liberty receives precisely that.

Why is it that we value liberty? According to Phillips, it is because liberty is essential to designing and living out one's own, individual plan of life (Mill's language), that liberty is essential to the successful pursuit of one's own conception of the good (Rawls's language). To have liberty is to be free from interference; it is for others not to act in ways that inhibit or thwart the successful pursuit of one's conception of the good, one's plan of life. Thus, Phillips adopts a conception of liberty as negative liberty, a libertarian conception not unlike Narveson's.

However, although liberty is *necessary* to the carrying out of one's plan of life, it is by no means sufficient. In addition to freedom from interference, the successful pursuit of one's conception of the good requires material resources: "Liberty alone will not be sufficient to secure this good life for us; I may be entirely free from interference, but if I have insufficient food and no opportunity to obtain it, I am in no position to live the good life. . . . To make liberty valuable we need to make it effective. . . . My liberty is valuable only if it is effective. The same is true of everyone else." No one's liberty is valuable—at least, not *very* valuable—unless it is accompanied by sufficient material wealth to make it truly *effective* liberty. "Hence, one who values liberty must also favor [some measure of] egalitarian redistribution." Highlighting the contrapositive: our prereflective impulse in favor of liberty must presuppose effective liberty; were we to think of liberty as the absence of interference but also the absence of the resources needed to use that liberty, we would *not* in fact value liberty very much. Thus, "to maximize the value of liberty, we need to give as many people as possible effective liberty. And that is likely, under many kinds of social conditions, to require a fairly equal distribution of resources."

Essential to Phillips's argument for the compatibility of liberty and equality is this: in addition to wanting for myself sufficient resources to make my liberty effective, in addition to acknowledging the fact that others too need resources to make their liberty effective, I must subscribe to the position that effective liberty ought to be maximized. I must believe that from the moral point of view, the more people whose liberty is made effective, the better. Phillips argues for this by adopting (what he calls) "the impartial consequentialist perspective" and defending it against competing perspectives—including Narveson's contractarian strategy.

In his contribution to this volume, Steven Lee seeks to resolve the (apparent) conflict between liberty and equality by *deriving* equality from liberty. As we shall see, Lee's starting point is very different from Phillips's. Very quickly, however, their arguments converge—and then arrive at the same destination, a conclusion in support of redistribution.

Lee subscribes to "the familiar idea that people should have the maximum degree of freedom of action consistent with everyone else's having the same degree of freedom." The next step of his argument is the selection of a particular conception of liberty. As identified by Lee, there are two competing conceptions of liberty. One competitor is "formal liberty," "freedom from interference." Lee notes that this is often labeled "negative liberty," the conception to which Narveson subscribes and the starting point of both Sterba and Phillips. Lee, however, *rejects* this conception in favor of what he considers its more worthy competitor: "effective liberty." He chooses effective liberty instead of negative liberty because "the moral basis of liberty, the value of liberty, is the contribution it makes to human development, and that effective liberty is preferable to formal liberty because effective liberty better realizes this value. . . . The conception of liberty I endorse is effective liberty. Liberty is realized in society when everyone has equal freedom of action and that freedom involves effective choices." And in specifying the conception of equality he will derive from liberty, Lee writes that "material resources should be more equally distributed than they are currently. In particular, material starting points must be more equal, and some degree of ongoing redistribution will be necessary, for example, through progressive taxation for social programs or 'negative' income taxes."

Finally, in returning to the general topic of this volume, Lee states, "Effective liberty, unlike formal liberty, makes reference to how material resources are distributed, because without access to material resources, important choices will often not be effective. If the distribution effective liberty requires is at least roughly the same as the distribution our notion of equality requires, liberty will be shown to entail equality and the apparent conflict between liberty and equality will be resolved."

Thus, Phillips subscribes to negative liberty but believes redistribution must occur in order to make liberty effective, and thus truly valuable. Lee sees negative liberty and effective liberty as competing conceptions, and chooses effective liberty because only it is truly valuable.

A question raised by Narveson ought to be asked of both Phillips and Lee: How much redistribution does morality require? As we have seen, Phillips uses the expression "fairly equal." Lee argues that material resources should be "more equally distributed" than they are, and advocates "ongoing redistribution." But surely the successful pursuit of different plans of life will require different amounts of resources; some persons will need relatively more, and others will need relatively less. Even if we subscribe to Phillips's "impartial consequentialism," the maximizing of effective liberty could well be consistent with substantial disparities in wealth.

Any doubts that remain about our claim that there are diverse conceptions of liberty and equality will be dispelled by the contribution of Alistair M. Macleod. Many of the disputes typically cast as conflicts between liberty and equality, he argues, can be *re*cast as disputes *within* either the "liberty ideal" or the "equality ideal." What is more, the precise nature of these conflicts is oftentimes more clearly revealed when so constructed; as such, the conflict is more susceptible to philosophical progress. Consider this revealing example:

> The freedom to contribute to political campaigns is valued because it is one of the ways in which the members of a democratically organized society can exercise the

> right to participate in political decision-making processes. . . . If no contribution limits are imposed on what individuals may contribute, then, in a society in which individual members have (vastly) unequal economic resources, the political participation prerogatives of the wealthier members will be greater in practice than the prerogatives of the poorer members. A law limiting contributions can therefore be seen as a device for reducing inequality in the political freedom enjoyed by the members of a society. Disagreement about the defensibility of such a law is misrepresented when it is said to involve a conflict between freedom and equality. The dispute should be seen, rather, as involving a clash between those who are not unhappy about inequality in the distribution of political freedom and those who favor measures to diminish such inequality.

This is an important perspective on the issue of political campaign contributions. And in focusing on the *value* of liberty, Macleod's work resonates nicely with that of Phillips and Lee. Whether the "recasting" of other liberty/equality conflicts as conflicts *within* either liberty or equality actually clarifies them will have to be determined separately. To some extent, perspicuity is in the eye of the beholder.

All the chapters discussed thus far focus on the controversy between liberalism and libertarianism. As such, all presuppose—assume without comment, much less argument—a particular metaphysics of the "self." All presuppose an independent, very "individualistic" self, a self that is the bearer of rights (though of course *which* rights it bears is a matter in dispute), a self that is concerned with its own liberty (and maximizing it), a self that seeks equality with others, or fears that others will take from it to achieve equality. From this perspective, the work of Patricia H. Werhane is the most "radical"; she calls into question the concept of self that is the unexamined "given" of the Western political tradition. Writing in the spirit of the later Wittgenstein and drawing on the texts of Michael Walzer and Emmanuel Levinas, Werhane offers a metaphysics of the self in social context that, she believes, resolves the (apparent) conflict between liberty and equality. Of course, that resolution differs markedly from the preceding resolutions.

No one begins life as the disembodied, abstract "self" of liberal political theory. We all begin life imbedded in a particular context: a particular family (of some description), a particular culture, a particular economy, a particular historical era. This is the so-called thick self, a being enveloped by its context. Only later—in that social context—does the "thin self," the self of Western liberal theory, develop. "In the first instance, there is no self-as-such as a precritical, transcendental cogito, or totally ideal spectator. Self-reflection and self-criticism, what Walzer calls a 'thin self,' does develop, but only later out of the thick socialized self." Essential to this development is a phenomenon of interaction between selves, what Levinas calls "face to face"; "how liberty and equality are defined become realized only in this confrontation." Because freedom is *derived* from social relationships, it cannot be separated from responsibilities for other people. In consequence, positive freedom "entails responsibility for others." The apparent conflict between liberty and equality is thus resolved: "On this level of abstraction, freedom and equality are not incompatible since negative freedom comes out of the confrontation between equals, and my freedom entails, and is entailed by, yours." However, the resolution occurs not at the level of political theory but at the level of metaphysics. Whether a resolution at this level is sufficient for political theory is a matter for continuing discussion.

In concluding, let us return to Narveson's rhetorical question. It is uncontroversial that any state institution whose mission is to reduce inequalities will *take* from those with relatively more and *give* to those with relatively less. It is not implausible to consider this as a clash between liberty and equality; it is not inappropriate to insist that something be said, by way of justification, to those from whom material wealth is taken. Comparing and contrasting the responses of our six philosophers on this matter will constitute a succinct summary of this set of papers.

Jan Narveson does consider this a conflict between liberty and equality, a conflict in which liberty ought to prevail. All such takings violate the rights of the rich—the rights to acquire and to keep private property. Any such taking, which inevitably will be coercive, is morally offensive. James P. Sterba urges us to see this *not* as a conflict between liberty and equality but as a conflict between two different liberties. When we ask which liberty ought to be respected, the answer is clear: for reasons of rationality and morality, the "right" of the rich to surplus possessions must give way to the right of the poor not to be interfered with in taking from those surplus possessions to satisfy their basic needs. To become morally upright, the rich will establish institutions that function as if the poor had a positive right to welfare. Despite quite different starting points—David Phillips accepts the libertarian conception of liberty, and Steven Lee rejects it—these two philosophers are in agreement on this: to be truly valuable, to be a social ideal worthy of our veneration, liberty must be "effective." And liberty cannot be effective without some (yet to be specified) amount of material wealth. To be a champion of liberty is to be a champion of *effective* liberty; to champion effective liberty is to acknowledge the need for redistribution. Liberty and equality do not conflict; indeed, liberty *demands* equality. Alistair M. Macleod shows that various conflicts can be considered conflicts *within* either liberty or equality rather than *between* liberty and equality. Both the rich and the poor want to influence the political process; because influence requires resources, this clash is most perspicuously seen as a problem of more equal versus less equal political liberty. Finally, Patricia H. Werhane believes that this dispute itself "starts in the middle"; it presupposes a very abstract and individualistic theory of the self. Were we to step back from the debate and acknowledge the fact that everyone begins life deeply imbedded in a community—the disembodied self of philosophizing getting abstracted only later—we would see ourselves as beings with responsibilities as well as rights. Liberty and equality would not be conceived in the same way—nor would there be so apparent an inconsistency.

It is not our place to judge the sufficiency of any of these responses. Surely, there is a libertarian/incompatibilist response to each; just as surely, a rejoinder to each response will be forthcoming. However, the goal of this section is to *advance* the philosophical conversation about liberty, equality, and justice—not to conclude it.

—Jonathan Schonsheck

Chapter 1

Liberty, Equality, and Distributive Justice

Jan Narveson

Equality Principles

My subject is the consistency of liberty and equality. But to talk of the "consistency" of two concepts, just like that, is not sensible: what are consistent or inconsistent with each other are not concepts but propositions—in the present case are principles, specifically, political and social principles. The question is whether liberty principles are consistent with equality principles.

More specifically, such principles, in turn, are principles of justice. Such principles concern what we must do, what is required of us, and not what might merely be nice. Should there be laws, or what amount to laws, enforcing liberty(ies), or equality(ies) in some respect(s) or other? In this chapter I argue, first, that, in the senses that are specifically in contention, liberty and equality are fundamentally inconsistent; and second, that of the two, liberty is preferable. Society may indeed compel us to respect one another's liberty; it may not compel us to bring it about that we are equal, or more nearly equal, in any material respect.

This thesis is in need of clarification, however. Each of these concepts needs to be brought into sharper focus, starting with equality. It is essential to distinguish a wider and narrower meaning of this notion for present purposes.

1. It is often said that each of us is entitled to a presumption of equality before the law, that we must all be presumed to be moral equals. The "equality" in question is *sameness*—identity—of underlying principles. All are to be subject to treatment under the same principles; the same rules apply to all.

I take it to be uncontroversial, because definitive of morality, that its principles hold for all. And to hold this is, no doubt, to hold that there is some respect or other in which, for moral purposes, different individuals are the same: some abstract features of persons, present in all, are the ground for this sameness of principle. If this were what is meant by "equality" for present purposes, then we could all go home. But of course it is not. One principle—the same for all—can call for equality in respect F; another principle—again, the same for all—can permit indefinite inequalities in that same respect. *Everything*, then, turns on what respects we are talking about. This one is irrelevant, for it is uncontroversial common ground.

2. This narrower sense of "equality" is what we are concerned with here. To say of two things that they are equal or unequal in this second sense is *not* to say that they are "the same," or identical. To say that two things are equal is, instead, to suppose (a) that there is some feature or respect, variable *in degree* and at least roughly commensurable, found in both, and (b) such that *the measure* in the two is the same—the number that measures them is identical (or nearly so) in each: one piece of cake each, both 5 feet 10¾ inches, and so on. Until we know what aspects of persons, inherently commensurable, are such that their equal or unequal incidence in those persons is what is in question, we are not discussing equality. In normative matters, we are always discussing whether this or that principle applies to such-and-such a range of cases. But we are not always discussing whether people exemplify or should initiate the same degree of some commensurable variable.

To affirm that justice is about equality, then, is to affirm that justice has to do with coercively imposed redistributions of something in the direction of equality. The advocate of an equality principle, then, must tell us which quantity is to be equalized, and, of course, among which set of people it is to be so. When general theories of justice are in question, I take it, the presumptive answer to the latter is "everybody," so the focus must be on what it is that is to be equalized. Principles and policies of that kind are *egalitarian:* they call for equalizing welfare, income, health, "opportunity," and so on. Once we know what it is that is to be equalized, we must ask, Why force people to distribute that quantity equally, or even, merely, more nearly equally, to all?

Equalization is variable in degree, of course. Most contemporary theories, I am sure, favor equality "in moderation": Let's take *some* from the "haves," maybe only those near the top, and give it only to those have-nots who are near the bottom, of the favored spectrum. Different motivations for stopping short of full equalization are possible. The theorist might conclude that noble though it may be, it is not practicable to go whole-hog. Or the theorist might attach some weight to equalization and some weight to another principle that conflicts with equalization, giving us a "mix" of the two. In that case, though, we have to ask whether the reason for proposing the redistribution is that the results are more nearly equal. If so, the challenge to be put is, why should we allow that as any reason at all to do the thing in question? My thesis is that it is not or, at any rate, that no one has shown that it is, and that there is excellent reason for *not* allowing it.

Let me also point out that no matter how restrained one might be in this regard, what one is advocating will necessarily cut into liberty, so that there will remain the question whether liberty should not have, as Rawls used to insist, "lexical" priority over all sorts of equality, partial or out-and-out. I will argue that it should indeed. Aggressive takings from one person to give to another are, prima facie, thefts; small ones are no more defensible, as such, than large ones.

I must emphasize, in view of many reactions received to early revisions of this paper, that the arguments that follow do not in any way depend on assuming what might be called "fanaticism" about egalitarian principles. If the theorist thinks we should have some equality in his favored respect but wants to stop well short of 100 percent, that is his business. But this chapter calls for the supplying of a reason for going as far as he does, no matter how far that is. If Jones has a million and Smith has zero, and the theorist thinks that therefore we ought to transfer, say, ten from Jones to Smith, my question is, Why is that a reason? How is that supposed to follow? Is there any reason at all, from the sheer fact of disparity, to require any transfers at all? The person who says yes but wishes to limit the transfer to something less than precise equality has two jobs, not one. One is to tell us why we should go in that direction at all; the other is to tell us why we should stop just where he wants us to and not somewhere else. The theorist's response to the first might make the second an awkward business, but that is not my concern here. It is the first job that this chapter is concerned with. There is a genuine and compelling argument for liberty. I see no such argument for equality.

Of course, many readers will say, "Well, equality just *is* a duty, or a value." To which I reply that it surely does not look like that to me—or, what is more important, to most of the people from whom the transfer is to be involuntarily extracted. And so I ask, Can the egalitarian do any better? I shall argue that the answer to this question in all cases is no.

Liberty Principles—Negative and Positive

Next let us look at principles oriented toward liberty. In the largest sense, to say that person A is "at liberty" to do something is to say that whether he does it is up to him: that A does x if A chooses to do x—nothing stops[1] A from doing x. For purposes of moral and political philosophy, however, we are concerned only with a certain subclass of possible obstructions to A's doing as A wants: namely, the intentional actions of other persons. This we may call "social liberty." Person A has this when, within the area in which A has it, no other person, B, acts so as to prevent A from doing as A chooses to do (or, A can reasonably expect B to refrain from doing so); in short, it is A's choice, not B's, that is sufficient to make x occur, if A is otherwise able to do x.

What if A is not in fact able to do x? Then we are into a different subject, which I will discuss later. Attributions of liberty normally presume ability to do the thing in question; when that is lacking, the subject, A, may wish that somebody else would do something about it. But what this other person, B, would do would not be, merely, to respect A's liberty; instead it would consist in actively helping A in some way—bringing it about that A has more capability, more powers. But only if one's assistance took the form of removing certain humanly imposed obstacles—the mafia, say, or certain official actions—would it simply consist in promoting A's liberty.

We usually speak of liberty in contexts where the ability or capacity to do the action in question is not in doubt. Not always, to be sure. Still, it is obviously a very different thing to say that Jones is not at liberty to pole-vault twenty feet because he does not have the physical capacity to do it, and to say that he is not at liberty to do so because, though he is quite capable of it, the police will nab him if he tries. Our question is whether any interventions of that kind—that is, forcible interventions—are ever justified by the sheer fact of inability in the former sense. That the inability could be rectified by others, who could supply the individual in question with the means enabling him to do it, hardly suffices to show that such interventions are perfectly all right.

Another relevant case is where the individual, though perhaps possessed of the ability and the desire, cannot afford it. In that case, a transfer of funds from others would presumably enable him to do it. But how is the transfer to be effected? If the others simply decide, out of pity or interest, to make a donation, there is no problem. But if they do not, and social philosophers or legislators propose to compel them to supply the needed funds, that is another matter, for to invade someone else is to interfere with his liberty, the domain in which he acts as he pleases. And, we assume, the potential donor has earned his money by various mutually agreed transactions with others, none of whom were compelled to participate. Where that is so, a compulsory transfer interferes with the liberty to engage in such activities.

A principle calling for liberty in some domain enjoins us all to refrain from interfering with a person who wishes to act in the domain in question: within the area in which he is to have liberty, nobody may intervene to prevent him from doing whatever he chooses to do. This identifies the kind of principle that invokes a *negative right* to act in some domain. Such a right imposes a *negative duty* on others: a duty to refrain from doing something, namely, interfering, either in general or in ways to be specified, with the doing of the things in question.

We may also define the notion of *positive rights*. Such rights call upon others not merely to refrain from doing something but also to do something. We may refrain by doing nothing—by going to sleep, say. But if we must also do something, for example, supply A with certain goods or create for A certain opportunities, then inaction is not enough. Professor Sterba has, in recent years, made much of insisting that when starving S comes to the door of well-to-do W, it is S's purely negative right to "do what would satisfy his minimum needs" that would be infringed upon by W's refusal to leave the door to his larder open for S. But that is quite wrong. It is W's right to do as he likes that allowed him to grow a superfluity for whatever purposes W had in mind in doing so. If one of those purposes is not feeding S, then forcing W to leave his door open for S is forcing W to act on a new purpose, not his own, namely, that of feeding S—not merely forcing S to refrain from something that he could do without the involuntary cooperation of W. Indeed, W in keeping his door locked simply defends his own negative right to basic liberty in this case. (See also discussion below.) It is quite possible to formulate principles proclaiming positive rights, not only to such substantive goods as wealth or health but also, as we will see below, to liberty itself. Such principles would call upon people to provide conditions, hitherto lacking or in short supply, that would enable the persons supplied them to be in the position to have their choice to do or get x be effective. Such principles are radically different from principles invoking only negative rights. To illustrate, consider a right to freedom of movement. A negative right to walk is a right that others not prevent one from walking where one pleases in the domain in question. But consider the lame and halt, whose negative right to walk does them little good because they cannot. A positive right to walk would require others to supply them with, say, crutches or prostheses.

The question whether people have *any* kind of right is the question whether there is adequate reason to impose what it requires. At this point, I am concerned only to distinguish types. But we must now emphasize an important point about positive rights, or rights to "positive liberty": any such positive principle is strictly incompatible with others remaining at liberty in the respect described. If I must supply you with a crutch, then I am not at liberty to decline to do so. It is also true, of course, that if you have the negative right to walk, I am not at liberty to trip you up. All rights impose requirements—that's what they are all about. But positive rights inherently impose further requirements than negative ones. For positive rights entail negative ones: a right that others help you do x makes no sense if at the same time they are not forbidden to prevent you from doing it. But the reverse does not hold: a right requiring you not to prevent them need not also require you to help them out. That is a central conceptual point in this debate.

When the general area of ethics we are concerned about is "distribution," to claim that justice calls upon us to see to it that various persons are equal in some respect, F, is to say that (1) it is possible for people to be either equal or unequal in respect F; (2) that it is possible for others to do something to (help) bring it about that those people are more nearly or less nearly equal in that respect; and, finally, (3) that they are required, where possible, to do what promotes equality of F or promotes it to the prescribed extent either by taking steps to reduce or prevent the onset of what would otherwise become an inequality or by supplying amounts of F to persons in such a way that they end up (more nearly) equal in respect of F-possession.

The Incompatibility of Equality and Liberty

The foregoing analysis makes it clear that principles calling for liberty and equality respectively, in the only senses that are relevant to this inquiry, are, by definition, incompatible. There is no question of identity or even compatibility: an egalitarian principle imposes an obligation on people to do certain of the very things that liberty denies there is such an obligation to do.[2] And this is true whether the obligation is to go some small distance in the direction of equality or to go all the way.

Why do theorists such as James Sterba and Alistair Macleod insist that equality and liberty are compatible? (See this volume.) What must be meant is that persons acting as they want to *could*, as it happens, act in the very ways that the corresponding equality principle would compel them to if they were not so inclined. Thus, it is logically possible that every voluntarily chosen action in the domain in question should turn out to be precisely the one called for by the egalitarian principle. If that is the point, then it should be appreciated that, although perfectly true, it is also quite remarkably uninteresting and certainly totally ineffectual as a conceptual defense of egalitarianism. Principles of justice are coercively prescriptive, requiring us to do or refrain. Although it is always possible that we would have done that anyway, we have to point out that if it were always so, there would not be any point to the prescription in question. We do not need to tell people to breathe; we do need to tell them to refrain from cheating, stealing, lying, injuring, and so on—and we would most certainly need to tell them that half of their income must go to somebody else, whether they like it or not. That people have motivation for performing the forbidden acts is a practical precondition of forbidding them. Claims of extensional equivalence in this field are, in short, not credible.

Can Sterba, Macleod, and others really mean this? If they do, then they face an interesting challenge, for they should then be happy to adopt a libertarian constitution! After all, if equality and liberty were equivalent, it should be true that a libertarian constitition would have exactly the same result as the compulsory programs egalitarians actually recommend. This, the reader will appreciate, is fantastic. The egalitarian requires what the libertarian merely allows because he knows perfectly well that people will not, even typically—let alone always—act as his principle requires. For the world as we know it, then, the principles proposed by the two theorists are inconsistent *as principles*, and the sorts of societies that would be determined by them respectively are sure to be very, very different.[3] One must make a choice. The question is which is better—more reasonable. I argue that the libertarian option is.

Equal Liberty

So far, I have left generally open the question of just what is to be equalized in an egalitarian scheme. We may formally sketch an egalitarianism by means of the following formula:

(E) Everyone is required to attempt to bring it about that all persons are equal in respect F.

We then specify an equality principle by supplying values for the variable F. But there seems to be one possible substituend that would indeed make liberty and equality compatible: liberty itself. And indeed, an "equal liberty" principle occupies much space in the writings of current philosophers, notably John Rawls. Does this confirm the egalitarian's assertion that we must all be egalitarians of one kind or another? It does not.

As has already been hinted at, there are two very different versions of liberty principles. One version does say precisely what (E) says, with "Liberty" substituted for "F":

(EL) Everyone is required to attempt to bring it about that all persons are (more nearly) equal in respect of liberty.[4]

But the other does not do any such thing. It says, instead:

(L) Everyone is required to refrain from interfering with anyone else's liberty.

The latter does not say, or imply, that we must all see to it that everyone has an equal amount of something we can distribute, even if it is liberty. We could try to construe it as such, for example, by reading it as "It is equally true of all that they have the obligation to . . . ," or "Everyone is equally required to . . . " But as we saw at the outset, that trivializes the issue, reinvoking the first of the two senses of equality distinguished—and rejected as irrelevant: *Every* moral principle propounds some basic set of rules, the same for all, but they need not be rules requiring that certain commensurable magnitudes be equal or equalized. Prescribing to all that they are to do such and such is not engaging in an action that need have any clear measure conceptually associated with it. If I say, "I hereby prescribe that everybody refrain from eating Wheaties!" then the only sense in which the concept of "measurable magnitude" is applicable would be if we wanted to decide how much a given person might have deviated from it.

Nor does a liberty principle call for an equal amount of enforcement of itself. How best to bring about compliance—for example, how much enforcement is necessary, if any—is a separate issue. Justice is enforceable, in principle. But how much enforcement and who supplies it are separate questions. (Failure to appreciate this point refutes the thesis, recently popular among Anglo-American philosophers, that the distinction of negative and positive is invalid.[5]) Our question is what people *may* be forced to do. A liberty principle's answer is, only refraining from interfering with others' voluntary performances of the kinds of action specified. Forcing them to produce and/or distribute equal, or any, quantities of anything is not on its agenda.

Should we, though, not say that the intent of such a principle is to bring it about that the "quantity of interference" with the acts in question is equal, namely nil? Well, zero for all is, no doubt, one sort of equality. A principle prescribing that the incidence of x should be zero is, in this way, a residual equality principle: the "amount" we are to do to each person in conformity with the principle in question is in a curious sense the same. But that is misleading. In the first place, the amount of psychological effort it might cost to follow this principle would no doubt vary greatly from one person or occasion to another: refraining from socking some very annoying person might take a lot of psychological effort, but for mild-mannered folk like us, the cost of similar refraining in regard to random persons on the street is negligible. Yet, we each observe the same requirement when we refrain.

The other thing to say is that the proposed equivalence is simply wrong, for nondoing rather than doing is not inherently the bringing about, on the part of all, of *any* commensurable magnitude of anything. (Try it: Which state of affairs would it be the bringing about *of*? Answer: The state of affairs in which one does not do the thing in question!) Nor is complying with a principle calling for nondoing the same as bringing about enforcement of the principle enjoining that.

The Argument for Liberty

It has become popular among philosophers, such as Ronald Dworkin and the later Rawls, to deny that there is any such thing as a general right to liberty. Instead, they hold, only specified liberties should have standing in the principles of the just society. This departs from the classic idea that each person is entitled, in Rawls's earlier words, to the "*most extensive* liberty compatible with a like liberty for all" (my italics).[6] On such a principle, liberty is to be limited only by liberty: Citizen A is confined to activities that do not curtail the free activities of any other person, B. I will assume for present purposes that this formula does make sense—recognizing that there is a major job to do to show that. I shall also assume, without further explanation and defense, that the general liberty principle leads directly to a general right of private property: not only may we do as we please with ourselves, but we may also use whatever we can find in external nature, as we please, short only of such use as would conflict with the previously initiated uses of things by others.[7] This principle is fully universal. And it is monopolistic, for all other principles forbid some activities that are inherently compatible with a like liberty for all. Thus, this maximal principle has reasonably come to be called libertarianism. To argue that libertarianism is preferable is to argue that egalitarianism is a mistake: that we, as a society, will do better to allow people to act on their own in the respect(s) in question rather than to enforce actions of the type(s) the egalitarian has in mind, namely, actions aimed at reducing or eliminating disparities in respect of the sorts of goods we have considered.

I now present a brief argument for a general liberty principle's claim to acceptance. This will also prove a useful occasion for explaining my dissent from Sterba, whose thesis is misleadingly (as we have seen) described as asserting equivalence of the main options about justice. As we have seen, it cannot really be that. Instead, it is the quite different, but certainly very important, claim that the one proper sort of argument for any social principle leads to just one result: *his*. I, for my part, quite agree that it is the one proper sort of argument and agree that it leads to just one result: *mine*—which is very different from his!

That common argument is a social contract one: principles of justice are those principles concerning the use of coercion that all would agree to, upon a rational consideration of their own best interests, in their own view of what constitutes "best" in the long run. If no agreement is reached, there are *no* principles, and we both suppose that this would be worse for all. The question is, then, this: Would we, as I claim, contract for liberty, and if so, why? Why would we not go for at least some elements of the welfare state or some other redistributive state?

Here is the answer. Liberty (for present purposes) is the absence of obstacles intentionally imposed by others to one's doing what one prefers and is within one's powers. As such, it is important to appreciate, liberty is *not* an *intrinsic good*. What's good about liberty is only that if one does not have it, one is not able to do as one wants. For any given noninvasive action that someone else would prevent one from doing on some alternative principle, the reason for being a libertarian is that a liberty principle lets one do it. No doubt some could acquire desirable things by subjecting others to coercion: theft—including theft from the rich by the poor—can pay. But the social contract is universal: all must sign if any principle is to be valid. So consider the proposal from the point of view of the coerced. What interest have they in such behavior? The prima facie answer is none—as is suggested by the fact that if they did have such an interest, the liberty principle allows them to go right ahead and pursue it, for instance, by making arrangements with their bankers to deduct periodic payments to cover the cost. No problem!

But, manifestly, many of them do not and would not do that. How, then, could Sterba suppose that *all* of us would go for a system imposing that as a *requirement* on *all?* Unanimity is possible only for the liberty scheme: everyone benefits from the nonaggression of others, compared to a condition where we are at one another's disposal. Rich or poor, intelligent or stupid, strong or weak, everyone is liable to depredations from others. No one, however badly off, is incapable of being made still worse off by the aggressions of others. All other schemes, by contrast, impose costs on some to provide benefits for others. When that is so, the providers are either happy to provide voluntarily or, if not, then they will not accept an involuntary imposition of a duty to provide. For this reason, as I have argued elsewhere,[8] liberty is the only principle that can straightforwardly claim to represent the common good. All other principles may be accused of bias toward some and against others.

Sterba's preferred principles, then, will not receive unanimity. The rich would not agree to any scheme compelling them to open their cellars to the poor should the latter be in need. If the motive is to save the costs of fighting, those are costs that the poor would pay in as full measure as the rich: all parties lose from war. The alternative in which neither is allowed to coerce the other is better for both—even when the poor are starving. If general coercion had been allowed, the poor would not have got even as far as they have, or if coercion is allowed against the productive, then there will be no production to distribute. The only general principle on which all do the best they can, given that everyone is subject to the same requirements, is general liberty. Contrary to the prevailing view, no redistributive principle makes sense in these terms. But these are the only reasonable terms there are. I conclude that no coercively enforceable redistributive principle makes any sense.

Can anything be said against this case? Let us now consider the arguments for the other side.

Arguments for Egalitarianism

Egalitarianism holds that all are required, at least prima facie, to do what they can to bring about an equal, or more nearly equal, distribution of some sorts of goods or services, independently of any consideration of desert, and regardless of who produced the goods in question. Such theories deny that one may do whatever one likes with such things.[9] How does one argue for this? I briefly survey several of the leading arguments.

1. The unwary will appeal to the *impartiality* of moral principles. It being, near enough, a defining feature of morals that moral principles cannot arbitrarily favor some over others, this would be conclusive if it worked. But impartiality does not entail egalitarianism. Liberty principles are impartial, imposing the same restrictions on all. And, far from being paradigmatically impartial, egalitarianism is partial, for in calling for the uncompensated taking of what some have produced in order to make others more nearly equal to them, it favors the unproductive at the expense of the productive.

2. Then there is the "veil-of-ignorance" idea: principles are to be such as would be chosen if we had no idea who we were. In fact, it is not really clear what this idea is. If it is the requirement that principles must be acceptable to all, no matter what their situation, then that is precisely what the social contract idea says, and that way, I hold, lies libertarianism. But in another reading, it would ignore individuals' interests in using their own powers for their own purposes. In choosing for "myself" when "I" do not know who I am, "I" choose for Homogenized Anybody: say, assigning the same probability to my being any actual person as to my being any other. On this view, morality favors "people" who do not know who they are! Small wonder that it has an egalitarian (or at least utilitarian)[10] output. But why should we pay any attention to principles that could appeal only to people who do not know who they are? To be a person, one must know who one is. The assertion that the "moral point of view" assumes the opposite is completely tendentious (and, surely, would be a conclusive reason for rejecting the moral point of view if it were so—a view's entailing what is false is fatal for that view). At the same time, moral principles must, of course, be the same for all, and so, in the social contract, A's choice of principles must be the same as B's, however much the two individuals may differ.[11]

3. The most influential of all recent egalitarian arguments appeals to the moral arbitrariness of desert—due, again, to Rawls in its modern form.[12]

Its key principle is what we may call the Transitivity of Nondesert: if you claim to deserve G (the scholarship, say) by virtue of being F (the superior violinist), then if your being F is not deserved (you were born a musical prodigy), then neither is G. The argument, then, is that we are all fundamentally entitled to equal ministrations because we are not fundamentally entitled to unequal ones.

Clearly, the premise is right: we cannot be thought to deserve our natural assets, stemming as they are said to do from the "natural lottery"; nor can we deserve inherited wealth, and so on. But Transitivity of Nondesert says that we also do not deserve whatever differential advantages we may claim as a result of the working of such undeserved factors.

It is instructive to appreciate that this famous argument is entirely fallacious for this purpose. Egalitarians intend the positive conclusion that everyone ought to get *some* G—an equal, but, it is hoped, sizable amount. Yet, the argument's premise is only that nobody deserves any more G than anyone else—a purely negative premise. What follows? On one reading, that we should not give anybody any G—hardly what the egalitarian wants! Obviously, he cannot accept that version, for he wants to give everybody *something*—as much as possible, so long as it is the same.[13]

In another, "weaker" reading, on the other hand, the argument says merely that justice does not require giving A some G—but does not forbid it, either. The weak version, in fact, leaves wide open what we should actually do with the things whose "distribution" is in question. If justice won't allow that Jones deserves something, but I want to give it to him anyway, what is to keep me from doing so? Not this argument! Again, then, no support at all for egalitarianism.

Of course, contemporary philosophers would like to draw some "intermediate" conclusion from Rawls's argument. For example, it may be said, "When once we realize that our natural assets and advanced starting place are not deserved, and when once we realize that the lack of natural assets and the disadvantageous starting place of others [are] also not deserved, we will not take the position that we are entitled to the entirety of the benefits that can be realized from developing and marketing our talents. We deserve much of the benefits . . . but not every last sou."[14] Well, why? Alas, no reason is given. Certainly nothing follows from the premises in question, other than that if you want to give money to your kids, you had better not do so on the basis that they deserve it. But as to how much you should give them or anyone else for any other reason, the argument provides no answer at all. Unless, of course, it supplies the wrong one, which would call for depriving everyone of everything.[15] Humans are sympathetic and inclined to help one another. Liberty lets them do so, of course. The only question is whether charity is properly to be enforced. That is what needs arguing. But this famous argument actually implies nothing about that.

We may agree with the argument in one way: the principles of justice themselves may not, indeed, single out anybody for special favor—no matter how well he plays the violin. They cannot require everyone or anyone to put forth effort and skill to supply the favored persons, the "deserving," with special privileges or goods. That we are all morally entitled to none of such things from society is perfectly true. But, then, neither are the needy or the less educated or the hapless—which is exactly what libertarianism says: any individual is obliged to do or produce something for someone *only* if both individuals agree to the transfer, for example, by means of a suitable contract—exactly what egalitarianism denies. As an argument for egalitarianism, then, the Rawlsian argument is a washout; in its only plausible interpretation it supports libertarianism instead.

4. A more promising argument at first sight appeals to the idea of cooperation. Richard Norman, for instance, holds that equality principles are "appropriate to co-operative organisations, because they are principles on which everyone committed to such co-operation can agree."[16] He proposes two: "(a) that power should be shared equally, and (b) that benefits and burdens should be so distributed that everyone benefits equally overall" (73). But a more careful examination shows that those conclusions are either misleading or wrong. He defines "co-operation" as "any interaction or association between a number of people producing a result which they could not have produced individually" (74). Slaves operating cotton gins would fit that description, though. What rules them out is that "a co-operative community is contrasted with a coercive form of association" (74). Just so. But the members of Norman's groups are also "fully committed to working together"—they look to group advantage only (70). Yet, voluntary members of productive groups need not think in this way: coinvestors in a mutual fund think only of their own good. Nor will cooperators' products be divided equally. That would be so only if they entered as equals. If they do not—the usual case—then those who bring more will also get more: each voluntary coproducer will get not an equal share but his marginal product, which may vary greatly.

In any case, society is not a voluntarily cooperating group in the sense required. It is just a lot of people who happen to be in touch with one another. Norman might insist that it *ought* to be more (90), but he would need an argument for that; he cannot just assume that society *already is* cooperative in this larger sense. But what could that argument appeal to, if not mutual benefit?[17] Which, however, is libertarian—*not* egalitarian. Why does appeal to mutual benefit yield libertarianism *rather than* egalitarianism as a principle, instead of, say, both? Because appeal to mutual benefit is appeal to *whatever* benefits the individuals concerned—be that "whatever" equal or unequal. Certainly cooperation for mutual benefit could sometimes yield an equal return in dollars, say, to both A and B. But more often, it will not. For example, the manager of some very popular movie star arranges her appearance in a certain movie, she to get $6,000,000, and the agent $600,000. This is mutually beneficial—all parties gain. But the amounts they gain are extremely disparate. We all make such arrangements, entering into schemes of cooperation that benefit all concerned, but unequally. As usual, appeal to mutual benefit cannot yield egalitarianism because it is a special case. If the appeal is made generally, as intended, then it will instead yield the principle that each should be able to do the best he can with his resources, whatever they may be. This forbids acting at the expense of others but does not in the least forbid acting for unequal benefit.

What about equality of political power? Could it, for instance, be wielded to prevent the more productive from producing? If so, it would conflict with the other principle: it would prevent mutually beneficial reallocations of resources. Those contemplating joining an association and knowing that this could eventuate would have ample reason for thinking twice about it. They would want strong constraints against such uses of equal political power—constraints *against* egalitarianism, then. Norman himself agrees that voting would have to be constrained by a provision against exploitation of minorities by the majority. But if no majority could ever overrule anyone, then we would have a society with no politics at all:[18] everything would be done by agreement among the parties concerned, with due care that third parties not be negatively affected, and that would be that. Libertarianism, again! Let us remember that political power is coercive power over others—not a good at all, but an evil. If there must be some political power, perhaps it should be equal. But should it not also be *minimized*, ideally at zero?

A Note on Democracy

Democracy is the equal distribution of political power, and thus a kind of egalitarianism. Why would we want democracy? With any other form of government, the rulers are not identified with their subjects. The solution, then, is to make everyone the ruler . . . Or is it? Is my participation in ruling, on an equal basis with all others, a sufficient condition for decent government, from my point of view? No. For that requires the assumption that a 1/n share of political power over everybody, where I am one of the n, is as good as 100 percent power over myself and none over anyone else. That is a great blunder, as a moment's reflection will show.

In principle, democracy would have it that x is right if x is in accordance with majority wishes, no matter what the subject, and no matter what the basis of majority wishes. No sensible person could accept such a principle. What makes x right in moral matters is obviously not the arbitrary will of a majority. It is, if we can have it, *freedom*, not dictatorship by irrelevant millions.

Free exchange is treating according to productive powers. So far as I, Everyman, am concerned, your productive powers are your powers to effect good for me. Now, when we evaluate each other's output, we are in effect deliberating about what I would be willing to do for the other in view of what he has to offer. In free exchange, parties use their own values to assess each other's contributions, and act accordingly. If the asked price is too high, I do not buy; if it is too low, you do not sell. Exchange occurs at the point of maximal mutual advantage. In such a system, all are restricted to whatever they have acquired by their own work and by voluntary transfers. (Some suppose that we need government as a centralized enforcement agency to uphold the rights in question. That belief is unfounded, as it turns out[19]—but in any case, the sort of government thus called for is utterly different from the totalitarianism of unrestricted democracy.)

Appeals to cooperation, then, yield no support for egalitarian justice.[20]

Conclusion

The foregoing reflections have suggested that there is no genuine reason for substantive egalitarianism, whereas there is much to be said for general liberty in human relations. Of course, there are always those who claim that we do not need, perhaps because we cannot have, a reason for a moral/political view. But I deny that. Egalitarianism imposes on those to be cut down to size: the rich, the talented, whoever. And impositions *always* need to be justified—no matter how unpopular the candidates for imposition, such as the wealthy, may be. Those who claim that there can be no argument, and thus that none is needed, are really using "But I *like* equality!" or "I clearly see that equality has a unique nonnatural property!" as their argument. I suggest that this compares with "But I want it!" said by a five-year-old. I remind my colleagues that we are discussing principles, not tastes; a metatheory that cannot even distinguish the two is unhelpful.

Three Fatal Flaws of Egalitarianism

The egalitarian inherits three insoluble problems. First, egalitarians can supply no sensible criteria on the subject of just what it is that is supposed to be equalized. Second, they cannot explain why equality stops at the border. And third, they cannot rationally motivate the idea.

1. What are we supposed to equalize in the name of justice? Prominent candidates are welfare and wealth, opportunity and resources. These are an unruly set, of course; if you equalize one, you are likely to disequalize others. Thus, equal opportunity normally results in inequality: when persons of unequal capacity compete on equal terms, the more able will come out ahead. In the cases of welfare and opportunity (and, really, all of the candidates), there are huge problems of commensurability. Declaring that two persons' welfares are similar when the persons in question are markedly dissimilar—as they always are—is one problem whose solution inevitably involves departing from liberal criteria and relying on the ideological sense of the estimator. As to resources, a resource for one person is not such for another; the world is full of things that some find infinite uses for, while others stand by blankly. Resources require human resourcefulness, which varies all over the map. Wealth? Equalizing wealth by equalizing income runs quickly into a major coherence problem:[21] the value of money—the only reasonable measure of wealth—can be determined only in a market, which egalitarians abolish. Proposing to equalize wealth by coercion buys into a contradiction. And so on.

2. If there were egalitarian human rights, we should be equalizing the situations of all persons everywhere. Actual egalitarians rarely go for that. What they want is that "the" government, meaning their own government, should aim at equalizing F among these people, the citizens of this government.

Equality, billed as a "human right,"[22] ends up a right of Americans, Swedes, and so on—regardless of the outcome for Swedes, Americans, and so on. Canadians get fabulously high welfare payments at the same time that poor Mexicans, Ethiopians, and others are frozen out by Canadian immigration laws. That someone needs something is held to be sufficient reason to take it from somebody who has it and giving it to him—unless he happens to be a citizen of somewhere else. Curious!

Seriously proposing to equalize F around the globe in light of North American ideas of the "minimum" is, for the popular values of F, a job far exceeding the resources of the wealthiest countries. Yet, drawing a line around our own citizens is utterly arbitrary. It would not be if our citizens owed this to each other because, say, of what they have done for each other. But it is never true that *all* citizens have "done" *anything* for each other; instead, particular people have done things for some other particular people, the terms of exchange being variably settled between those individuals. There is no room left for an argument covering all and only the citizens of a particular state. Moreover, this argument presupposes that F should go to those who have done something to *deserve* F—which egalitarianism cannot allow: "all" and "deserve" do not mix well.

3. Most fundamental, however, is that egalitarianism is irrational as a general social doctrine. What is to be equalized is a *good;* for each person, more of it is better than less. Yet, my having more whether or not you do is, on the face of it, still a good thing for me: how am I to be persuaded that I should have more *only* if you have a similar amount? Reasons that have any prospect of appealing to those who don't happen to have the same "intuitions" or feelings as egalitarians are not forthcoming. The theory is literally groundless.

There are those who seem to think that large wealth in the hands of a few is somehow bad for others. One might wonder what sort of examples they have in mind. Consider the case of Microsoft's Bill Gates, one of the world's richest people today. Well, who has the mild-mannered Mr. Gates murdered lately? Or chiseled, cheated, defrauded, or stolen from? On the other hand, the number who have benefited enormously from his highly ingenious activities is legion—which, in fact, is exactly *why* he is so wealthy. Certainly there can be people who have become wealthy through fraud or political violence. But both of those ways of attaining wealth, it will be remembered, are *proscribed* by respect for liberty. In the cases permitted by the theory, all will be seen to be people whose activities are beneficial to a great many others—not surprisingly, for if exchanges to mutual advantage are the only permissible ones, then wealth gained on the free market has necessarily benefited many people.

It has also been popular to appeal to the superior political power of the wealthy as a reason for preventing people from becoming so in the first place. This argument overlooks a number of things, such as the fact that there simply is no necessary connection between wealth and the exercise of political power. Being apolitically wealthy is perfectly possible—even today, despite the burgeoning panoply of restrictions on business activities imposed by today's politicians, which virtually demand counterlobbying, as well as opportunities created by politicians for rent-seeking businessmen. But it is a fault of democratic politics and not of immoderate wealth that the wealthy have more influence—if they do—than the poor. (And the poor, or rather their representatives among academics and lobbyists, have done exceedingly well for themselves in terms of influencing politicians to spend the public's money on them.)

It is a framing feature of libertarianism that no one is permitted to injure, harm, or in general worsen the situation of others as a means of securing his own advantage. One can pass that test easily and yet make a great deal of money—or write many concertos, or do any number of other things that show one to be singularly unequal to others. Those attempting to tar the prospect of great wealth with the very brush libertarians themselves advocate against the violent and the fraudulent are grasping at straws. To make immoderate wealth generally illegal, forbidding *any* from prospering in order to make sure that there are no mafiosi among the prosperous, is to throw out the babies with the bathwater in about as wholesale a way as could readily be imagined. Those who think this way must be supposing that the "division" of wealth in society is a genuinely "distributive," zero-sum game—more for some entailing less for others. It simply is not so, as any economist can point out.[23] More for some, in a society in which all are confined to making their money *by free exchange*, is, *necessarily, more* for others, not less. And the more for some it is, the more there must be for the others who are the source of that wealth for the "some" in question. If such are the only arguments egalitarians can find, then the balance lies decisively on the libertarian side.

Why Equality Is Popular

If the preceding arguments are sound, then why is egalitarianism so popular? It is easy to see why those below the point above which egalitarians propose to transfer from the "above" to the "below" might favor efforts at equalization. But by the same token it is hard to see why those above should accept this. The theorist may invoke "altruism." But does he mean that everyone is altruistic or only that they ought to be? If the latter, then we must ask him, Why? And off he will go into question-begging answers. To be sure, those are fashionable nowadays: "Basic values" are in the dime-a-dozen rack. Such affirmations are fine, if one hopes to bamboozle—but not if rational support is the aim.

So it is easy to see why egalitarianism should appeal to the majority—who are unlikely to know much about public goods theory. But how are we to account for its popularity among intellectuals? Alas, the answer is not far to seek. Indeed, it could seem a mystery only to those averse to attributing anything but the most (question-beggingly so-called) exalted motives to their fellows. The short answer is that egalitarianism, unlike liberty, requires administration—lots of it. Because it consists in "doing down" a great many people—those on the upper end of the to-be-equalized scale, who, needless to say, would not voluntarily submit to being done down—the doing down has to be done by someone. Who will that be? The articulate, the visionary, the ambitious, and, of course, those happy to serve, at quite good salaries, in the sizable armies of civil servants needed to carry out the work. Egalitarians, most of them middle class, see the goal of equality as taking from those above them and "giving to" those below; it just happens that cushy middle-class jobs in the bureaucracy await the many who are needed to carry out the task.[24]

That those engaged in these amiable labors work on the basis of incoherent theories advanced by a kind of studied inarticulateness—intuited nonnatural qualities, "basic norms," and so on (replacing former-day appeals to the will of the Almighty and the like)—is not entirely surprising. If we were instead required to show those we are purportedly benefiting just how they are supposed to benefit by making war on the suppliers of what they want, we should have a more difficult time of it. But we do not have to; after all, they do not understand—they just collect the checks.

The final irony of egalitarianism, then, is that its basic functional motive is an inequality after all: it disequalizes power, redistributing it toward the theorist and assorted administrators of his favored programs, and away from everyone else—especially those better off or, as it turns out, worse off than himself.

Some will be a bit shocked, perhaps, at the above words. I invite them to respond, preferably by showing some genuinely good reason that egalitarianism should be accepted, and second, by being willing to search under all leaves for the truth, whatever and wherever it may turn out to be. So far as I can see at present, it lies with the "classical" liberals, that is, the libertarians, rather than their egalitarian descendants. Liberty and equality inherently conflict, and there is inherent reason from the social point of view to prefer the former.

Notes

I am indebted to AMINTAPHIL editors for raising this issue.

I have decided, after many years of concession to current fashion, to stick resolutely to standard English in this paper. "He" will be used in the formerly familiar way, that is to say, as gender-neutral unless the context calls for a gender-specific usage, or unless distinct personal pronouns are useful in context, saving me the nuisance of talking of "he or she." Accusations of sexism will be firmly rejected, and the accuser asked to show solid reason for his or her accusation.

1. We table the further question whether his choice must in turn be in some sense unconstrained. Many wish to make much of this. Had I space, I would point out that virtually all claims of this kind turn out to be question-begging. The main thing, though, is that they are almost always irrelevant. If I want a first-rate performance of the Sibelius violin concerto, and you can do it, I do not, as such, care whether what led you to be able to produce it was an exercise of Kantian free will or a violin-playing gene you happen to have, or umpteen years of hard work.

2. This was noted by Hobbes: "Law, and Right, differ as much, as Obligation, and Liberty; which in one and the same matter are inconsistent" (*Leviathan*, chap. 14).

3. To purists who do not like this, we need merely point out that Principle L says, "You are welcome to equalize F *if you like*, but if you do not like, then you need not," whereas principle E says, "You must do what equalizes F *whether you like to or not.*" L denies that force is legitimate in cases in which E says it is legitimate. This is a flat conflict in principle.

4. One can also attach another predicate variable: "Liberty to perform acts of type H." Libertarians, however, want to defend liberty as such, liberty, in principle, to do *whatever* one wants to do, that is, with variable H, deriving restrictions on liberty exclusively from the universality of the principle: A's liberty to be restricted only on the ground that what he does restricts the liberty of others. Whether the libertarian can succeed in explaining that in a plausible and noncircular way is, of course, one of that theory's major problems. But because that is what he is trying to say, I omit the complication of introducing a variable H into these formulae at this point.

5. See Henry Shue, "The Bogus Distinction—'Negative' and 'Positive' Rights," in *Making Ethical Decisions*, ed. Norman E. Bowie (New York: McGraw-Hill, 1985),

223–31. Shue's argument simply *identifies* the right to liberty with the positive version, so it is no surprise to find him concluding that there is no distinction.

6. John Rawls, "Justice as Fairness," in *Philosophy, Politics and Society,* ed. Peter Laslett and W. G. Runciman, 2d ser. (Oxford: Basil Blackwell, 1962), 133.

7. Among various places I have pressed the argument, see especially Jan Narveson, *The Libertarian Idea* (Philadelphia: Temple University Press, 1988).

8. This was argued in my "Rights, Laws, and the Common Good" (paper presented at the AMINTAPHIL conference, Allentown, Pa., 1992).

9. One popular way to do this is to claim that nobody actually does produce anything—by himself, anyway. I assume but do not here argue that that is untenable.

10. Rawls denies the utilitarian implication, and many have gone along with him on this, to be sure. I suspect that it is due to the confusion of interpretation mentioned. See Narveson, "Rawls and Utilitarianism," in *The Limits of Utilitarianism*, ed. H. Miller and W. Williams (Minneapolis: University of Minnesota Press, 1982), 128–43. For the point about the ambiguity of the idea, see Narveson, "A Puzzle about Economic Justice in Rawls' Theory," *Social Theory and Practice* (1976).

11. See David Gauthier, *Morals by Agreement* (New York: Oxford University Press, 1986), 266; more generally, chap. 8, "The Archimedean Point."

12. See John Rawls, *A Theory of Justice* (Cambridge: Harvard University Press, 1970) 15, 18, and chaps. 17 (100–108) and 48 (310–15). Note this passage, for instance (100–101): "Undeserved inequalities call for some redress . . . the idea is to redress the bias of contingencies in the direction of equality."

13. Nor will it do to insist that the idea applies only to "differential" deserts. If an asset cannot underwrite differential desert when it is not deserved, how can common assets fare any better? After all, Transitivity of Nondesert entails that *they* are not deserved, either.

14. Supplied by an anonymous AMINTAPHIL reader of the first submitted version of this chapter.

15. I have discussed the subject of desert in detail in "Deserving Profits," in *Profits and Morality*, ed. Robin Cowan and Mario Rizzo (Chicago: University of Chicago Press, 1994). I there make the point that the locus of "desert" has been completely misunderstood by social philosophers, who fail to take into account that to deserve is to be such as to serve the relevant interests of the *distributor* of whatever "rewards" and so on are in question.

16. Richard Norman, *Free and Equal* (Oxford: Oxford University Press, 1987), 69.

17. David Gauthier argues that, in the first place, each person entering into cooperation must expect to get at least what she could get in her best alternative; and then, with regard to the "co-operative surplus," each will get an equal *proportion* of her maximal marginal claim. Such a principle does not afford a basis for a general social reinforcement of equality in the distribution of anything in particular. See Gauthier, *Morals by Agreement*, chap. 5.

18. It might be argued that there is an exception to this: politics by *consensus*. Unfortunately, however, such politics is invariably a fake. If we insist on consensus, what we do is to put pressure on those who would normally dissent not to do so, by the threat of prolonging meeting times beyond what the putative dissenters are willing to endure. With consensus politics, power passes into the hands of those who are both articulate and have a generous budget of patience or tolerance for meetings.

19. The most important recent sources: David Schmidtz, *The Limits of Government* (Boulder: Westview Press, 1991), and Anthony de Jasay, *Social Contract, Free Ride* (New York: Oxford University Press, 1989).

20. A more complicated argument very roughly along Norman's lines is found in Gauthier's brilliant *Morals by Agreement*. Gauthier is far from an egalitarian anyway, but he does hold that "society may be viewed as a single cooperative enterprise" (274). I complain about this in "Gauthier on Distributive Justice and the Natural Baseline," in *Contractarianism and Rational Choice*, ed. Peter Vallentyne (New York: Cambridge University Press, 1991), 127–48. Society is clearly no such thing, in any positive sense. In its negative sense, of course, we may agree: the terms of cooperation in the general "social agreement" call for nonviolence.

21. Jan Narveson, "Equality vs. Liberty: Advantage, Liberty," *Social Philosophy and Policy* (fall 1984): 33–60.

22. Unless, of course, he is one of those more thoroughgoing egalitarians who wish to equalize the situations of humans in relation to animals while at it.

23. The hitherto uninitiated can hardly do better than to pursue the highly readable little book by James Gwartney and Richard L. Stroup, *What Everyone Should Know about Economics and Prosperity* (the Canadian edition is published by the Fraser Institute, Vancouver, 1993). Their larger book, *Introduction to Economics: The Wealth and Poverty of Nations* (New York: Harcourt Brace, 1993), may prove useful to those with a greater time budget.

24. A referee refers to this last sentence as "gossip." It is, of course, the defining feature of *egalitarian* redistribution that what is redistributed go from those with *more* to those with *less*. Insofar as the American middle class today is subject to high taxes, it is not, of course, in the cause, as such, of egalitarian redistribution of income; much of it is a kind of social insurance, whose intended beneficiaries are themselves mostly members of the middle class, or goes to expenditures having no particular bearing on equalizing incomes or anything else. A pure redistributive tax for income equalizing that was levied on those in the middle class makes no sense.

Chapter 2

Reconciling Liberty and Equality, or Why Libertarians Must Be Socialists

James P. Sterba

The central contrast between libertarians and socialists is usually put this way: Libertarians take the ideal of liberty to be the ultimate political ideal, from which they think it follows that only a minimal or night-watchman state can be justified, whereas socialists take the ideal of equality to be the ultimate political ideal, from which they think it follows that only a state that socializes the means of production can be justified. Libertarians, however, tend to agree with socialists that when the ideal of equality is interpreted in the manner favored by socialists, it would justify a socialist state. Libertarians simply contend that the socialist interpretation of the ideal of equality is morally contestable. Why not interpret the ideal in the manner favored by libertarians as equality before the law or equality of basic rights so that the ideal is at least consistent with if not required by the libertarian's own ideal of liberty? Why not indeed! But obviously an analogous question could be directed at libertarians. Why not interpret the ideal of liberty in the manner favored by socialists as a positive rather than a negative ideal so that it would justify the greater equality in the distribution of goods and resources that is characteristic of a socialist state?

To either of these questions, no convincing answer seems forthcoming. Both the interpretations of the ideals of liberty and equality favored by libertarians and those favored by socialists appear morally contestable. Consequently, the dispute between libertarians and socialists seems irresolvable. I wish to argue, however, that this is not the case. I will show that the dispute can be resolved, for all practical purposes, by proceeding from premises that libertarians endorse to a conclusion that socialists endorse. Specifically, I will argue that libertarians, given their ideal of liberty, must be socialists because they must endorse the equality in the distribution of goods and resources required by a socialist state.

I

To see that this is the case, suppose we interpret the ideal of liberty as a negative ideal in the manner favored by libertarians rather than as a positive ideal in the manner favored by socialists.[1] So understood, liberty is the absence of interference by other people from doing what one wants or is able to do. Interpreting their ideal in this way, libertarians claim to derive a number of more specific requirements, in particular, a right to life, a right to freedom of speech, press, and assembly, and a right to property. Here it is important to observe that the libertarian's right to life is not a right to receive from others the goods and resources necessary for preserving one's life; it is simply a right not to be killed unjustly. Correspondingly, the libertarian's right to property is not a right to receive from others the goods and resources necessary for one's welfare but, rather, a right to acquire goods and resources either by initial acquisition or by voluntary agreement.

Of course, libertarians would allow that it would be nice of the rich to share their surplus goods and resources with the poor. Nevertheless, according to libertarians, such acts of charity should not be coercively required. For this reason, libertarians are opposed to coercively supported welfare programs. By contrast, socialists would certainly interpret their ideal of equality to require not only coercively supported welfare programs but also considerable equality in the distribution of goods and resources as well.

To see why libertarians are mistaken about what their ideal requires, consider a typical conflict situation between the rich and the poor. In this situation, the rich have more than enough goods and resources to satisfy their basic needs.[2] By contrast, the poor lack the goods and resources to meet their most basic needs, even though they have tried all the means available to them that libertarians regard as legitimate for acquiring such goods and resources. Under circumstances like these, libertarians usually maintain that the rich should have the liberty to use their resources to satisfy their luxury needs if they so wish. Libertarians recognize that this liberty might well be enjoyed at the expense of the satisfaction of the most basic needs of the poor; they just think that liberty always has priority over other political ideals, and because they assume that the liberty of the poor is not at stake in such conflict situations, it is easy for them to conclude that the rich should not be required to sacrifice their liberty so that the basic needs of the poor may be met.

Of course, libertarians allow that it would be nice of the rich to share their surplus goods and resources with the poor. Nevertheless, according to libertarians, such acts of charity cannot be required because the liberty of the poor is not thought to be at stake in such conflict situations.

In fact, however, the liberty of the poor is at stake in such conflict situations. What is at stake is the liberty of the poor not to be interfered with in taking from the surplus possessions of the rich what is necessary to satisfy their basic needs.[3]

Needless to say, libertarians would want to deny that the poor have this liberty. But how could they justify such a denial? As this liberty of the poor has been specified, it is not a positive right to receive something but a negative right of noninterference. Nor will it do for libertarians to appeal to a right to life or a right to property to rule out such a liberty because, on the view under consideration, liberty is basic and all other rights are derived from a right to liberty.[4] Clearly, what libertarians must do is recognize the existence of such a liberty and then claim that it conflicts with other liberties of the rich. But when libertarians see that this is the case, they are often genuinely surprised—one might even say rudely awakened—for they had not previously seen the conflict between the rich and the poor as a conflict of liberties.[5]

When the conflict between the rich and the poor is viewed as a conflict of liberties, either we can say that the rich should have the liberty not to be interfered with in using their surplus goods and resources for luxury purposes or we can say that the poor should have the liberty not to be interfered with in taking from the rich what they require to meet their basic needs. If we choose one liberty, we must reject the other. What needs to be determined, therefore, is which liberty is morally preferable: the liberty of the rich or the liberty of the poor.

Two Principles

To see that the liberty of the poor not to be interfered with in taking from the surplus resources of the rich what is required to meet their basic needs is morally preferable to the liberty of the rich not to be interfered with in using their surplus goods and resources for luxury purposes, we need to appeal to one of the most fundamental principles of morality, one that is common to all political perspectives. This is the "ought" implies "can" principle:

> People are not morally required to do what they lack the power to do or what would involve so great a sacrifice that it would be unreasonable

to ask them to perform such an action, and/or in the case of severe conflicts of interest, unreasonable to require them to perform such an action.

For example, suppose I promised to attend a departmental meeting on Friday, but on Thursday I am involved in a serious car accident that leaves me in a coma. Surely, it is no longer the case that I ought to attend the meeting now that I lack the power to do so. Or suppose instead that on Thursday I develop a severe case of pneumonia for which I am hospitalized. Surely, I could legitimately claim that I cannot attend the meeting, on the grounds that the risk to my health involved in attending is a sacrifice that it would be unreasonable to ask me to bear. Or suppose the risk to my health from having pneumonia is not so serious that it would be unreasonable to ask me to attend the meeting (a supererogatory request), it might still be serious enough to be unreasonable to require my attendance (a demand that is backed up by blame or coercion).

Now, applying the "ought" implies "can" principle to the case at hand, it seems clear that the poor have it within their power willingly to relinquish such an important liberty as the liberty not to be interfered with in taking from the rich what they require to meet their basic needs. Nevertheless, it would be unreasonable to ask or require them to make so great a sacrifice. In the extreme case, it would involve asking or requiring the poor to sit back and starve to death. Of course, the poor may have no real alternative to relinquishing this liberty. To do anything else may involve worse consequences for themselves and their loved ones and may invite a painful death. Accordingly, we may expect that the poor would acquiesce, albeit unwillingly, to a political system that denies them the right to welfare supported by such a liberty, at the same time that we recognize that such a system imposes an unreasonable sacrifice upon the poor—a sacrifice that we cannot morally blame the poor for trying to evade.[6] Analogously, we might expect that a woman whose life was threatened would submit to a rapist's demands, at the same time that we recognize the utter unreasonableness of those demands.

By contrast, it would not be unreasonable to ask and require the rich to sacrifice the liberty to meet some of their luxury needs so that the poor can have the liberty to meet their basic needs.[7] Naturally, we might expect that the rich, for reasons of self-interest and past contribution, might be disinclined to make such a sacrifice. We might even suppose that the past contribution of the rich provides a good reason for not sacrificing their liberty to use their surplus for luxury purposes. Yet, unlike the poor, the rich could not claim that relinquishing such a liberty would involve so great a sacrifice that it would be unreasonable to ask and require them to make it; unlike the poor, the rich could be morally blameworthy for failing to make such a sacrifice.

Notice that by virtue of the "ought" implies "can" principle, this argument establishes that:

> (1a) Since it would be unreasonable to ask or require the poor to sacrifice the liberty not to be interfered with when taking from the surplus goods and resources of the rich what is necessary to meet their basic needs, (1b) it is not the case that the poor are morally required to make such a sacrifice.
>
> (2a) Since it would not be unreasonable to ask and require the rich to sacrifice the liberty not to be interfered with when using their surplus goods and resources for luxury purposes, (2b) it may be the case that the rich are morally required to make such a sacrifice.

What the argument does not establish is that it is the case that the rich are *morally required* to sacrifice (some of) their surplus so that the basic needs of the poor can be met. To establish that conclusion clearly, we need to appeal to a principle that is, in fact, simply the contrapositive of the "ought" implies "can" principle. It is the conflict resolution principle:

> What people are morally required to do is what is either reasonable to ask them to do or, in the case of severe conflicts of interest, reasonable to require them to do.

Although the "ought" implies "can" principle claims that if any action is *not reasonable to ask or require* a person to do, all things considered, that action is *not morally required* for that person, all things considered [–R(A v Re) → –MRe], the conflict resolution principle claims that if any action is *morally required* for a person to do, all things considered, that action is *reasonable to ask or require* that person to do, all things considered [MRe → R(A v Re)].

The conflict resolution principle accords with the generally accepted view of morality as a system of reasons for resolving interpersonal conflicts of interest. Of course, morality is not limited to such a system of reasons.

Most surely, it also includes reasons of self-development. All that is being claimed by the principle is that moral resolutions of interpersonal conflicts of interest cannot be contrary to reason to ask everyone affected to accept or, in the case of severe interpersonal conflicts of interest, unreasonable to require everyone affected to accept. The reason for the distinction between the two kinds of cases is that when interpersonal conflicts of interest are not severe, moral resolutions must still be reasonable to ask everyone affected to accept, but they need not be reasonable to *require* everyone affected to accept. This is because not all moral resolutions can be justifiably enforced; only moral resolutions of severe interpersonal conflicts of interest can and *should* be justifiably enforced. Furthermore, the reason why moral resolutions of severe interpersonal conflicts of interest should be enforced is that if the parties are simply asked but not required to abide by a moral resolution in such cases of conflict, then it is likely that the stronger party will violate the resolution and that would be unreasonable to ask or require the weaker party to accept.

When we apply the conflict resolution principle to our example of severe conflict between the rich and the poor, there are three possible moral resolutions.

I. A moral resolution that would require the rich to sacrifice the liberty not to be interfered with when using their surplus goods and resources for luxury purposes so that the poor can have the liberty not to be interfered with when taking from the surplus resources of the rich what is necessary to meet their basic needs.

II. A moral resolution that would require the poor to sacrifice the liberty not to be interfered with when taking from the surplus goods and resources of the rich what is necessary to meet their basic needs so that the rich can have the liberty not to be interfered with when using their surplus resources for luxury purposes.

III. A moral resolution that would require the rich and the poor to accept the results of a power struggle in which both the rich and the poor are at liberty to appropriate and use the surplus goods and resources of the rich.

Applying our previous discussion of the "ought" implies "can" principle to these three possible moral resolutions, it is clear that 1a (it would be unreasonable to ask or require the poor . . .) rules out II, but 2a (it would not be unreasonable to ask and require the rich . . .) does not rule out I. But what about III? Some libertarians have contended that III is the proper resolution of severe conflicts of interest between the rich and the poor.[8] But a resolution, like III, that sanctions the results of a power struggle between the rich and the poor is a resolution that, by and large, favors the rich over the poor. So all things considered, it would be no more reasonable to require the poor to accept III than it would be to require them to accept II. This means that only I satisfies the conflict resolution principle by being a resolution that is reasonable to require everyone affected to accept. Consequently, if we assume that however else we specify the requirements of morality, they cannot violate the "ought" implies "can" principle or the conflict resolution principle, it follows that despite what libertarians claim, the basic right to liberty endorsed by them, as determined by a weighing of the relevant competing liberties according to these two principles, actually favors the liberty of the poor over the liberty of the rich.[9]

Yet, couldn't libertarians object to this conclusion, claiming that it would be unreasonable to require the rich to sacrifice the liberty to meet some of their luxury needs so that the poor could have the liberty to meet their basic needs? As has been pointed out, libertarians don't usually see the situation as a conflict of liberties, but suppose they did. How plausible would such an objection be? Not very plausible at all.

Consider: What are libertarians going to say about the poor? Isn't it clearly unreasonable to require the poor to sacrifice the liberty to meet their basic needs so that the rich can have the liberty to meet their luxury needs? Isn't it clearly unreasonable to require the poor to sit back and starve to death? If it is, then there is no resolution of this conflict that would be reasonable to require both the rich and the poor to accept. But that would mean that libertarians could not be putting forth a moral resolution because according to the conflict resolution principle, in cases of severe conflict of interest, a moral resolution resolves conflicts of interest in ways that it would be reasonable to require everyone affected to accept. Therefore, as long as libertarians think of themselves as putting forth a moral resolution for cases of severe conflict of interest, they cannot allow that it would be unreasonable *both* to require the rich to sacrifice the liberty to meet some of their luxury needs in order to benefit the poor and to require the poor to sacrifice the liberty to meet their basic needs in order to benefit the rich. But I submit that if one of these requirements is to be judged reasonable, then, by any neutral assessment, it must be the requirement that the rich sacrifice the liberty to meet some of their luxury needs so that the poor can have the liberty to meet their basic needs. There is no other plausible resolution if libertarians intend to be putting forth a moral resolution.

It should also be noted that this case for restricting the liberty of the rich depends upon the willingness of the poor to take advantage of whatever opportunities are available to them to engage in mutually beneficial work, so that failure of the poor to take advantage of such opportunities would normally cancel or at least significantly reduce the obligation of the rich to restrict their own liberty for the benefit of the poor.[10] In addition, the poor would be required to return the equivalent of any surplus possessions they have taken from the rich once they are able to do so and still satisfy their basic needs. Nor would the poor be required to keep the liberty to which they are entitled. They could give up part of it, or all of it, or risk losing it on the chance of gaining a greater share of liberties or other social goods.[11] Consequently, the case for restricting the liberty of the rich for the benefit of the poor is neither unconditional nor inalienable.

Of course, there will be cases in which the poor fail to satisfy their basic needs, not because of any direct restriction of liberty on the part of the rich but because the poor are in such dire need that they are unable even to attempt to take from the rich what they require to meet their basic needs. In such cases, the rich would not be performing any act of commission that would prevent the poor from taking what they require. Yet, even in such cases, the rich would normally be performing acts of commission that would prevent other persons from taking part of the rich's own surplus possessions and using it to aid the poor. And when assessed from a moral point of view, restricting the liberty of these allies or agents of the poor would not be morally justified for the very same reason that restricting the liberty of the poor to meet their own basic needs would not be morally justified: it would not be reasonable to require all of those affected to accept such a restriction of liberty.

In brief, I have argued that a libertarian ideal of liberty can be seen to support a right to welfare through an application of the "ought" implies "can" principle and the conflict resolution principle to conflicts of liberty between the rich and the poor. In this interpretation of libertarianism, these principles support a right to welfare by favoring the liberty of the poor over the liberty of the rich. In another interpretation of libertarianism (developed elsewhere), these principles support this right to welfare by favoring a conditional right to property over an unconditional right to property.[12] In either interpretation, what is crucial to the derivation of this right is the claim that it would be unreasonable to require the poor to deny their basic needs and accept anything less than this right to welfare as the condition for their willing cooperation.

Now, it might be objected that the right to welfare that this argument establishes from libertarian premises is not the same as the right to welfare endorsed by socialists. This is correct. We could mark this difference by referring to the right that this argument establishes as "a negative welfare right" and by referring to the right endorsed by socialists as "a positive welfare right." The significance of this difference is that a person's negative welfare right can be violated only when other people through acts of commission interfere with its exercise, whereas a person's positive welfare right can be violated not only by such acts of commission but by acts of omission as well. Nonetheless, this difference will have little practical import, for in recognizing the legitimacy of negative welfare rights, libertarians will come to see that virtually any use of their surplus possessions is likely to violate the negative welfare rights of the poor by preventing the poor from rightfully appropriating (some part of) their surplus goods and resources. So, to ensure that they will not be engaging in such wrongful actions, it will be incumbent on them to set up institutions guaranteeing adequate positive welfare rights for the poor. Only then will they be able legitimately to use any remaining surplus possessions to meet their own nonbasic needs. Furthermore, in the absence of adequate positive welfare rights, the poor, either acting by themselves or through their allies or agents, would have some discretion in determining when and how to exercise their negative welfare rights.[13] In order not to be subject to that discretion, libertarians will tend to favor the only morally legitimate way of preventing the exercise of such rights: they will set up institutions guaranteeing adequate positive welfare rights that will then take precedence over the exercise of negative welfare rights. For these reasons, recognizing the negative welfare rights of the poor will ultimately lead libertarians to endorse the same sort of welfare institutions favored by socialists.

II

Now, it is possible that libertarians convinced to some extent by the previous argument might want to accept a right to welfare but then deny that this would lead to anything like a socialist state. After all, the fundamental rights recognized by libertarians are universal rights, that is, rights possessed by all people, not just those who live in certain places or at certain times. Of course, to claim that these rights are universal rights does not mean that they are universally recognized. Obviously, the fundamental rights that flow from the libertarian ideal have not been universally recognized. Rather, to claim that they are universal rights, despite their spotty recognition, implies only that they ought to be recognized at all times and places by people who have or could have had good reasons to recognize these rights, whether or not they actually do or did so. Nor need these universal rights be unconditional. This is particularly true in the case of the right to welfare, which, I have argued, is conditional on people doing all that they legitimately can to provide for themselves. In addition, this right is conditional on there being sufficient goods and resources available so that everyone's welfare needs can be met. So where people do not do all that they can to provide for themselves or where there are not sufficient goods and resources available, people simply do not have a right to welfare. Still, libertarians might grant that there are universal rights, even a right to welfare, that can be supported by the libertarian ideal of liberty but still deny that such rights lead to a socialist rather than a welfare state. But to see why this is not the case, consider what would be required to recognize a universal right to welfare.

Consider that at present there is probably a sufficient worldwide supply of goods and resources to meet the normal costs of satisfying the basic nutritional needs of all existing persons. According to a former U.S. secretary of agriculture, Bob Bergland, "For the past 20 years, if the available world food supply had been evenly divided and distributed, each person would have received more than the minimum number of calories."[14] Other authorities have made similar assessments of the available world food supply. Needless to say, the adoption of a policy of supporting a right to welfare for all existing persons would necessitate significant changes, especially in developed countries. For example, the large percentage of the U.S. population whose food consumption clearly exceeds even an adequately adjusted poverty index would have to alter their eating habits substantially. In particular, they would have to reduce their consumption of beef and pork in order to make more grain available for direct human consumption. (Currently, the amount of grain fed to U.S. livestock is as much as all the people of China and India eat in a year.) Thus, at least the satisfaction of some of the nonbasic needs of the more advantaged in developed countries would have to be forgone if the basic nutritional needs of all persons in developing and underdeveloped countries are to be met. Of course, meeting the long-term basic nutritional needs of these societies will require other kinds of aid, including appropriate technology and training and the removal of trade barriers favoring developed societies.[15] Furthermore, to raise the standard of living in developing and underdeveloped countries will require substantial increases in the consumption of energy and other resources. But such increases would have to be matched by substantial decreases in the consumption of these goods in developed countries; otherwise, global ecological disaster would result from increased global warming, ozone depletion, and acid rain, lowering virtually everyone's standard of living.[16]

In addition, once the basic nutritional needs of future generations are also taken into account, the satisfaction of the nonbasic needs of the more advantaged in developed countries would have to be further restricted in order to preserve the fertility of cropland and other food-related natural resources for the use of future generations. Obviously, the only assured way to guarantee the energy and resources necessary for the satisfaction of the basic needs of future generations is to set aside resources that would otherwise be used to satisfy the nonbasic needs of existing generations.

Once basic needs other than nutritional needs are taken into account as well, still further restrictions would be required. For example, it has been estimated that presently a North American uses fifty times more goods and resources than a person living in India. This means that in terms of resource consumption, the North American continent's population is the equivalent of 12.5 billion Indians. So unless we assume that basic goods and resources, such as arable land, iron, coal, oil, and so forth, are in unlimited supply, this unequal consumption would have to be radically altered if the basic needs of distant peoples and future generations are to be met. Accordingly, recognizing a universal right to welfare applicable both to distant peoples and to future generations would lead to an equal sharing of goods and resources over place and time. In short, socialist equality is the consequence of recognizing a universal libertarian right to welfare.

In brief, I have argued that when a libertarian ideal of liberty is correctly interpreted, it leads to a universal right to welfare and further that the recognition of this right leads to the equality in the distribution of goods and resources that is characteristic of a socialist state. Of course, the libertarian ideal, unlike the socialist ideal, does not directly pursue the goal of (substantive) equality.[17] Nevertheless, I contend that the practical effect of both ideals is much the same.

III

In his book *Individuals and Their Rights*, Tibor Machan criticizes the preceding argument that a libertarian ideal of liberty leads to a right to welfare, accepting its theoretical thrust but denying its practical significance.[18] He appreciates the force of the argument enough to grant that if the type of conflict cases that we have described between the rich and the poor actually obtained, the poor would have a right to welfare. But he denies that such cases—in which the poor have done all that they legitimately can to satisfy their basic needs in a libertarian society—actually obtain: "Normally," he writes, "persons do not lack the opportunities and resources to satisfy their basic needs" (107).

But this response virtually concedes everything that the preceding argument intended to establish, for the poor's right to welfare is not claimed to be unconditional. Rather, it is said to be conditional principally upon the poor doing all that they legitimately can to meet their own basic needs. So it follows that only when the poor lack sufficient opportunity to satisfy their own basic needs would their right to welfare have any practical moral force. Accordingly, on libertarian grounds, Machan has conceded the legitimacy of just the kind of right to welfare that the preceding argument hoped to establish.

The only difference that remains is a practical one. Machan thinks that virtually all of the poor have sufficient opportunities and resources to satisfy their basic needs and that, therefore, a right to welfare has no practical moral force. In contrast, I think that many of the poor do not have sufficient opportunities and resources to satisfy their basic needs and that, therefore, a right to welfare has considerable practical moral force.

But isn't this practical disagreement resolvable? Who could deny that most of the 1.2 billion people who are currently living in conditions of absolute poverty[19] "lack the opportunities and resources to satisfy their basic needs"? And even within our own country, it is estimated that some 32 million Americans live below the official poverty index, and that one-fifth of American children are growing up in poverty (29). Surely, it is impossible to deny that many of these Americans also "lack the opportunities and resources to satisfy their basic needs." Given the impossibility of reasonably denying these factual claims, Machan would have to concede that the right to welfare, which he grants can be theoretically established on libertarian premises, also has practical moral force.

If we turn to Narveson's recent work on libertarianism, we find a number of points of disagreement with my preceding analysis and argument. First, Narveson starts out with a slightly different definition of liberty.[20] Second, he seems to deny that one person's liberty can come into conflict with another person's liberty.[21] Third, he rejects my use of the "ought" implies "can" principle and the conflict resolution principle in favor of a Hobbesian social contract to determine what legitimate liberty people have.[22] Fourth, he maintains that the ideals of liberty and equality are incompatible because liberty is a negative ideal requiring that people not do certain things while equality is a positive ideal requiring that people do certain things.[23] Let me consider each of these points in turn.

In his recent work, Narveson offers a slightly different definition of liberty that further restricts liberty to the absence of *intentional* interference by other people.[24] Now, it is true that people are clearly more responsible for actions they do intentionally, and this may be why Narveson restricts liberty in this way. Nevertheless, people can still be responsible for actions they do unintentionally, especially if they were morally negligent and should have foreseen the consequences of their actions. Given, then, that moral responsibility can extend to both intentional and unintentional interference with a person's life, it seems best to consider both types of interference to be restrictions of a person's liberty.

Narveson also seems to deny that one person's liberty can come into conflict with another person's liberty. He states that "in a libertarian state, nobody's liberty 'takes precedence over' anybody else's, rich or poor, tall or short."[25] Thus, Narveson seems to deny that there is a conflict between the liberty of the rich and the liberty of the poor on which my previous argument depends. However, elsewhere Narveson does admit to conflicts of liberty of a certain sort. He writes:

> We should, of course, bear in mind that all rights restrict liberty. In saying that someone has a right to do something, what we are saying is that someone else may not do certain things, and if necessary may be compelled to refrain from them. The libertarian case is that the fundamental right is a right to liberty, but in being so it is automatically a prohibition of the liberty to do certain things: namely, acts that infringe liberty. It has been difficult, down through the years, for critics of libertarianism to understand this point, and I regret to say that it appears that Sterba likewise, despite his rather clear characterization of much of the theory, does not fully appreciate it either. The fact that it is the liberty of the poor to take from the rich

> that is being restricted, then, it does not follow that what we have is a clash of liberties in the relevant sense: namely a clash of liberties that the theory protects. It is, instead, a clash between a familiar kind of liberty that it is the very essence of the theory to forbid and another kind of liberty that it is the very essence of the theory to protect.[26]

Actually, it turns out that Narveson and I are really in agreement here. We agree that there is a sense in which there is, and a sense in which there is not, a conflict of liberty between the rich and the poor. We think there is a conflict because we agree that either the rich or the poor is going to be interfered with. We think there is not a conflict because we agree that only one of them has the relevant legitimate liberty. Of course, Narveson and I disagree over who it is who has the relevant legitimate liberty—Narveson claims the rich have it; I claim the poor have it—yet we both agree that this legitimate liberty does not conflict with any other legitimate liberty.

It is also important to note that the liberty of the poor, the legitimacy of which Narveson and I are contesting, is more precisely characterized as "the liberty of the poor not to be interfered with in taking from the surplus possessions of the rich what the poor require to meet their basic needs" rather than simply as "the liberty of the poor to take from the rich." The advantage of this more precise characterization is that it makes it abundantly clear that we are trying to determine the legitimacy of a negative rather than a positive liberty of the poor.

In trying to determine what legitimate liberty people have, Narveson, at least initially, did not realize that he and I are appealing to different standards.[27] This is because he interpreted my "ought" implies "can" principle and its contrapositive, the conflict resolution principle, to be equivalent to his Hobbesian social contract. To some degree this is understandable, given that Narveson has formulated his Hobbesian social contract standard in ways that resemble my two principles.[28] He says, for example, "To have the *right* to something you are using is for there to be good and sufficient reasons why everyone ought to let you do so."[29] And, in another place, he says that the "criterion of betterness is that better principles are more acceptable to people" (15). And, in still another place, he suggests that "we should expect support for our theory from the people to whom it is addressed: namely, everybody" (7). So in light of these statements, one might think Narveson is agreeing with me that the proper distribution of liberties cannot be unreasonable to require the rich and the poor to accept (as my "ought" implies "can" principle demands), or put positively, that the proper distribution of basic liberties must be reasonable to require both the rich and the poor to accept (as my conflict resolution principle demands). The crucial difference, however, is that my two principles, as I interpret them, impose a moral constraint on what legitimate liberty people have, whereas Narveson's Hobbesian social contract imposes only a self-interested constraint on what legitimate liberty people have.[30] According to Narveson, a distribution of liberty in society passes muster only if it does not work against the self-interest of anyone, whereas my two principles, as I interpret them, approve of distributions of liberty even when they work against the self-interest of some, provided that the degree of self-sacrifice or altruism that is required happens to be morally acceptable.[31]

Nor is my interpretation of the "ought" implies "can" principle and its contrapositive, the conflict resolution principle, in any way unusual in this regard. Most philosophers, libertarians included, do not think, as Narveson does, that morality can be founded on Hobbesian self-interest, and so they would be inclined to interpret my two principles so that they do require a certain degree of altruism.[32]

Moreover, even if we wanted to ground political obligation on Hobbesian self-interest, it is far from clear that we would end up with a justification for the libertarian society that Narveson envisions. Narveson is quick to point out that from his Hobbesian premises the needs of the poor may not, and usually will not, be a consideration to which the rich give any credence. But, for similar reasons, the fact that the rich got somewhere first and were first to mix their labor with something will not be considerations that from a Hobbesian perspective the poor must give any credence to either. From a Hobbesian perspective, everything is determined by the payoffs to each from various forms of cooperation and noncooperation. So unless the rich have invested heavily in their defense, it may turn out to be in the self-interest of the poor to take from the rich as much as they want. From a Hobbesian perspective, everything is determined by one's relative threat advantage. So, on Narveson's view, whether the poor have a right to welfare depends on what power relations happen to obtain between the rich and the poor, and what the rich and the poor have to gain or lose from using the power they have. Thus, Narveson, commenting on an example that I used in an earlier paper, claims that D (a she that Narveson for some reason turns into a he) is lucky that A, B, and C don't run an arrow through her to eliminate any possible threat to what they claim to be their property.[33] But a similar argument could be made whenever the poor are powerful enough to threaten or dominate the rich or talented effectively. So it seems that even on Narveson's view, a welfare state, or possibly even a socialist state, could emerge, depending on the prevailing power relations.

Fortunately, there is a way to show the preferability of the moral standard of the two principles over the Hobbesian standard that Narveson endorses. What needs to be shown is that the morality of the two principles is rationally preferable to Hobbesian self-interest. To show this, I have argued at length elsewhere that a conception of rationality that is acceptable to rational egoists because it presupposes nothing more than non-question-beggingness requires that we strike a compromise between egoism and altruism and favor high-ranking altruistic reasons over low-ranking self-interested reasons and high-ranking self-interested reasons over low-ranking altruistic reasons. More specifically, this conception of rationality requires the rejection of pure egoism in favor of the degree of altruism found in the two principles as I interpret them.

Although I cannot restate this argument here, I should point out that Narveson's only response to it is to claim that we must address our justification to people where they are, and since where at least some people are is committed to pure egoism, Narveson claims we must show that whatever rights we propose best serve the interests of these pure egoists.[34] Yet, in response, it can be argued that either pure egoists are committed to rationality or they are not committed to rationality. If they are committed to rationality, at least to the minimal rationality of non-question-beggingness, then what my argument shows is that they need to abandon their commitment to pure egoism. And if they are not committed to rationality, even to the minimal rationality of non-question-beggingness, then it is not clear how we could justify anything to them. Thus, insofar as it is possible to justify anything to pure egoists, I claim that my argument from non-question-beggingness succeeds in showing that they must abandon their pure egoism in favor of the degree of altruism found in my two principles as I interpret them.

Narveson thinks that the ideals of liberty and equality are incompatible because the ideal of liberty is a negative ideal requiring that people not interfere in certain ways with one another, whereas the ideal of equality is a positive ideal requiring that people *do* certain things to bring about equality in society.[35] But even accepting for the sake of argument that it is proper to characterize liberty as a negative ideal and equality as a positive ideal,[36] what the argument of this paper shows is that the two ideals can still be reconciled in practice. This is because the pattern of commissions or interferences that the ideal of equality requires is in fact justified or required by the pattern of omissions or noninterferences that the libertarian ideal requires. As I argued before, in recognizing the legitimacy of negative welfare rights, libertarians will come to see that virtually any use of their surplus possessions is likely to violate the negative welfare rights of the poor by preventing the poor from rightfully appropriating (some part of) their surplus goods and resources. Consequently, to ensure that they will not be engaging in such wrongful actions, it will be incumbent on them to institute adequate positive welfare rights for the poor. Only then will they be able to use legitimately any remaining surplus possessions to meet their own nonbasic needs. Likewise, in the absence of adequate positive welfare rights, the poor, either acting by themselves or through their allies or agents, would have some discretion in determining when and how to exercise their negative welfare rights. Thus, in order not to be subject to that discretion, libertarians will tend to favor the only morally legitimate way of preventing the exercise of such rights: they will to set up institutions guaranteeing adequate positive welfare rights that will then take precedence over the exercise of negative welfare rights. In this way, the negative rights of the libertarian's ideal of liberty will justify or require the positive rights of a socialist ideal of equality.

In sum, what I have argued is that the libertarian ideal of liberty supports the practical requirements that are usually associated with the socialist ideal of equality, and for this reason, libertarians must be socialists. I have also attempted to show that recent work done by libertarians Tibor Machan and Jan Narveson neither undercuts nor is incompatible with this argument for reconciling liberty with equality.

Notes

I would like to thank Joan Callahan, David Duquette, Joseph Ellin, Sidney Geldin, Carol Gould, Larry May, Jan Narveson, David Phillips, Jonathan Schonsheck, and Carl Wellman for helpful comments on earlier versions of this chapter.

1. See John Hospers, *Libertarianism* (Los Angeles: Nash Press, 1971).

2. Basic needs, if not satisfied, lead to significant lacks or deficiencies with respect to a standard of mental and physical well-being, Thus, a person's needs for food, shelter, medical care, protection, companionship, and self-development are, at least in part,

needs of this sort. For a discussion of basic needs, see my *How to Make People Just* (Totowa, N.J.: Rowman & Littlefield, 1988), 45–48.

3. It is not being assumed here that the surplus possessions of the rich are either justifiable or unjustifiably possessed by the rich. Moreover, according to libertarians, it is an assessment of the liberties involved that determines whether the possession is justifiable.

4. There is another interpretation of libertarianism, according to which a particular set of rights are basic, and liberty is interpreted as the absence of interference with these rights. But as I have argued elsewhere, the same sort of argument works against both forms of libertarianism. For this interpretation, see "From Liberty to Welfare," *Ethics* (1994): 89–109, and my *How to Make People Just*, chap. 5.

5. See Hospers, *Libertarianism*, chap. 7; and Tibor Machan, *Human Rights and Human Liberties* (Chicago: Nelson-Hall, 1975), 231ff.

6. See James P. Sterba, "Is There a Rationale for Punishment?" *American Journal of Jurisprudence* 29 (1984): 29–43.

7. By the liberty of the rich to meet their luxury needs, I continue to mean the liberty of the rich not to be interfered with when using their surplus possessions for luxury purposes. Similarly, by the liberty of the poor to meet their basic needs I continue to mean the liberty of the poor not to be interfered with when taking what they require to meet their basic needs from the surplus possessions of the rich.

8. See, for example, Eric Mack, "Individualism, Rights and the Open Society," in *The Libertarian Alternative*, ed. Tibor Machan (Chicago: Nelson-Hall, 1974).

9. Because the conflict resolution principle is the contrapositive of the "ought" implies "can" principle, whatever logically follows from the one principle logically follows from the other. Nevertheless, by first appealing to the one principle and then the other, as I have here, I maintain that the conclusions that I derive can be seen to follow more clearly.

10. The employment opportunities offered to the poor must be honorable and supportive of self-respect. If otherwise, the poor would be offered opportunities to meet some of their basic needs at the cost of denying some of their other basic needs.

11. The poor cannot, however, give up the liberty to which their children are entitled.

12. For this other interpretation, see note 4, supra.

13. When the poor are acting collectively in conjunction with their agents and allies to exercise their negative welfare rights, they will want, in turn, to institute adequate positive welfare rights to secure a proper distribution of the goods and resources they are acquiring.

14. Bob Bergland, "Attacking the Problem of World Hunger," *National Forum* 69, no. 2 (1979): 4.

15. Henry Shue, *Basic Rights* (Princeton: Princeton University Press, 1980), chap. 7.

16. For a discussion of these causal connections, see Cheryl Silver, *One Earth, One Future* (Washington, D.C.: National Academy Press, 1990); Bill McKibben, *The End of Nature* (New York: Anchor Books, 1989); Jeremy Leggett, ed., *Global Warming* (New

York: Oxford University Press, 1990); Lester Brown, ed., *The World Watch Reader* (New York: Nelson, 1991).

17. Here I agree with Narveson that there are formal notions of equality, like equality before the law and equality of basic rights, that libertarians will frequently aim to achieve.

18. Tibor Machan, *Individuals and Their Rights* (La Salle, Ill.: Open Court, 1989), 100–111.

19. Alan Durning, "Life on the Brink," *World Watch* 3, no. 2 (1990): 24.

20. Jan Narveson, *The Libertarian Idea* (Philadelphia: Temple University Press, 1988), 20–21, and in his contribution to this volume.

21. Jan Narveson, "Revisiting the Excursion from Liberty to Equality with Jim Sterba" (circulated paper, 1994), 2.

22. Narveson, *The Libertarian Idea,* chap. 14.

23. Ibid., 61, 266–67, and in his contribution to this volume.

24. Narveson, *The Libertarian Idea,* 20–21, and in his contribution to this volume.

25. Narveson, "Revisiting the Excursion from Liberty to Equality with Jim Sterba," 2.

26. Jan Narveson, "Comments on Sterba's Ethics Article" (circulated paper, 1994), 7. See also Narveson, *The Libertarian Idea,* 35.

27. Jan Narveson, "Sterba on Reconciling Conceptions of Justice" (circulated paper, April 24, 1992), Narveson's commentary on my symposium paper presented at the Central Division American Philosophical Association Meeting, Louisville, 1992.

28. I was so struck by the resemblance that in some of my recent work I claimed that Narveson was actually endorsing these two principles the way I interpret them, for example, in my 1992 APA symposium paper "Reconciling Conceptions of Justice," which was published in James P. Sterba et al., eds., *Morality and Social Justice* (Totowa, N.J.: Rowman & Littlefield, 1994).

29. Jan Narveson, "Property Rights: Original Acquisition and Lockean Provisos" (circulated paper, 1991), 11.

30. I made this abundantly clear in my response to Narveson at the Central Division American Philosophical Association Meeting in 1992. Unfortunately, he persists in making this same misinterpretation; for example, see his contribution to this volume.

31. Narveson criticizes political moralities for not satisfying the interests of rational egoists. I criticize rational egoism for not meeting its own rationality requirements. For my argument, see *How to Make People Just,* chap. 11, "From Rationality to Morality."

32. For example, John Rawls simply dismisses Hobbesian egoism out of hand in *A Theory of Justice* (Cambridge: Harvard University Press, 1971), 124, 130–36, and many philosophers have followed his lead, despite its arbitrariness. Among libertarians, I think the work of Tibor Machan is typical here. He distinguishes between an Aristotelian grounding for libertarian rights, which he accepts, and a Hobbesian grounding for these rights, which he rejects. See his *Individuals and Their Rights,* 35.

33. Narveson, "Sterba on Reconciling Conceptions of Justice," 10.

34. Jan Narveson, "Comments on 'From Rationality to Morality'" (circulated paper, December 23, 1993). This response has been reiterated in subsequent conversations.

35. Narveson, *The Libertarian Idea*, 61, 266–67, and in his contribution to this volume.

36. As I noted before, liberty can be characterized as a positive ideal. Likewise, equality can be characterized as a negative ideal, as in interpretations of equal opportunity where the ideal is that certain unfair constraints not be imposed on candidates for various positions.

Chapter 3

The Foundations of Ethics and the Conflict between Liberty and Equality

David Phillips

In this chapter I formulate and consider the presuppositions of an important argument linking liberty to equality. The argument claims that liberty is valuable only if it is effective and that under many kinds of social conditions, some measure of egalitarian redistribution is required to maximize the overall value of liberty. Hence, one who values liberty must also favor such redistribution. To make this argument is to accept a certain kind of moral perspective,[1] which I shall call "the impartial consequentialist perspective." Some libertarians, like Loren Lomasky,[2] accept this perspective and still try to argue that liberty is specially valuable. I shall criticize such arguments. Others, like David Gauthier[3] and Jan Narveson,[4] reject this perspective and argue for an alternative "foundationalist" moral perspective. I shall argue that this kind of foundationalism should be rejected because it cannot justify enough of (what we ordinarily think of as) morality. Thus, I will argue that someone who values liberty and adopts the most plausible moral perspective must also favor some measure of egalitarian redistribution.

The Argument That Valuable Liberty Requires Equality

The egalitarian principles I have in mind are principles mandating equality in wealth and income, the kind of clearly redistributable goods that are useful in pursuing many different forms of the good life. But not only principles mandating equality (no matter what) should be thought of as egalitarian. Instead, in accordance with an important and familiar understanding of these matters, I suggest we count as egalitarian any principle that legitimates the overriding of the liberty or property rights of some to provide wealth and/or income for others. There are, then, egalitarian principles of various "strengths." The principle built into many utilitarian and consequentialist views, that everyone's interests count equally in evaluating the goodness of states of affairs, is in this sense an egalitarian principle. Another relatively weak sort of principle requires that everyone get a decent minimum of resources. There are, then, a number of versions of broadly Rawlsian difference principles,[5] including ones that count *only* the interests of the worst-off group and ones that give the satisfaction of these interests *lexical priority* over the interests of the next-worst-off group, and so on. Weaker than these, and in some respects weaker than the principle requiring a decent minimum, is one that merely gives *great weight* to the interests of the worst-off group.

I shall use *liberty*, in accordance with the usual understanding of "negative" liberty, to refer to various sorts of freedom from interference and coercion. Let us assume that such liberty is (sometimes) valuable. We then need an account of *why* and *under what conditions* liberty, so defined, is valuable. The obvious kind of answer is, liberty is valuable because it helps us live a life good according to our own conception.[6] This idea is suggested, among others, by Mill, when he writes: "The only freedom which deserves the name is that of pursuing our own good in our own way,"[7] and by Rawls in placing liberties among the "primary goods," which "normally have a use whatever a person's rational plan of life."[8] But if we give this sort of answer,[9] then we see that liberty alone will not be sufficient to secure this good life for us; I may be entirely free from interference, but if I have insufficient food and no opportunity to obtain food, I am in no position to live a good life. What makes liberty valuable is that it contributes to our ability to achieve our goals and live a good life. But coercion and interference are not the only things that stop us from achieving our goals. A lack of resources may have just the same effect. So, the (familiar kind of) argument goes, to make liberty valuable, we need to make it effective. My liberty to do something is effective if I am prevented from doing it by neither coercion nor interference, *nor* by lack of resources.[10] My liberty is valuable only if it is effective. The same is true of everyone else. Hence, to maximize the value of liberty, we need to give as many people as possible effective liberty. And that is likely, under many kinds of social conditions, to require a fairly equal distribution of resources.

The perspective from which I make this argument is an impartial and consequentialist one. If liberty (*contra* my argument) is to be shown to be uniquely important, or liberty rights to be uniquely justifiable,[11] this must be done by showing that the greatest *overall* amount of valuable liberty will be secured by giving liberty this unique importance, or by recognizing *only* liberty rights. I allow the proponent of liberty to give any plausible account of what makes liberty valuable, then ask if privileging liberty or liberty rights will secure the greatest overall amount of this sort of value. This impartial consequentialist perspective is attractive, partly because of its apparent weakness. If liberty cannot be shown to be uniquely valuable from this perspective, that is a significant blow to libertarianism. But the impartial consequentialist perspective certainly does require one crucial presupposition: the presupposition that one can do moral theory and moral justification by thinking about value, that is, value "*from the point of view of the universe*" (as Sidgwick puts it).[12] An important alternative "foundationalist" perspective, taken by contractarians, rejects the notion of impartial value, at least as a basic notion in moral theory. The basic notion is instead one of value *to an individual*, and moral justification of some scheme must then amount to showing that that scheme is advantageous to each individual.

Responses to the Argument within the Impartial Consequentalist Perspective

Libertarians might pursue at least three different strategies in response to my argument that if it is to be valuable, liberty requires some measure of equality. The first two strategies might be taken while accepting the impartial consequentialist perspective. First, libertarians might deny the sort of account of the value of liberty I suggested and argue that liberty (noninterference) is valuable on its own. Second, they might argue that even though liberty is valuable only when it is effective, there is still good reason to accord rights to noninterference a special status. The third strategy is to reject the impartial consequentialist perspective, and to argue for an alternative approach to moral theory.[13]

I see no plausibility whatever in the first strategy. Freedom from interference certainly is valuable. But it is just as certain that freedom from interference is of little value in isolation: if I am starving and desperate, it may be of some comfort to me to be protected from interference and coercion,[14] but this liberty will not alone make my life valuable or even worth living. It is difficult to conceive of a view on which freedom from interference does not become part of an immensely more valuable whole when combined with sufficient resources to pursue a range of kinds of life reasonably considered to be valuable.

The second strategy is a more interesting one. It is developed by Loren Lomasky in *Persons, Rights and the Moral Community*.[15] Lomasky considers an argument for "welfare liberalism" that has the same flavor as the argument I have been considering:[16]

> To judge an interest *important* is to judge that it should be *met*. Simply to eliminate a group of obstacles to its attainment will be of value only when those are the only obstacles. It is small comfort to a person who lacks some vitally important good G to be informed that he hascomplete liberty to pursue G if possession of that liberty is insufficient to ensure his attainment of G. Liberties that are unaccompanied by the ability to make effective use of the liberty are of negligible value. (93)

Lomasky then argues that "if a cogent case is to be made for classical liberalism, it will have to meet the charge that assigning favored status to liberty rights is morally arbitrary" (94).

Lomasky pursues two lines of argument. The first asserts that liberty rights are typically *less costly* than welfare rights: "An argument for a liberty right can go through in circumstances where the argument for a corresponding welfare right does not . . . when a bona fide interest has been established" (94–95) but where the cost to a representative individual of acknowledging a welfare right to some good G exceeds the cost to a representative individual of acknowledging a liberty right to G, and the moral weight to the representative individual of the interest in G falls in between. Lomasky goes on to give some intuitively plausible examples of cases where the cost of welfare rights *does* apparently exceed the cost of liberty rights. But he acknowledges that there are cases where welfare rights are *not* severe impositions. For someone who accepts the impartial consequentialist perspective, it will be a partly empirical question to what extent the value of liberty can be maximized by overriding the liberty rights of some to secure to others the basic resources required for their liberty to be effective. Many will be persuaded that such liberty rights will need often and systematically to be overridden to secure the most overall value of the kind to which liberty contributes.

Lomasky doesn't limit his argument for the primacy of liberty rights to these claims about cost. He also argues that liberty has a combination of properties that make it a unique good: it "must be provided by others if it is to be enjoyed at all" (97); it is *universal* "in the sense that it is of value to every project pursuer"; it is *general* "in the sense that it is valued irrespective of the nature of the ends one intends to advance"; and "it is needed *from everyone*" (98).

Let us grant that liberty is unique in combining these features; the question still remains what this shows about the unique *value* of liberty or place of liberty rights. Lomasky's argument (99)[17] appeals to a conception of practical reason, according to which if I have an end, you have some reason to promote this end, but not as weighty a reason as I have. Let "C" be a condition necessary for the attainment of this end. Then Lomasky argues that if C is something I *could* provide myself, then giving me a right against you for its provision puts an equal burden on you to provide it, and that to do this is "at odds with the essentially individuated character of practical reason." The same objection cannot be made with respect to liberty because liberty isn't something I could provide myself.

This argument is unconvincing. The problem is that the fact that it is *logically possible* for me to provide a certain kind of good myself seems to matter little if it is *impossible in practice* for me to do so. The argument for welfare rights that Lomasky has been considering claims plausibly that it is sometimes impossible in practice for people to gain the resources to make their liberty rights effective. If it is, that seems a good justification for welfare rights; observations about the logical character of resources vis-à-vis liberty seem beside the point. It should also be noticed that in its reliance on an agent-relative conception of reason, this argument abandons the impartial consequentialist perspective.

Foundationalism versus the Impartial Consequentialist Perspective

The third strategy available to the person who wishes to reject the argument we are considering and to assert the primacy of liberty rights is to reject the impartial consequentialist perspective and take an alternative approach to moral justification. Such is the foundationalist and contractarian strategy adopted by Gauthier and Narveson.[18] The foundationalist[19] rejects any basic appeal to value *simpliciter* and holds that one must justify moral constraints in terms of value *to individuals;* the contractarian holds that morality consists of the rules all individuals would rationally agree to accept. As Gauthier puts it: "Proponents of the *maximizing* conception of rationality, which we endorse, insist that . . . the rational person . . . seeks the greatest satisfaction of her own interests. . . . Morals by agreement offer a contractarian rationale for distinguishing what one may and may not do. Moral principles are introduced as the objects of a fully voluntary *ex ante* agreement among rational persons."[20] Narveson writes: "The one proper sort of argument for any social principle . . . is a social contract one: principles of justice are those principles concerning the use of coercion that all would agree to, upon a rational consideration of their own best interests, in their own view of what constitutes 'best' in the long run."[21]

I cannot here give a full discussion of the merits of foundationalism and contractarianism. I will limit myself to the following. First, I sketch an important reason to think that contractarianism cannot provide an adequate account of the foundations of ordinary morality. The contractarian, though, can certainly legitimately ask what account of moral justification and the rationality of moral commitment can be given by someone who accepts the impartial consequentialist perspective. To meet this challenge, I sketch *one* conception of moral rationality and moral justification with which one might fill out the alternative, impartial consequentialist, account of morality. I claim that this conception of moral rationality and moral justification—which is not the only one a consequentialist might adopt—allows the consequentialist to overcome the contractarian challenge without understating the genuine force of that challenge.

That foundationalist contractarians cannot give a proper account of what we ordinarily understand by morality is a large and controversial claim. In brief defense of this claim, consider impartiality and its role in ordinary moral reasoning. A certain kind of impartiality and a certain kind of impartial reasoning are at the core of ordinary understanding of morality. Questions basic in moral training, like "How would you like it if someone did that to you?" are not threats that someone will do it to you. They're appeals to the idea that others have interests like yours, and if your interests ought to be respected, so ought theirs. It is a basic move in ordinary moral argument to appeal to what are taken to be morally relevant similarities, and features of individual identity don't count. Contractarians can't allow that such inferences are straightforwardly acceptable. According to contractarianism, others' interests that look relevantly similar to mine count as relevantly similar to mine for the purposes of moral reasoning only if it is to my advantage to enter into cooperative arrangements with those others. That contractarian idea entirely misrepresents moral impartiality and ordinary moral reasoning. An adequate philosophical account of a problematic area should do as well as possible at solving the philosophical problems of that area without just being an account of some different area. I think contractarianism, though it has the appealing feature that it provides a strong answer to the question Why should I be moral? fails this test.[22] (I shall henceforth refer to ordinary morality as I understand it tendentiously as "morality.") Given the choice between abandoning morality and abandoning foundationalism, we should abandon foundationalism.

We certainly need, though, to be able to give an alternative account of moral justification to fill out the impartial consequentialist perspective. I shall suggest one way to fill out the impartial consequentialist perspective, which I think both plausible and appropriately sensitive to the force of foundationalism. To do this filling out, we need to distinguish two questions: a question about rationality, and a question about motivation. The question about rationality is, Do we have *reason* to accept the moral point of view and to do what morality requires? The question about motivation is, Can we realistically expect people to be motivated to act, and in fact to act, as morality requires?

Consider first the question about reason. To answer this question, we need to appeal to a certain reading of Sidgwick.[23] He famously held that although the conflict between the method of utilitarianism and the method of intuitionism *can* be resolved, the conflict between the method of utilitarianism and the method of rational egoism cannot. There is controversy about how to understand Sidgwick's view.[24] On the interpretation I want to invoke here (for these purposes whether it is the right interpretation is irrelevant), Sidgwick holds that there are two competing, equally valid, accounts of what we have most reason to do. The first holds that we have most reason to promote our own interests (it is thus at least very close to the account accepted by contractarians like Gauthier and Narveson).[25] The second holds that we have most reason to promote everyone's interests, considered impartially. Sidgwick could not resolve this conflict. I further claim (though I cannot defend this claim here) that later writers have not succeeded in resolving the conflict.[26]

If matters are as Sidgwick (on this interpretation) suggests, we can make the following claims. We can, first, claim that it *is rational* to care about morality. That is, there's a defensible account of rationality according to which it's rational to care about morality. But another defensible account of rationality says it's only rational to care about *your* doing better on your own terms (as opposed to everyone's doing better on their terms). If the argument I sketched earlier is persuasive, this latter version of rationality cannot justify morality, but it is still a powerful, though not compelling, account of rationality.

There remains the question about motivation. It is an important question. I'm sympathetic to the thought that it's pretty silly for moral philosophers to spend their time arguing about whether people have reason to do something they could not or do not have any motivation to do. So it is important to have some story about how people might be motivated to act as morality requires. This story will have two parts. The first part involves appeal to just the sort of motivation to which Narveson's foundationalist appeals. The vast majority of moral theorists have reason to welcome the idea that (significant parts or aspects of) morality serve everyone's interests, because there certainly isn't a problem about expecting people to be motivated to look out for their own interests. The second part appeals to some one or more kinds of "social sentiment," which clearly are also a part of our makeup. Among them might be affection for relatives and friends, and dispositions to feel guilt and other putatively morally useful emotions.[27]

In saying this, I am not arguing (as someone might, and some do) that the moral point of view is uniquely rational. I'm also conceding that the foundationalist project is an important one. For the sort of motivation to which it is, according to the foundationalist, uniquely rational to appeal is certainly important and reliable; the social sentiments to which I referred are also important and prevalent, but one hopes that morality does not have to rely too much on them.

One might worry now about the practical force of my original argument, that to maximize the value of liberty we need some measure of equality. The worry would be that given what I just said about moral motivation, one could not expect to sustain a society in which welfare rights were accorded the same status as liberty rights because the requisite motivation did not exist. Fortunately, though, I think the empirical evidence is that societies that accord strong welfare rights do survive and indeed flourish.

It remains important to ask what sort of egalitarian principle is justified by the argument from the value of liberty. The answer is that the impartial consequentialist perspective only, as one would expect, requires maximizing the overall amount of the kind of value to which liberty contributes. In the usual utilitarian way (provided there are diminishing returns in terms of the value of liberty from more resources), this gives a strong but defeasible empirical presumption in favor of equal distribution. To get anything stronger, we would need more egalitarian assumptions; the libertarian and the defender of the incompatibility of equality and liberty could reject such assumptions much more easily than they can reject the impartial consequentialist perspective.

Conclusion

I have argued that it is misleading to say that liberty and equality are incompatible, for to make an individual's liberty maximally valuable, you must make her liberty effective; to maximize the overall value of liberty in a society, you need to maximize the effectiveness of liberty; and one cannot maximize the overall effectiveness of liberty, under most social conditions, without some measure of egalitarian redistribution. The moral perspective from which it is natural to make this argument is an impartial consequentialist perspective. I argued against Lomasky that one could not take the impartial consequentialist perspective and maintain the special value of liberty rights. I then contrasted the impartial consequentialist perspective with the foundationalist and contractarian view adopted by Gauthier and Narveson and argued that the foundationalist cannot give an adequate account of the content and logic of ordinary morality, and that the impartial consequentialist perspective can be developed so as to include a plausible account of moral justification. Thus, I think, a familiar argument that liberty requires equality—in the sense explained above—is essentially correct. To show that it is essentially correct, one needs to address some quite basic issues in moral theory.

Notes

I want to thank Jan Narveson, Bill Nelson, and the AMINTAPHIL publications committee for helpful advice and comments on earlier versions of this chapter.

1. I use "moral perspective" to mean a basic view about what morality is and how moral claims are to be justified.

2. See Loren Lomasky, *Persons, Rights and the Moral Community* (New York: Oxford University Press, 1987).

3. See David Gauthier, *Morals by Agreement* (New York: Oxford University Press, 1986).

4. See Jan Narveson, *The Libertarian Idea* (Philadelphia: Temple University Press, 1988), esp. 105–84.

5. I intend these principles to apply only to income and wealth.

6. There are complexities here. (1) The account of the value of liberty I give seems to me not only the most plausible one but also the one likely to find favor with enthusiasts for liberty. It is in the spirit of the Millian idea that self-determination is an essential component of a good life rather than (as a kind of cruder utilitarianism might

suggest) just an instrument often useful in attaining a good life. (2) One might ask whether living a life good according to one's own conception is an agent's *only* good. (3) If liberty is valuable because it is part of a complex whole that is valuable, we face the question (to which there is no obvious answer) how to assess the separate value of each part of the valuable whole. I work on the assumption that any plausible answer to this question will be such that the value of liberty is overwhelmingly constituted by its contribution to the value of this complex whole.

7. John Stuart Mill, *On Liberty* (1859; reprint, Indianapolis: Bobbs-Merrill, 1956), 16.

8. John Rawls, *A Theory of Justice* (Cambridge: Harvard University Press, 1971), 62.

9. Which is explicitly suggested also by Lomasky in *Persons, Rights and the Moral Community*. He suggests that liberty rights are valuable because they allow us to "pursue projects."

10. Rawls plausibly suggests (in *A Theory of Justice*, 202) that "liberty can always be explained by reference to three items: the agents who are free, the restrictions or limitations which they are free from, and what it is they are free to do or not to do." In terms of this characterization, I reserve "liberty" in the text (in accordance, I think, with the everyday understanding in debates about liberty and equality, and with libertarian usage) for the absence of restrictions or limitations that are the product of coercion or interference. My liberty is "effective" if, in addition, I am free from restrictions and limitations that are the product of a lack of resources. Even effective liberty does not, of course, guarantee my ability to achieve possible goals; many of us, for example, are effectively free to slam dunk but still cannot. But political philosophy should be most concerned with politically malleable restrictions on the achievement of people's central goals; these goals are typically more attainable than slam dunks are for most of us, and the most important politically malleable restrictions preventing their attainment are matters of lack of liberty or of effective liberty.

11. I mean by calling the impartial consequentialist perspective "broadly consequentialist" to allow that this perspective may generate rights in the ways in which consequentialists do: rights may, for instance, have great utility in securing basic interests.

12. See Henry Sidgwick, *The Methods of Ethics* (1874; 7th ed., 1907; reprint, Bloomington, Ind.: Hackett, 1981). Sidgwick uses the phrase when discussing utilitarian arguments against egoism, pp. 382, 420–21.

13. I certainly do not mean to suggest that my dichotomy between the impartial consequentialist perspective and the contractarian perspective exhausts the options in moral theory. Kantianism, virtue theory, or intuitionism, for instance, might well be taken to be alternative moral perspectives in my sense. It is also important to note, though, that both the perspectives I mention encompass a lot of territory. One can take the impartial consequentialist perspective at a basic level and still allow for a pretty robust notion of rights at a less basic level, and one can take what I have called the contractarian approach to justification while (paradoxically) denying that any social contract turns out to be mutually advantageous and thus morally justifiable.

14. Though if Sterba is right, this comfort will not be worth enough to me for me to be willing to buy it at the expense of giving similar comfort to the well-off. See, among others, his contribution to this volume.

15. Lomasky, *Persons, Rights and the Moral Community*, chap. 5. It is an oversimplification to regard Lomasky as accepting the impartial consequentialist perspective, but he comes much closer than Gauthier or Narveson to accepting it. In general, the force of the arguments of Lomasky's I consider here is not undermined by simply treating him as accepting the perspective; I note otherwise when it *does* make a difference.

16. The arguments considered in this paper and by Lomasky contrast interestingly with Henry Shue's important argument that subsistence rights are "basic rights" (see his *Basic Rights* [Princeton: Princeton University Press, 1980], esp. 18–29). Both sorts of argument oppose the idea that (all) liberty rights are more important than (any) "economic" rights. But the strategies differ. Shue's argument utilizes a notion of "basic rights." For Shue, a right is basic "only if enjoyment of [it] is essential to the enjoyment of all other rights" (19). The claim that a right is basic is not the claim that "the right is more valuable or intrinsically more satisfying to enjoy than other rights" (20). The overall form of the argument is, given the definition of basic rights, anyone who acknowledges *any* rights must acknowledge basic rights (and subsistence rights are basic rights). By contrast, the argument considered here and by Lomasky works with a notion of the value of liberty. It begins with the presupposition (a presupposition one might think libertarians and enthusiasts of liberty should accept) that liberty is valuable and that *ceteris paribus* the value of liberty should be maximized.

17. Lomasky here, then, is appealing to something other than the impartial consequentialist perspective. But that (I think) makes no difference to the cogency of my counterarguments.

18. Narveson would carry out this project somewhat differently than Gauthier. For these differences, see Narveson, *The Libertarian Idea*, and Narveson, "Gauthier on Distributive Justice and the Natural Baseline," in *Contractarianism and Rational Choice*, ed. Peter Vallentyne (Cambridge: Cambridge University Press, 1991). The differences do not make a difference to my critique, so in the critique I will focus largely on Gauthier.

19. The term "foundationalism" is used in this context by Narveson (in a way that properly accords with its standard use in other philosophical contexts).

20. Gauthier, *Morals by Agreement*, 7, 9.

21. Narveson, this volume. In *The Libertarian Idea*, Narveson puts the idea thus: "Generally speaking . . . the foundation of morality is the interests of those party to it, given the facts of social life. Morality is a set of requirements that will make us all better off if they are met by everyone" (145).

22. Of course, contractarianism provides a strong answer to the "why be moral?" question only if the other parts of (some) contractarian theory work. If, for instance, there is really no satisfactory means to ensure compliance or no satisfactory solution to bargaining problems, then contractarianism fails anyway.

23. See Sidgwick, *The Methods of Ethics*, esp. 418–21, 496–509.

24. See David Brink, "Sidgwick and the Rationale for Rational Egoism," in *Essays on Henry Sidgwick*, ed. Bart Schultz (New York: Cambridge University Press, 1992).

25. The difference is that Sidgwick's account is, of course, explicitly egoistic, while Gauthier and Narveson are careful to suggest that the foundationalist need not presuppose the unique rationality of egoism. Gauthier writes: "On the maximizing conception it is not interests in the self, that take oneself as object, but interests of the self, held by oneself as subject, that provide the basis for rational choice and action" (*Morals by Agreement*, 7). This difference is not vital because for Sidgwick, too, the basic idea is to contrast universalistic justification with justification from an agent's perspective.

26. A particularly distinguished attempt to do so, using resources suggested by Sidgwick himself, is Derek Parfit, *Reasons and Persons* (New York: Oxford University Press, 1984).

27. Rawls discusses these issues in part 3 of *A Theory of Justice*, esp. 490–504. He is concerned with the "stability" of a society governed by justice as fairness, in face of the threat that individuals will pursue individual advantage instead of justice. He gives a theory of moral development designed to show how, in a society governed by justice as fairness, individuals will acquire motivation to be just.

Chapter 4

The Conflict Resolved? Dworkin on Liberty and Equality

Steven Lee

One common view of the left-to-right political spectrum in the United States is that those on the left favor distributional equality over liberty; those on the right favor liberty over distributional equality; and those in the middle seek a balance between the two political ideals. This view assumes that liberty and distributional equality come into conflict and that when they do, a choice must be made between them or they must in some way be balanced off against each other. Much of our political life is animated by the acceptance of this assumption, in the partisan battles between defenders of liberty and defenders of distributional equality and in the making of the painful choices that the conflict of the two ideals is seen to entail. But is this assumption correct? Although liberty and distributional equality certainly appear to conflict, is this mere appearance? (Henceforth, I will refer to distributional equality simply as equality.)

Ronald Dworkin argues that liberty and equality do not ultimately conflict, that properly understood they are, rather, different aspects of a single political ideal. The case for this is made in his article "What Is Equality? Part 3: The Place of Liberty," one in a series of four articles that set out his notion of political equality, a notion that, for him, lies at the heart of liberalism.[1] His claim is that under the conception of equality that is most defensible, most philosophically justifiable, a conception he refers to as equality of resources, the conflict disappears because liberty is properly seen as an aspect of equality. He seeks to derive liberty from equality as the most effective way of demonstrating that there is no conflict between them.

Even if his argument is sound, however, the results are not as far-reaching as they might at first appear because the erstwhile conflict between liberty and equality would simply be displaced into a conflict over the correct conception of equality. For example, a dispute between a leftist and a rightist over some policy matter, which would normally be viewed as a conflict over the relative importance of equality and liberty, would, accepting Dworkin's argument, be transformed into a conflict over differing conceptions of equality.[2] But this is not to say that an argument such as Dworkin's can make no advance, because some conceptions of equality may be more defensible than others. As a result, political theory may well gain from the resulting shift in the focus of discussion. But though political theory may gain, everyday policy analysis is less likely to gain. Concrete policy differences normally run deep and often focus on less abstract matters than liberty or equality.[3] Thus, the search for a foundational conception of equality is unlikely to do much to advance the policy debates.

Because political theory may gain, however, I endorse the motivation behind Dworkin's efforts to bring about a shift in the focus of discussion. But there are problems with the argument for the particular shift he proposes. There is a different way of shifting the ground in the debate, one that is in some respects preferable to the one Dworkin proposes. One could come at the problem from the opposite direction. Instead of arguing that there is a conception of equality from which one can derive our notion of liberty, as Dworkin does, one could argue that there is a conception of liberty from which one can derive our notion of equality. Both approaches would remove the conflict between liberty and equality, but the second approach may be preferable to the first. If so, it could be that liberty, rather than equality, is more accurately seen as the notion at the heart of liberalism.[4]

In the first section of this chapter, I examine Dworkin's proposal for resolving the conflict between liberty and equality. In the second section, I consider some problems with his argument for this proposal. In the third section, I develop the idea that the tension between liberty and equality can be resolved by taking liberty rather than equality as the primary concept.

I

The foundation of Dworkin's liberal political theory is the abstract egalitarian principle, sometimes referred to as the principle of equal concern, that "government must act to make the lives of those it governs better lives, and it must show equal concern for the life of each" (7). But this general concept of equality may be understood through different specific conceptions, and the particular conception Dworkin argues for is equality of resources. Under this conception, "equal concern requires policies that aim to provide each citizen, so far as this is possible, with an equal share of the resources the economic structure distributes to them, measured by fixing the value of the resources each person has as the cost to others of that person's having them" (10–11).[5]

The ideal egalitarian distribution is defined as one that satisfies an envy test, as one under which no one envies the share of resources held by another. No one prefers "someone else's bundle of resources to his own bundle."[6] Dworkin argues that such a distribution could ideally be achieved by dividing up available resources through a special auction in which each person begins with equal bidding resources. The auction is allowed to run repeatedly until all are satisfied with the outcome, indicating that no one envies the share of another. It is a crucial feature of the auction that it brings about a distribution in which "the resources available to any one person depend so far as possible on the opportunity costs of those resources to others" (18). Dworkin believes that a constrained form of the market, both in the guise of the hypothetical auction and as a real-world institution, is essential to equality because a market is necessary to determine such opportunity costs.[7] In any case, the question is whether the conflict between liberty and equality can be shown to be merely apparent under equality of resources, so understood.

Dworkin argues that there are, in general, two kinds of strategy one might employ in seeking to resolve the conflict between liberty and equality, an interest strategy and a constitutive strategy. An interest strategy (typically employed, for example, by utilitarians) defines an ideal distribution as one based in some way on an equal concern for people's interests, and then seeks to show that, given those interests, part of that distribution would be an appropriate set of liberties possessed by each person, thus reconciling liberty and equality. Dworkin's objection to the interest strategy is that it holds liberty hostage to debatable empirical claims about what people's interests actually are. A constitutive strategy, on the other hand, avoids this kind of problem because it "builds liberty into the structure of its chosen conception of equality from the start" (13) thereby guaranteeing a reconciliation between liberty and equality. The problem with a constitutive strategy is that it seems ad hoc, a reconciliation by definition.

Nevertheless, Dworkin adopts a constitutive strategy. Any attempt to apply an interest strategy to equality of resources, he argues, would misunderstand that notion and, in particular, the nature of the auction it involves. An interest strategy applied to equality of resources would see liberties as among the resources to be auctioned, on which individuals would bid based on their interests. But the very idea of an auction makes no sense in the absence of what Dworkin calls a baseline liberty/constraint system as a background condition. The reason is that "no one can intelligently, or intelligibly, decide what to bid for in an auction, or what price to bid for it, unless he makes assumptions about how he will be able to use what he acquires" (21). As a result, liberty enters conceptually into the auction scheme, as part of the definition of that scheme, prior to the expression of interests involved in the bidding. Hence, equality of resources must adopt a constitutive strategy. But the question, in addition to whether this avoids ad-hocness, is whether the liberties the auction thus presupposes are "the morally important liberties—freedom of speech, religion, and conviction, and freedom of choice in important personal matters, for example." It is these liberties that "liberals are most concerned to protect" (2, 3). If the auction does not presuppose these liberties, then it has not effected a meaningful resolution of the liberty/equality conflict.

To determine which liberties the auction presupposes, Dworkin argues, the abstract egalitarian principle must be brought back into the discussion. He refers to this procedure as the bridge version of the constitutive strategy. The question is what baseline liberty/constraint system builds the best bridge between equality of resources and the abstract egalitarian principle, that is, which baseline system treats people with equal respect. This should avoid ad-hocness because the liberties built into the scheme result from the foundational egalitarian notion.

But what are the liberties that result? The first thing to notice about the auction, in this regard, is that the distribution it achieves is a function of the form in which the resources are offered for bid, for example, the size of the lots of property offered. Thus, before the auction begins, the auctioneer must choose the form in which the resources are offered, and this choice turns out to be related to the question of which liberty/constraint system the auction entails. Because the cost of the resources distributed by the auction is measured in terms of the opportunity costs involved in others lacking those resources, Dworkin argues that the choice of the form in which the resources are offered for bid should be determined by which form will yield a distribution reflective of what he calls *true* opportunity costs. True opportunity costs result when the form in which the resources are offered for bid is as sensitive as possible "to the discrete plans and preferences people in fact have" (28). This is the case when the resources are offered for bid in as abstract a form as possible. Hence, this line of argument yields what Dworkin calls the principle of abstraction. The bridge to the abstract egalitarian principle in this argument is apparently the claim that a distribution is fairer, a better expression of equal concern, when it is more sensitive to individuals' plans and preferences.

What are the implications of the principle of abstraction for liberty? What does this principle, which concerns the form in which goods are offered in the auction, have to do with a baseline liberty/constraint system? The connection is established through an observation about the use one will be entitled to make of the resources one receives when they are offered for bid in their most abstract form. The point is that a distribution is more sensitive to individuals' plans and preferences when it recognizes their right to do whatever they want with the material resources distributed to them, consistent with what Dworkin calls the principle of security, which is the idea that there must be appropriate limitations on the ability of people to interfere with the safety and property of others. In other words, the most abstract form in which the resources are offered for bid is one in which the purchaser is free to do whatever he or she wants with the resources, consistent with the principle of security. This freedom, Dworkin argues, is the foundation of liberty that the principle of abstraction implies. The principle establishes "a general presumption of freedom of choice at the core of equality" (29).

But the principle of abstraction is by itself inadequate to yield a proper theory of liberty. Dworkin characterizes this inadequacy by claiming that the principle "does not discriminate among liberties by ranking some as more basic or fundamental than others" (34). What should be discriminated are the morally important liberties referred to earlier. Dworkin seeks to find such discriminatory power primarily in another principle, which, like the principle of abstraction, is implied by the bridge strategy, namely, the principle of authenticity. The auction is meant to reflect preferences, but preferences are subject to change. Moreover, one can distinguish between more authentic and less authentic preferences. More authentic preferences are those that are formed in a context in which people have the opportunity to be exposed to new ideas, so that they can exercise effective choice in assessing the preferences they have, deciding whether to keep them, alter or abandon them, and/or adopt new ones. Presumably, it is the abstract egalitarian principle that favors an auction scheme involving authentic preferences, though Dworkin is not clear about the argument for this. In any case, he claims that the auction scheme favors authentic preferences and that the resulting principle of authenticity would protect the morally important liberties. A combination of the principles of abstraction and authenticity, Dworkin argues, shows that a large part of an adequate notion of liberty can be derived from equality of resources by means of the bridge version of the constitutive strategy.[8]

II

Does Dworkin succeed in his attempt to derive an adequate notion of liberty from the theory of distributional equality under equality of resources? There is an important weakness in his case. Though his account may be adequate to economic liberties, it is not adequate to civil liberties, the morally important liberties that Dworkin argues are derivable from equality of resources. If he has not provided an adequate derivation of civil liberties from his notion of equality, he has not succeeded in eliminating the conflict between equality and liberty.

Civil liberties are liberties concerned with areas of activity such as belief, expression, and association. Economic liberties are liberties to do as one chooses with the resources one possesses (while respecting the safety and property of others). Although the two kinds of liberty are distinct, there is a large area of overlap in their exercise; many actions are exercises of both kinds of liberty. Civil liberties are often exercised by means of one's resources, so that the act in question is an exercise of economic liberty as well. For example, one can exercise freedom of speech by donating money to a political campaign, exercising both a civil and an economic liberty. But not all exercises of civil liberty are exercises of economic liberty. Speaking, meeting others, or praying on a street corner do not necessarily require the use of one's material resources. Likewise, not all exercises of economic liberty are exercises of civil liberty. Purchasing a six-million-dollar yacht is an exercise of economic liberty but not normally an exercise of civil liberty. Because civil liberty can be exercised independently of economic liberty, guarantees of economic liberty are not sufficient by themselves to protect civil liberty.

This is precisely the weakness in Dworkin's argument. He seeks to derive civil liberties from a mechanism, the auction, that can guarantee only economic liberties. Consider the principle of abstraction. In order that the resources at auction be offered for bid in a form most sensitive to individuals' plans and preferences, this principle guarantees individuals freedom of choice (consistent with the principle of security) in the use of the resources distributed to them. This is economic liberty. The principle of abstraction would protect the choice of someone to donate his or her resources to a political campaign, but only as an exercise of economic liberty, not as an exercise of the civil liberty of free speech. The principle would not protect the choice of someone who, through no expenditure of resources, seeks to speak, meet others, or pray on a street corner. Dworkin provides two main arguments to show, on the contrary, that the auction mechanism of equality of resources does protect civil liberties. The first is that the principle of abstraction indirectly protects civil liberty by avoiding legal moralism. The second is the argument discussed in section I: that the principle of authenticity, which directly protects civil liberty, is derivable from the auction mechanism.[9]

In the first argument, Dworkin admits that the principle of abstraction seems to entail the negation of "the liberal thesis that legal prohibitions cannot be justified on the sole ground that the conduct prohibited is offensive to some dominant religion or moral orthodoxy." The reason is that freedom of religion, for example, has opportunity costs for the orthodox majority, who desire to live in a society committed to their orthodoxy, just as the lack of freedom of religion has opportunity costs for the nonorthodox minority, so that a choice must be made between them or some kind of balance struck between their interests. The upshot might be a partial or complete denial of freedom of religion. "The objection claims to find an antiliberal impulse in the idea of opportunity costs and therefore at the heart of equality of resources" (29, 30). Dworkin denies this. He introduces the analogy of the "imperial connoisseur," someone who wishes to assemble "massive collections of masterpieces in a private storehouse." Such a person would fail to achieve this wish because with equal bidding resources, he or she could not offset the opportunity costs of the many others who would thereby be deprived of access to the art. Likewise, the orthodox individual could not achieve the wish of legalized religious intolerance because his or her equal bidding resources could not offset the opportunity costs this would entail for the nonorthodox.

The problem with this response is the same as the problem Dworkin discusses with the interest strategy, namely, that it secures its result, in this case a respect for civil liberty, only by appeal to debatable empirical assumptions. The reason is that numbers count. In terms of the analogy, if only a few people cared for the artworks in question, and not very much, the imperial connoisseur might well be able to acquire those works with his or her initial bidding resources because the opportunity costs in that case would be relatively low. Likewise, if there were only a few nonorthodox individuals and their spiritual lives were not particularly important to them, the opportunity costs for religious intolerance might be low enough for the orthodox individual to bid successfully for it. More realistically, if the nonorthodox were few, even assuming that they cared deeply about their spiritual lives, the orthodox might well be able collectively to offset the opportunity costs of religious intolerance to the nonorthodox and to successfully bid for it.

Dworkin grants that the numbers count but seems not to appreciate the implications of this (31). He observes that connoisseurs, if sufficiently numerous, could establish museums for great artwork. Likewise, he argues, the orthodox, if sufficiently numerous, could band together into special religious communities within the larger society. But the relevant point concerning the connoisseurs is that the museums they secure through their bidding would not be public. What the connoisseurs want is exclusive access. If the connoisseurs successfully offset the opportunity costs involved in nonconnoisseurs' not having access to the art, the museums would be open only to the connoisseurs themselves. If the museums were public, there would be no opportunity costs for the nonconnoisseurs that the connoisseurs would need to offset.

Likewise, what the orthodox in our example want is a religiously intolerant society, that is, exclusivity for their religious views, which they can achieve only through legal enforcement of those views. Given sufficient numbers, they could succeed in offsetting the opportunity costs to the nonorthodox that this would involve. Dworkin characterizes the special religious communities he envisions as being "without the benefit of criminal law," which must be the case if religious liberty is to survive. But his justification for adding this qualification is not clear. The views of the orthodox being legally enforced is like the connoisseurs' museum being private: it is necessary for the exclusivity each group desires and each group might be able to afford the opportunity costs involved. Thus, the principle of abstraction does indeed have the illiberal implication that it provides no bar to legal moralism, no bar to the denial of civil liberty this entails.

Dworkin's second argument, that civil liberties may be derived from the auction mechanism, is that the auction yields the principle of authenticity, which provides a direct defense of those liberties. His argument, rehearsed earlier, is that the auction must be based on authentic preferences, which presupposes respect for important civil liberties, such as freedom of conviction and expression. In assessing this argument, it is important to note that the method for arriving at a distribution under equality of resources requires reference to individuals' actual preferences. Unlike Rawls's theory, which appeals "to counterfactual choices people would make . . . under circumstances of radical ignorance," Dworkin's theory provides a "here-and-now test," requiring that "people with full knowledge of their plans, projects, and attachments not prefer the resources assigned to someone else. Equality of resources insists that people be allowed to deploy all aspects of their personality in making the judgments on which the envy test depends" (19).

But the goal of authenticity—that is, the goal of opening up one's preferences to critical assessment—is itself a matter about which people have preferences, and these preferences are not always favorable. As a second-order preference, some prefer authenticity in this sense and some do not. Some prefer to open their first-order preferences to criticism and possible alteration, and some are quite content with their existing first-order preferences, which they would prefer not to have subject to criticism and possible alteration. Some are open to acquiring new tastes and new ideas; some are not. Given this difference and the importance for Dworkin of individuals' actual preferences in determining the ideal distribution, it is not clear how he justifies imposing a scheme that, through the principle of authenticity, favors the preferences of some and disregards the preferences of others. Nor is it simply a matter of individuals being able to take or to leave the opportunities to have their preferences challenged that the civil liberties would provide, for those who dislike such a challenge may also dislike living in an atmosphere in which such a challenge is possible. Dworkin himself points out, in his criticism of the interest strategy, that people's preferences often run more toward a closed than an open society (16–17). Thus, it seems that if Dworkin is going to be neutral among actual preferences, as he wishes to be, his theory cannot include the principle of authenticity as a constitutive element of the ideal distribution scheme.

My conclusion is that the principle of abstraction, which can be included as a proper constitutive element in Dworkin's theory, cannot adequately ground a defense of civil liberties, and that the principle of authenticity, which could provide such a ground, cannot be included as a proper constitutive element. The only defense of civil liberties that remains is through an appeal to the interest strategy, and Dworkin has shown clearly how such an appeal is not adequate.

III

The apparent conflict between liberty and equality can be resolved in the spirit of Dworkin, I now argue, if we turn his specific proposal on its head, that is, if we take liberty rather than equality as the prior notion. The strategy is to seek to derive an adequate notion of equality from an adequate conception of liberty.

Consider the case Dworkin makes in his essay for the priority of equality. In speaking of the common understanding of our left-right political spectrum, Dworkin remarks that it is "deeply misleading as an account of the range of views available within our political culture." In support of this claim, he offers the following rather startling assertion: "No theory that respects the basic assumptions which define that culture could subordinate equality to liberty, conceived as normative ideals, to any degree. Any genuine contest between liberty and equality is a contest liberty must lose." The reason is that "we are now united in accepting the abstract egalitarian principle" (7).

What are we to make of his claim that it is an assumption of our political culture that equality is never to be subordinated to liberty? To the extent that the claim is true, it seems to be merely verbal rather than substantive. Dworkin denies that the claim is empirically empty, arguing that although virtually no one in our political culture would deny the abstract egalitarian principle, it is possible to do so, for example, by holding the view that one person should be treated better than another merely because the two differ in race (8). One may dispute this defense of the claim,[10] but there is a more important basis for regarding the claim as lacking empirical content. The claim is empty because the abstract egalitarian principle admits of differing conceptions, that is, it is empty for the same reason that his overall argument for resolving the liberty/equality conflict amounts simply to focusing our disagreements in a different way. The consensus for equality Dworkin sees in our political culture is merely a different way of understanding our disagreements. Erstwhile partisans of liberty and equality now become partisans of differing conceptions of equality. The political spectrum has not disappeared; rather, its endpoints have been renamed.

Dworkin has not unearthed an unrecognized fundamental agreement among us but, rather, has proposed a new way of talking about how we disagree. One could, with as much warrant, claim that we are united in accepting the concept of liberty, formulated in some abstract way, but that the political disagreements among us are to be explained by our adhering to differing conceptions of this concept. This claim and Dworkin's are equally matters of mere redescription.

That Dworkin's claim lacks empirical content is important because it shows that his focus on equality, at least to the extent that it is based on this claim, is arbitrary. One could, with as much warrant, treat liberty as the prior concept, asserting there to be a consensus in our political culture around an abstract concept of liberty, while admitting that we still differ over how the concept is to be interpreted. But this is not to say that there would be no basis for favoring equality or liberty as the prior concept. The appropriateness of the choice would be governed by pragmatic considerations. Which works best? Which turns out to be theoretically more fruitful? As claimed earlier, political theory can gain from such a discussion. We have already considered the theoretical difficulties Dworkin encounters in treating equality as the prior concept. I provide the sketch of an argument that finds it more fruitful to treat liberty as the prior concept.

There are four steps to the argument. We need, first, to choose an abstract principle of liberty, a concept of liberty. Second, we need to specify a conception of this concept. Third, the notion of equality we seek to derive from the conception of liberty must be indicated. Fourth, with equality and liberty so understood, we must see if we can derive equality from liberty. (This set of steps parallels those in Dworkin's argument, except that the roles of equality and liberty are reversed.) If we can make it satisfactorily through the four steps, we will have some reason, in light of the weaknesses in Dworkin's attempted derivation, to regard an approach via the priority of liberty as more fruitful than an approach via the priority of equality.

For the abstract principle of liberty, I suggest the familiar idea that people should have the maximum degree of freedom of action consistent with everyone else's having the same degree of freedom. As Dworkin does in regard to equality, I claim that there is a consensus in our political culture that liberty, in the sense of this abstract principle, is not to be subordinated to equality. Though this concept of liberty will be interpreted in different ways, no one, with the specific conception of liberty he or she has, would regard it as appropriate to place equality above liberty in any apparent conflict between them. Although it is true that people often assert that equality must take precedence over liberty in some situations, I will not allow such assertions to count as counterexamples to my claim, anymore than Dworkin does in his argument. Like him, I will reinterpret such assertions, for example, by regarding them as involving a descriptive rather than a normative use of the term "liberty" or "equality" (5–6).

The second step is to propose a particular conception of liberty, a specification of the abstract principle. There are at least two dimensions on which such a conception might be drawn. One dimension concerns kinds of liberty, involving, for example, holding some liberties, such as civil liberties, to be more important than others, such as economic liberties. This dimension is the one in terms of which Dworkin characterizes liberty in the third step of his argument, that is, when he is choosing a notion of liberty to derive from his conception of equality. The second dimension in terms of which a conception of liberty might be drawn concerns the mode in which the liberty is enforced or protected, in particular, the distinction between formal and effective liberty.

The distinction between formal and effective liberty is a familiar one, discussed by a number of political and social theorists, often under the label of negative versus positive liberty. Formal liberty is freedom from interference. It is, roughly, a person's freedom of action when this freedom is secured by disallowing interference by others with that person's choices, so long as that person is respecting the formal liberty of others. Effective liberty is freedom to realize some of one's choices, to have some of one's choices be effective choices. Effective choices are those for which the options in regard to which the person is said to have freedom are eligible options, that is, options it is practically possible and not highly imprudent to choose. This sometimes requires providing the person with material means, in the absence of which the choices would not be effective. It is obvious that a system of effective liberty could not guarantee that all of everyone's choices be effective, including, for example, the choice to possess a six-million-dollar yacht or to spend one's life surfing. Some choices that a person makes are more important than other choices that person makes, and we want a system where people's important choices would be effective.

The point is that given the importance, for example, of a person's choice to communicate his or her ideas with others, freedom of the press should be an effective liberty. As an effective, not merely a formal, liberty, freedom of the press would require not only that the government not censor what I choose to publish but also that I have real access to the press, in particular, that my poverty is not a bar to my being published. It would be easy to caricature this idea by, for instance, claiming that it implies that the government has an obligation to buy a printing press for everyone who wants but cannot afford one. But I assume that there are ways to make freedom of the press an effective liberty without such extravagance. If not, freedom of the press would have to be redefined so that everyone would be guaranteed the means to make communicative choices. I do not have the space to provide an elaborate argument for my conception of liberty, to defend it against its competitor, formal liberty. But I believe that such an argument should appeal to the idea that the moral basis of liberty, the value of liberty, is the contribution it makes to human development, and that effective liberty is preferable to formal liberty because effective liberty better realizes this value. In any case, the conception of liberty I endorse is effective liberty. Liberty is realized in a society when everyone has equal freedom of action and that freedom involves effective choices, in the sense just explained.

The third step in the argument is to indicate the notion of equality I will seek to derive from the conception of effective liberty. The point is not to beg the question by choosing a notion simply because one suspects it is derivable from the conception chosen at the second step but, rather, to choose an "adequate" notion, one that is in its own right "an attractive political ideal" (24, 25).[11] The notion of equality should indicate the kind of goods the distribution will be characterized in terms of and what counts as equality in the distribution of goods so characterized. Dworkin's equality of resources takes the kind of goods to be resources (as opposed to utility or welfare) and distributional equality to be specified in terms of opportunity costs, which requires satisfaction of the envy test. The basic moral intuition behind Dworkin's conception of equality is, I believe, that everyone should be given an equal or fair opportunity to realize his or her chosen goals and projects. Because such realization requires material resources, there must be a corresponding equal division of such resources, and that division must be defined in terms of opportunity costs, for it is opportunity costs that allow the division to take account of each individual's own goals and projects. This implies that material resources should be more equally distributed than they are currently. In particular, material starting points must be more equal, and some degree of ongoing redistribution will be necessary, for example, through progressive taxation for social programs or "negative" income taxes.

This basic intuition, so understood, defines the rough notion of equality that I will seek to derive from the conception of effective liberty. Dworkin's equality of resources is a much more fully developed version of this basic intuition, with the envy test specifying the idea of equalizing starting points and an insurance scheme to compensate for bad "brute luck" specifying the idea of ongoing redistribution.[12] But I have no need to specify the notion of equality in anything like the detail Dworkin does because there is a difference between what is necessary at step two of the argument and what is necessary at step three. The conception deployed at step two, equality of resources for Dworkin and effective liberty for me, should be developed in detail, but the notion to be derived from the conception, deployed at step three, need not be specified in detail. All that is necessary is that the notion be an adequate one, that it represent an attractive political ideal (which is required to avoid the argument's begging the question). Thus, Dworkin does not go into detail on the notion of liberty he seeks to derive from his conception of equality, simply pointing out that civil liberties are more important than economic liberties. Likewise, the rough notion of equality of the preceding paragraph is all that is needed for the current argument.

Finally, does the derivation go through? Can this rough notion of equality be derived from the conception of effective liberty? The answer, it seems, is yes. Effective liberty, unlike formal liberty, makes reference to how material resources are distributed because without access to material resources, important choices will often not be effective. If the distribution effective liberty requires is at least roughly the same as the distribution our notion of equality requires, liberty will be shown to entail equality and the apparent conflict between liberty and equality will be resolved. Indeed, it seems that the distribution each recommends is at least roughly the same because the resources one needs to have an equal opportunity to realize one's projects are the same as the resources one needs to make one's important choices effective. One makes important choices in realizing one's projects, and one realizes one's projects by making important choices. Having equal freedom of action, when this is understood as effective freedom, and having an equal opportunity to realize one's projects amount to having the same thing. It is because of this conceptual connection that the conflict is resolved. The distributions' coming out the same is simply a token of this conceptual connection.

Early in his argument, Dworkin refers to a parallel conceptual connection. He argues that equality of resources depends "not on a bare outcome that can be measured directly, like preference satisfaction, but on a *process* of coordinated decisions" and that liberty "is essential to any process in which equality is defined and secured" (2, 3). Equality involves a process and this process requires liberty. This conceptual connection is at the heart of his argument for the resolution of the liberty/equality conflict. But the weaknesses discussed earlier in the details of that argument are the difficulties he has showing that this connection in fact holds, that is, that the process equality of resources involves is a process requiring liberty—in particular, civil liberties. The advantage of my approach is that the conceptual connection is more defensible. I claim that one can show that the idea of an equal opportunity to realize one's projects follows from the idea of equal effective freedom of action, and that one can show this by showing that the distributions come out roughly the same. In contrast, Dworkin fails to show that his asserted conceptual connection in fact holds. Thus, seeking to derive equality from liberty is a more fruitful way of attempting to resolve the liberty/equality conflict than Dworkin's approach of seeking to derive liberty from equality.

Notes

For helpful comments at the AMINTAPHIL meeting at which this chapter was presented, as a paper, I would like to thank Carol Gould and Bruce Landesman. I also received valuable comments from Andrew Altman and Jonathan Schonsheck.

1. Ronald Dworkin, "What Is Equality? Part 3: The Place of Liberty," *Iowa Law Review* 73 (October 1987): 1–54. Unless otherwise indicated, subsequent Dworkin citations will be to "The Place of Liberty." The other parts of the series are "What Is Equality? Part 1: Equality of Welfare," *Philosophy and Public Affairs* 10 (summer 1981): 185–246; "What Is Equality? Part 2: Equality of Resources," *Philosophy and Public Affairs* 10 (fall 1981): 283–345; and "What Is Equality? Part 4: Political Equality," *University of San Francisco Law Review* 22 (1987): 1–30.

2. In giving a list of possible conceptions of equality, Dworkin contrasts his own conception, equality of resources, with that of the "laissez-faire egalitarians" (10).

3. This point was made clear to me by Bruce Landesman.

4. It should be noted that Dworkin's case for the centrality of equality goes beyond the defense it receives in "The Place of Liberty."

5. Dworkin argues for equality of resources in the article by that name in the four-part series on equality (see n. 1, supra).

6. Dworkin, "Equality of Resources," 285.

7. Ibid., 284, 289.

8. Also involved in Dworkin's account of the derivation of liberty are the principles of correction and independence, which I will not discuss here. In addition, in Dworkin's understanding, some aspects of the notion of liberty implied by equality of resources follow not from its theory of distributional equality, which is the focus of "The Place of Liberty," but from its interpretation of political equality, which is the subject of part 4 of the series, "Political Equality."

9. For criticisms different from the ones I offer concerning these two arguments, as well as other valuable criticisms of Dworkin, "The Place of Liberty," see Gerald Postema, "Liberty in Equality's Empire," *Iowa Law Review* 73 (October 1987): 55–95.

10. Dworkin's defense seems open to empirical criticism. There certainly are racists in our political culture. Although it may be true that explicit racism is limited to the political fringes, there are what one might call implicit racists in the political mainstream who, though they would never explicitly avow racist doctrines in public, find ways to communicate their racism to racist voters by using certain code words that such voters recognize. Both these candidates and voters, however, may be, to a greater or lesser extent, in a state of denial or self-deception about their own racist views.

11. Also Dworkin, "Equality of Welfare," 185.

12. For a discussion of the insurance scheme and the redistribution it entails, see ibid., 292–304.

Chapter 5

Freedom versus Equality: A False Antithesis

Alistair M. Macleod

I

Freedom and equality are both multiversion sociopolitical ideals. Until they are specified in some reasonably determinate way, they cannot coherently be said to be either conflicting or complementary ideals. It is natural, therefore, to ask how the requisite specification is to be effected, with the question then having to be faced whether, once specified in this or that way, they are ideals that come into conflict with each other—either systematically or occasionally.[1]

With the freedom ideal, it is standard for three questions to have to be answered: Freedom to what? Freedom for whom? Freedom from what?

For our purposes, the second of these questions is of particular interest. If, for example, individual freedom—freedom, that is, for individuals (as opposed to, say, freedom for corporations or organizations)—is thought to be at issue, it is necessary to ask, for the sake of securing a suitably determinate specification, whether the ideal calls for freedom for all individuals. If, in response to this further question, sponsors of the freedom ideal indicate that what they are committed to is freedom for all, there will be at least one respect in which endorsement of the freedom ideal will require that the equality ideal be endorsed as well. In virtue of the answer being provided to the "Freedom for whom?" question, the freedom ideal has to be seen as incorporating a demand for the securing of freedom for all individuals, which is tantamount to the recognition of all individuals as enjoying equality of status vis-à-vis freedom-conferring or freedom-protecting institutional arrangements—precisely what would-be egalitarians are committed to saying in all those contexts in which the focus is on the desiderated distribution of freedom.

That there is indeed this sort of overlap between the freedom and equality ideals can be brought out by considering, expressly, what it takes to give specificity to the equality ideal. Here there are at least two questions to which answers must be supplied if the ideal is to be given a suitably determinate formulation: Equality of what? and Equality for whom? Suppose the answer—one answer; one standard answer—to the first turns out to be "freedom." It will then be necessary for sponsors of the equality ideal, in this version, to work toward institutional arrangements that will serve to protect freedom. There will thus be an essential connection between the equality and freedom ideals: crucial ingredients in these ideals will have been located that turn out on inspection to be identical in content. If freedom is what egalitarians are committed by their answer to the "Equality of what?" question to trying to safeguard, it makes no sense to wonder whether there's a conflict between freedom and equality. There cannot (logically) be a conflict because to be an egalitarian (of this sort) *is* to be committed to arrangements that foster freedom. And it makes no sense either—and for the same reason—for sponsors of the freedom ideal or of the equality ideal to wonder how much they value freedom and how much they value equality, with a view to determining what "mix" of these values it would be appropriate to aim at.

The same point can be reinforced by considering the second of the questions to which sponsors of the equality ideal must furnish an answer, namely, "Equality for whom?" Here too the natural answer for egalitarians—equality for all—points to the existence of an overlap in content between the freedom and equality ideals. Not only is it the case, as was noted earlier, that for both ideals it is individual freedom that institutions must be structured to promote; it can now be added that for both it is important that the freedom of all be promoted.

The upshot, so far, is that if we give content to the freedom and equality ideals by answering certain inescapable questions about each in the quite common ways indicated, there cannot logically be any conflict between freedom and equality. The sponsor of the freedom ideal understands that freedom is to be promoted, equally, for all, and the sponsor of the equality ideal is committed, too, to the promotion of freedom for all.

However, in the attempt hitherto to give content to the freedom and equality ideals, a simplifying assumption has been made. In discussion of the freedom ideal, it has been assumed that the freedom at issue—namely, freedom for individuals (as distinct from, say, groups or corporations)—can in principle be secured, simultaneously, for all who are "covered" by the ideal. And in discussion of the equality ideal, it has been assumed that if it is freedom that is to be equalized across society, this can be done simply by arranging for all the individual members of society to be protected in the enjoyment of freedom (that is, for all to be secured in the enjoyment of all the freedom there is, so to speak).

Notoriously, of course, this assumption is false. Talk of freedom (singular) is shorthand for talk about an assortment of freedom*s* (plural). Once we set about itemizing these freedoms with a view to giving content in a more precise way to the freedom ideal—now by supplying an answer to the "Freedom to what?" question—it becomes clear that the freedoms in question can and do come into conflict in constantly recurring situations and that therefore a state of affairs in which all the members of a society enjoy all the favored freedoms—and enjoy them all "without limit or restriction"—is in principle unachievable. A few examples will serve to show both that it is only to be expected that freedoms will collide and that the colliding-freedoms problem is a pervasive one. Thus, freedoms of the same general sort can collide, as they do when A's freedom to secure effective access to communications media (to television, e.g.) for the purpose of advocating this rather than that line on matters of public concern is pitted against B's freedom to secure such access. Freedoms of different sorts can, in the same general way, collide: A's freedom to play a musical instrument may be at odds in some particular situation with B's freedom to sleep in peace and quiet. And freedoms of different sorts can collide within a single person's life. For example, people can reasonably expect to be free to live their lives with some measure of security (i.e., engage in a wide range of mundane activities from day to day without running any great risk of being assaulted, robbed, or killed) only if they accept certain restrictions on the freedom they might otherwise wish to retain to spend (all) the money they earn in ways of their own devising (free of any requirement, e.g., that they pay the taxes needed to maintain for all an adequate system of security).

It would take us too far afield to attempt a taxonomy of the various freedoms that sponsors of the freedom ideal might want to see protected, or to try to plot the various ways in which these freedoms may conflict. It is clear, however, that once we have to reckon with the necessity of limiting even desirable forms of freedom in order to resolve these conflicts, the project of securing freedom for all—a project to which, as we have noted, advocates of the freedom and equality ideals are equally committed—ceases to be simply a matter of trying to arrange for every single person to enjoy all the freedoms "covered" by the ideals. To look at the emerging problem from the standpoint of the freedom ideal, questions have now to be faced not only about *whether* given freedoms are to be protected in the name of the ideal but also about *how far* the favored freedoms are to be protected: subject to what restrictions (or limits) is this or that freedom to be enjoyed by this or that individual? And if we look at the emerging problem from the standpoint of the equality ideal, it has now to be determined what more is meant by the equality-of-freedom formula than that all the members of a society are to be secured in the enjoyment of freedom.

In response to (what might be dubbed) the "freedom-rationing" problem, there is no reason to expect any systematic divergence between the solutions favored by sponsors of the freedom and equality ideals. Would-be egalitarians are likely to want to argue that where the freedoms they are committed to protecting cannot, without restriction or limit, be secured simultaneously for all, it is natural to regard the equality-of-freedom formula to which they are already committed as incorporating, even if only in a very general form, an answer to the question how much freedom of all the kinds at issue is to be guaranteed the members of a society. The general aim under this formula would be to arrange for all to be equally free, and all will be equally free in the requisite sense, presumably, if all are, to about the same degree, beneficiaries of freedom-conferring and freedom-protecting institutional arrangements. But it would be equally natural for the sponsor of the freedom ideal to want to argue that where freedom of a particular sort must for practical purposes be restricted to some degree, the freedom-limiting rules should be designed to restrict the freedom of any given person neither more nor less than the freedom of any other person. Would this not be a natural corollary of the commitment, already noted, to the desirability of securing freedom for all? Thus, if talk of "shares" can be permitted in the context of the freedom-rationing problem, sponsors of the freedom ideal might be expected to concur in the claim of sponsors of the equality ideal that what equality of freedom calls for is not only freedom for all but also equal shares for all of the various freedoms that are prized by all.

To sum up. One straightforward way of showing that freedom and equality can be ideals that overlap is to highlight the answers their sponsors might provide to certain questions they must answer if the ideals are to be given a suitably determinate formulation. If the sponsor of the freedom ideal is depicted as holding that the freedoms to be protected in the name of the ideal must be secured for all, then in one important even if somewhat minimal sense, the position being championed will be egalitarian as well: it will overlap in content with the equality ideal, provided the sponsor of the latter ideal specifies the equality to be aimed at as equality of freedom. Again, if the sponsor of the freedom ideal can be represented as holding that in cases where the various freedoms to be safeguarded have to be "rationed," the preferred rationing formula is one that ensures that all enjoy the freedoms in question to about the same degree, then, too, in a second sense, the position is going to be simultaneously egalitarian—provided, of course, the sponsor of the equality ideal is taken to hold that the equality-of-freedom formula calls for freedom-restricting rules to aim at ensuring that so far as is feasible, all the members of a society are guaranteed roughly equal "shares" of the various freedoms deemed worthy of protection.

II

The relationship between the freedom and the equality ideals will be somewhat different, of course, if freedom is represented as nothing more than an individual ideal—as an ideal, that is, that tells us what it would be desirable in principle for this or that individual to have in the way of freedom of various kinds but without any answer being returned to either of the questions we have had in view about the preferred distribution of freedom across society—either the question that asks whether it is desirable in principle, from the standpoint of the ideal of freedom itself, for valued liberties and freedoms to be secured for all the members of society, or the question that asks whether, if these freedoms cannot be fully (i.e., without limit) secured for all simultaneously, the preferred "rationing" principle is one that guarantees "equal shares" for all of the freedoms in question. (These are the questions I have hitherto been assuming sponsors of the freedom ideal would wish to answer in the affirmative. And, of course, it is precisely when these questions are taken on and answered in the ways indicated that the ideal of freedom can be characterized appropriately as a social or sociopolitical ideal. When these answers are part and parcel of the ideal, the ideal itself calls for institutional arrangements to be so structured as to help bring about a certain distribution of freedom across society.)

It is some such alternative view of the status of the freedom ideal that is taken note of in a glancing way by D. D. Raphael when, comparing freedom and equality as things we value, he writes that "there is a sense in which we can describe freedom as an individual value and equality as a social value." He goes on to explain the distinction: "Although freedom has to do with a man's relation to other people, what is *valued* in freedom is the scope that it gives to the individual person—to do what he likes, to exercise choice, to develop his talents, or even to go to rack and ruin. In the case of equality, the comparison with others enters into the thing valued; the similarity between different individuals is what is valued and sought."[2]

Rawls's terminology can be appropriated to mark much the same distinction between freedom as a (merely) individual ideal and freedom as a sociopolitical ideal. Freedom, it might be held, is a "primary good," not a sociopolitical ideal or principle. The view that freedom is something that it is desirable in principle for an individual to have is an important part of the doctrine of the good for the individual: it draws attention to one of the things individuals must have if, as individuals, they are to be in a position to live satisfactory lives. On this account of its status, freedom can be seen to be a desideratum for individuals without its being clear—yet—how social institutions are to be structured if freedom is to be secured for individuals. It is only when certain essentially distributive questions are tackled under the aegis of the freedom ideal—questions here about how freedom in its various forms is to be distributed across society—that the ideal can be seen to be a sociopolitical ideal. There is, of course, a sense in which, for Rawls, freedom (or liberty) is both an individual and a sociopolitical ideal. *Qua* primary good, freedom (or liberty) is an individual ideal. *Qua* principle of justice, freedom (or liberty) is a sociopolitical ideal. It should be noted, however, that when Rawls thinks of freedom (or liberty) in the second of these ways, the principle he sponsors is, strictly, an *equality* principle: the so-called liberty principle is the *equal liberty* principle.

When freedom is seen as a merely individual ideal in the sense explained, it ceases to be possible to claim that freedom and equality are overlapping ideals. They were overlapping ideals, of course, precisely because they were both representable as sociopolitical ideals, and because, *qua* sociopolitical ideal, the freedom ideal was held to incorporate answers to questions concerning the preferred distribution of freedom. But although the "overlap" hypothesis collapses if the freedom ideal is construed, narrowly, as the sort of individual ideal that is silent about the answers that ought to be returned to questions about the distribution of freedom, there's an obvious enough sense in which it is still impossible to represent freedom and equality as potentially conflicting ideals. The reason is that freedom, insofar as it is taken to have something like the status of a Rawlsian "primary good," is one of the things presupposed (in a sense) by sociopolitical ideals like the equality ideal: it is part of the function of such ideals to spell out how "primary goods" are to be distributed. Although there can be disagreement, of course, about which things deserve to be recognized as "primary goods"—and although there can be disagreement, too, about the content of the sociopolitical ideals that specify the preferred distribution across society of these "primary goods"—there can be no direct competition between "primary goods" and sociopolitical ideals. Where freedom is thought to be nothing more than a "primary good," there can be competing accounts of the particular freedoms it is in principle desirable for individuals to enjoy—and there can be competing accounts of the content of the sociopolitical ideals that specify the preferred distribution of these freedoms across society—but there cannot be any *direct* conflict between freedom *qua* "primary good" and the sociopolitical ideals that regulate its distribution. And this means that where the sociopolitical ideal in question happens to be the equality ideal, there cannot be any direct conflict between freedom and equality.

III

The argument set out in section I was to the effect that when the freedom and equality ideals are specified in certain commonly approved ways, there cannot be a conflict between them because they are overlapping ideals. If the freedom that sponsors of the freedom ideal endorse is freedom for all, and if the equality would-be egalitarians are committed to is equality of freedom, there simply cannot be any systematic conflict between freedom and equality.

But the argument in this form, it might be held, focuses our attention on too simple, and too unimportant, a set of answers to the questions to which we admittedly need answers if the freedom and equality ideals are to be given a suitably determinate formulation. What if, for example, the crucial "Equality of what?" question is not answered in the way presupposed by the overlap argument? What if would-be egalitarians want things other than freedom to be equalized—opportunity, for example, or welfare, or resources, or income and wealth? Once these—perhaps more important—versions of the equality ideal are before us, isn't the prospect of conflict between the demands of equality and the demands of freedom a near-certainty?

Although no full-scale response to these questions can be attempted here, a number of points can be made to deflect the challenge they present to the overlap argument. First, although it's true that the overlap argument requires that "freedom" be the favored answer to the "Equality of what?" question, no particular account of what in detail freedom amounts to or involves is presupposed by the argument. No position has been taken, for example, on the dispute between those who favor a fairly narrow definition of freedom (as is the case with defenders of the so-called negative freedom account when they claim that only deliberate acts of "interference" by others should be given recognition as impediments to the enjoyment of freedom) and those who favor a more expansive conception of freedom (as is the case with the defenders of various versions of the doctrine of "positive" freedom when they give recognition, in dealing with the "Freedom from what?" question, to a much broader range of obstacles to the effective enjoyment of freedom). Again, the thrust of the overlap argument is not affected by differences of view, among advocates of the freedom ideal, about the answers that should be returned to the crucial "Freedom to what?" question. Because both of these sets of questions can be—and in fact are—answered in a large number of different ways, and because the structure of the overlap argument is not affected by these disagreements, the overlap argument has a much broader range of application than might at first be thought. And, of course, disputes about the answers to these two sets of questions must be seen, from the standpoint of the overlap argument, as disputes internal to *both* the freedom ideal *and* the equality ideal—not as disputes generated by any conflict *between* them.

Second, and relatedly, egalitarians who want to see opportunity or welfare or resources or income and wealth equalized generally also have an interest in the equalization of freedom. Egalitarians who take this view fall into at least two classes. One class comprises egalitarians who try to distinguish between freedom on the one side and opportunity (or resources, or welfare, or income and wealth) on the other side, and then go on to claim—as Rawls does, for example—that a properly structured social order must secure for the members of a society equality of freedom *and* equality of opportunity *and* (some approximation to) economic equality, and so on. The other class comprises egalitarians who find that equality of freedom, equality of opportunity, equality of resources, and equality of welfare—either some of them or all of them—are inextricably interconnected objectives. The mutual entanglement of some of these versions of the equality ideal may reflect conceptual linkages, for example, between freedom and opportunity. (How *could* "freedom" to x be secured for someone in circumstances in which there is no "opportunity" to x?) In other cases, different versions of the ideal may be interconnected because the elimination of (at least certain kinds of) economic inequality in society may in practice be a necessary condition of successful pursuit of equality of freedom, or of equality of opportunity, or of political equality—or even of equality under the law. In yet other cases, it may be argued that the favored equality objective (equality of welfare, for example) is in practice unachievable in a society in which freedom and opportunity are unequally distributed.

Third, even if some freedom egalitarians are committed to maintaining—perhaps on the basis of a very narrow view of what counts as freedom in this context—that it is freedom and freedom alone that a society ought to try to secure on an equal basis for all, and even if (somewhat more implausibly) there are egalitarians on the other side who contrive to maintain that it is various things other than freedom (not including freedom itself) that a society ought to aim at equalizing, the disagreement is about how to give content to the ideal of equality, not about whether freedom is more important than equality or equality more important than freedom.

Finally, when it comes to differences as to the preferred formulation of the ideal of equality—differences, in particular, about the preferred answer to the "Equality of what?" question—any tension there may be between the view that it is freedom that ought to be equalized and the view that it is opportunity (or resources, or welfare, or income and wealth) that ought to be equalized is traceable to the relationship found to obtain between freedom and opportunity (or between freedom and resources, or freedom and welfare, or freedom and income and wealth). What is crucial, that is, to the existence of any such tension is how we conceive the relationship—or what, empirically, the relationship turns out to be—between freedom on the one side and, on the other, one or more of (a) opportunity, (b) resources, (c) welfare, and (d) income and wealth. Further exploration of the relationship between freedom and equality is precisely *not* what is called for.

IV

I turn now to cases where there does indeed seem to be a direct clash between freedom and equality but where the conflict can be seen to be of no real interest from the standpoint of a normative theory of freedom or equality. It is sometimes assumed, for example, that freedom as such is a good thing and that therefore any restriction on freedom is open to (at least prima facie) objection. Because it is undeniable that certain of these restrictions are thought to be necessary in that they are called for by an equality principle, they appear to provide evidence of direct conflict between freedom and equality. And it is true, of course, that unlimited freedom (freedom for individuals to do whatever they please) cannot be squared with any of an indefinitely large number of equality principles, whether they be principles that call for equalization of freedom across society or principles calling for equalization of opportunity, or of resources, or of welfare.

This sort of conflict between freedom and equality, although real enough, is, however, uninteresting. It is uninteresting because of the falsity of the assumption that freedom as such is a good thing—and the falsity, consequently, of the related assumption that there is a prima facie objection to any restriction on freedom. The falsity of these assumptions can be easily demonstrated. If freedom as such were a good thing, then for all values of x in "freedom to x" and for all values of A in "A is free to x," it would be a good thing, at least prima facie, for A to be free to x. However, there are values of A and values of x for which this is false. Thus, where A is a criminal organization bent upon making money by forcing store owners in crime-ridden neighborhoods to pay large sums for "protection," it is plainly not a good thing, even prima facie, for A to be free to perform acts of extortion. Indeed, in civilized jurisdictions, organizations like A will be illegal and there will be laws expressly prohibiting extortion, which means that organizations of this sort will not be free to engage in such activities.

We should not be tempted by the suggestion that, in such cases, there is a presumption in favor of A's being free to engage in acts of extortion, even though it is a presumption that is overborne—overborne, say, because it is not in the public interest for this particular freedom to be given legal recognition. If there were anything to this suggestion, then (on a perspicuous view of the status of the law forbidding extortion) the decision by legislators to enact a proscriptive statute would be grounded in an on-balance (or all-things-considered) judgment about whether or not this particular freedom should, in the name of the freedom ideal, be afforded legal protection. It is the sort of judgment that could be reached by weighing the importance of *not* interfering with the freedom of organizations to carry out acts of extortion (where this would be a consideration to which at least some weight would have to be held to attach) against the importance of protecting members of the public from the harm they suffer when this freedom is exercised. Talk of legislators having to balance such considerations before arriving at an all-things-considered judgment is, however, surely a mistake in this sort of situation. It is a mistake because it obliterates the difference between this sort of situation and situations in which considerations that have genuine independent weight pull legislators in different directions. Affording organizations the freedom to engage in extortion activities is something to which no weight need be given: the freedom in question is one to which no value whatsoever attaches. The decision to enact a law expressly prohibiting acts of extortion is thus in no way complicated by the thought that the law is restrictive of freedom. This is not because the law does not restrict freedom; it clearly does. It is because there is no reason to think that the freedom to perform acts of extortion is one of the freedoms that it would be a good thing, even prima facie, for a society committed to the ideal of freedom to endeavor to protect.

Notice that nothing hinges, in the case just cited, on the fact that it is the freedom of an *organization*—not the freedom of an *individual*—that is restricted. Much the same point can easily be made by taking cases in which the freedom of individuals is at stake. When individuals are subject to laws prohibiting murder or assault, they are not free to commit acts of murder or assault. But because there is no plausible presumption in favor of their being free to commit such acts, legislators who enact laws forbidding the acts should not be depicted as doing so because the case for having such laws (restrictive of individual freedom though they undeniably are) happens to be much weightier than the case for protecting the freedom to commit acts of murder and assault.

If it is false that freedom, in all the forms it can take, is something it would be desirable, at least prima facie, to protect, the fact that the equality ideal, in any of a number of versions, can be the source of restrictions on freedom cannot be cited as evidence that there is apt to be a direct conflict between the freedom and equality ideals. Whether the equality ideal clashes with the freedom ideal is quite different from whether there are ever situations in which freedom has to be limited because the equality ideal requires that it be limited.

A similar response is appropriate in all cases where evidence is presented that the equality ideal, if implemented, would serve to restrict the freedom to x of this or that individual or group. A proposed tax measure aimed at reducing sharp existing inequalities in the distribution of the tax burden may be objected to by certain individuals or groups, for example, on the ground that their freedom to dispose as they please of their own economic resources would be reduced by the measure. Again, a law designed to guarantee all political parties equal access to major communications media (e.g., through free-time political broadcasts) may be objected to on the ground that it restricts the freedom of those who own radio and television stations (or networks) to exercise exclusive control over the conditions of access to facilities they own. In cases of these kinds, there is an obvious enough sense in which equality-based provisions run counter to the claims to freedom of particular individuals or groups. The conflict is, however, of no real interest from the standpoint of normative political theory unless—and until—the freedom claims in question can be shown to be legitimate. To show that they are legitimate, the relationship in which they stand to (what are regarded as) legitimating principles or ideals will have to be brought out. And there will be the potential, thereafter, for a theoretically interesting clash between the principles or ideals in question and the version of the ideal of equality that provides the underpinning, ostensibly, for the objected-to measures or laws. But then it will have to be shown that this clash can be characterized, illuminatingly, as a clash between freedom and equality—something it may prove difficult to do. In the cases cited above, for example, no such demonstration seems likely to succeed. In the dispute about requiring privately owned radio and television stations to underwrite free-time political broadcasts, the fact that an important freedom—freedom to participate effectively in democratic political processes—is at stake on what would be represented as the equality side in the conflict undercuts any serious attempt to maintain that the crucial tussle is between advocates of the equality ideal on the one side and advocates of the freedom ideal on the other. And in the controversy about equality-based tax proposals, the awkward fact, for anyone anxious to represent it as a "freedom versus equality" dispute, is that the freedom to dispose as one pleases of one's own economic resources is at stake on both sides. Measures aimed at equalizing the tax burden across society can be expected to increase this sort of freedom for (at least many) members of the so-called middle class, even though the measures will reduce it for members of the economic elite.

V

That it is unhelpful to conceive of freedom and equality as competing ideals can be further confirmed by a brief examination of the view of the relationship between them urged by Narveson.[3] The conflict between equality and liberty that Narveson discusses—and that he thinks should be decided in favor of liberty—is between economic equality and economic liberty. That these ideals come into direct conflict in the economic sphere is, of course, consistent with the recognition that there is no grander conflict between equality and liberty—no conflict, for example, between equality as such and liberty as such. Indeed, Narveson notes in the opening paragraph of his article at least two senses in which he would be prepared to endorse an equality-emphasizing approach. In one of these senses, sociopolitical principles or ideals must apply to all. In the second (somewhat more substantive) sense, the package of rights (and so on) that they secure for individuals must be "the same" (package) for all.

It is worth asking, however, whether there is a direct clash between equality and liberty of the sort Narveson posits even in the economic sphere. On Narveson's account, the embattled principles are, on the one side, the principle of economic liberty, and on the other, the principle of economic equality. And the conflict between them is so stark, moreover, that a choice must in the end be made. Narveson's recommendation is, of course, that liberty be chosen and equality rejected.

Narveson is right, I think, about the starkness of the conflict between (what he calls) the economic liberty view and (what he calls) the economic equality view. He is right, that is, to hold that it is impossible simultaneously to endorse (1) institutional arrangements that ensure that all the members of a society are equal in wealth, income, or property, and (2) arrangements that confer on all the members of a society wide-ranging economic freedoms (of all the kinds associated with the free market ideal). The question I want to raise is whether it is reasonable to represent the conflict as between equality and liberty, even if it is made clear that the conflict between them is in the economic sphere only.

A more perspicuous[4] formulation of the conflict, I suggest, would take more seriously than Narveson does the simple point that *any* would-be egalitarian (i.e., *any* would-be sponsor of the equality ideal) must make clear *what* precisely would have to be equal across society for the ideal to be fully implemented. In the sort of economic context that is of interest to Narveson in his article, both those who champion (what he calls) economic liberty and those who favor (what he calls) economic equality can easily be represented as sponsoring versions—albeit incompatible versions—of the equality ideal. Thus, the champion of the economic equality view wants institutional arrangements that will bring about economic equality across society, arrangements that will ensure, that is, that all the members of society are equal in wealth, income, and possessions. By contrast, the sponsor of the economic liberty view wants a society in which all members, and all equally, are secured in the enjoyment of economic liberty (where "economic liberty" is shorthand for the various free-market freedoms). On this way of representing the conflict, it is a conflict between two versions of egalitarianism, a version that calls for "economic liberty" to be equalized across society, and a version that calls, instead, for wealth, income, and possessions to be equalized.

The dispute can also be represented, it is worth noting, as one between two versions of the liberty ideal. There is, plainly, disagreement between sponsors of the economic equality view and sponsors of the economic liberty view about the importance that attaches to economic liberty. But this is better represented as a disagreement about the content of the ideal of liberty than as one between those who value liberty and those who don't. If sponsors of the economic equality view reject the economic liberty view—and they do—this should not be taken to spring from any general hostility on their part to liberty, even to liberty in the economic domain. It reflects, rather, a disagreement about the relationship between *certain* of the economic liberties central to the economic liberty view and the many other (economic and noneconomic) liberties protected by the liberty ideal. The issues here are, of course, complicated, given (a) the diversity of the settings (economic and noneconomic) in which liberties of the many kinds individuals have reason to value may be at stake, and (b) the complexity of the (logical and causal) relations that obtain between liberties of these many kinds in these diverse settings. However, the disagreement cannot be represented—perspicuously—as involving a battle between those who assign precedence to liberty over equality and those who think equality is more important than liberty. As Narveson recognizes, his economic libertarian (if we may so denominate the sponsor of the economic liberty view in the debate) continues to be committed to the importance of equalization of economic liberty, so it is misleading to think of the pro-liberty position as anti-equality. ("Economic liberty for all" and "Equality of economic liberty" are slogans that could be used, unmisleadingly, by the Narvesonian sponsor of the economic liberty view.) Likewise, the economic egalitarian (if we may so label the sponsor of the economic equality view) is not committed, by virtue of the fact that he or she is in favor of economic equality, to adopting an anti-liberty stance. Lack of enthusiasm for certain free-market freedoms is consistent with firmness of commitment to all the other freedoms protected by the liberty ideal. Indeed, the sort of economic inequality that is the standard outcome of economic interaction in a free-market economy is arguably incompatible with equality in the distribution of some of the most important of these freedoms. Equality of freedom to participate in political decision-making processes, for example, cannot be secured in practice if there are large differences in the economic power of the participants.

If the dispute between sponsors of the economic equality view and sponsors of the economic liberty view can be represented both as a dispute about the content of the equality ideal and as a dispute about the content of the liberty ideal, it is at least misleading to treat it—as Narveson's rendition of what is at issue seems to do—as exemplifying, even if only in economic contexts, a tussle between equality and liberty.

VI

The view that it is a mistake to think that systematic conflict (or tension) between freedom and equality provides part of the backdrop to attempts by normative political theorists to give simultaneous recognition to the ideals of freedom and equality can be further supported by examining the situations in which there is purported to be such conflict. In Dworkin's important 1987 article in the *Iowa Law Review*,[5] three cases of purported conflict between freedom and equality set the stage for his discussion of "the place of liberty" within the kind of broadly egalitarian theory he favors: (1) the dispute over limiting individual financial contributions to political campaigns; (2) the dispute over the desirability of permitting a system of private health care to exist alongside a public system; and (3) the dispute over the defensibility of minimum-wage (and maximum-hour) legislation.

In all three cases, it might be said that the claims of freedom are in collision with equality-based claims. In the campaign contribution case, the freedom of individuals to contribute whatever they please is at odds with a statute that places limits on what individuals may contribute in order to bring about a greater measure of political equality. In the dispute about the place of private medicine in a society with a national health service, the freedom of individuals to purchase the medical services of their choice is in conflict with a system that aims at securing equality of access for all individuals to the health care they need. The disagreement about wage-and-hour legislation pits the advocates of "freedom of choice in contract and employment" against those who want to promote greater economic equality in society by restricting freedom of contract.

Is there, then, a genuine conflict in these cases between freedom and equality? In the campaign contribution case, there is undeniably a conflict between the freedom of individuals to contribute as much as they please to political campaigns and laws that place limits on individual contributions. But is the conflict illuminatingly described as a conflict between freedom and equality?

To see what is at stake in the conflict, one must ask what it is about the freedom to contribute that makes it a valuable freedom and why, despite its value, there is support for legislation to limit it. The first of these questions is easily answered. The freedom to contribute to political campaigns is valued because it is one of the ways in which the members of a democratically organized society can exercise the right to participate in political decision-making processes. The second question too has an obvious answer. If no contribution limits are imposed on what individuals may contribute, then, in a society in which individual members have (vastly) unequal economic resources, the political participation prerogatives of the wealthier members will be greater in practice than the prerogatives of the poorer members. A law limiting contributions can therefore be seen as a device for reducing inequality in the political freedom enjoyed by the members of a society. Disagreement about the defensibility of such a law is misrepresented when it is said to involve a conflict between freedom and equality. The dispute should be seen, rather, as involving a clash between those who are not unhappy about inequality in the distribution of political freedom and those who favor measures to diminish such inequality. But although there is indeed a disagreement about the value of (at least one important form of) political equality, there is no difference of view about the value of freedom. The disputants are in agreement on the importance in a democratic society of freedom to participate in collective decision-making processes. Those who oppose the law limiting campaign contributions want the members of a society to be in a position to exercise this freedom in as effective a way as their financial resources will permit. Those who favor such a law value the freedom to participate effectively in the democratic decision-making processes so highly that they want to ensure that all the members of a society—all *equally*—are in a position to exercise it. But if the dispute is not about the importance of political freedom but, rather, about the preferred answer to the question "Political freedom for whom?"—between those who want political freedom for those who can afford to exercise it and those who want political freedom for all—it cannot be represented, perspicuously, as involving a conflict between freedom and equality.

In the dispute about the desirability of having systems of private and public health care exist alongside each other, there is certainly, on the surface, a clash between those who favor (unrestricted) freedom of choice in health care contexts and those who think freedom of choice must be restricted in the interest of equality. Beneath the surface, however, the conflict is really between those who think it is all right (or even positively desirable) for people with money to be free to purchase medical services unavailable to others (or to be free to jump the queue for services that are in principle available to all) and those who think of freedom of choice in health care contexts as the sort of important freedom that all the members of a society ought to enjoy. It is a conflict between those who favor and those who oppose equality in the distribution of freedom of choice in the health care system. It is inaccurate to represent it as a conflict between the advocates of freedom (here freedom of choice in health care contexts) and the advocates of equality, as though freedom (but not equality) were on one side and equality (but not freedom) on the other. The truth is that although there is indeed disagreement about whether equality in the distribution of freedom of choice in health care contexts matters, there is no dispute about the importance of freedom of choice: freedom of choice in health care contexts is valued by *both* sides.

In the third of Dworkin's cases, laws that impose minimum-wage (or maximum-hour) requirements on employers are thought to be open to objection on the ground that they restrict the freedom of employers to set the terms of employment contracts. However, the dispute about the defensibility of such laws cannot be represented—perspicuously—as involving a tug-of-war between freedom and equality. Freedom of one sort—and for one subclass of the population (namely, employers)—is certainly restricted by laws of these kinds. But freedom is also at stake on the other side: minimum-wage (and maximum-hour) laws enhance the freedom of ordinary working people to secure employment on fair terms. The dispute is better seen as one between partisans of one sort of freedom and partisans of another sort of freedom: freedom for employers to set the terms of employment contracts is in competition with freedom for employees to secure fair terms of employment. One reason, then, that the conflict cannot be represented as between freedom and equality is that the disputants are at odds with each other, in part at least, about how precisely the freedom ideal should be articulated. A second reason is that on the equality front, the difference of view has to do not with whether equality in any of its versions is an acceptable principle but, rather, with which is the preferred version. Those who oppose minimum-wage (and maximum-hour) legislation in the name of freedom of contract hold that there should be equality in society for all to secure, on the basis of voluntary interaction, whatever is yielded by the agreements they can reach through exploitation of the advantages they happen to possess. The proponents of minimum-wage (and maximum-hour) laws, on the basis of a different answer to the "Equality of what?" question, want (some approximation to) equality of bargaining power in the economic domain, or, if that should be unachievable, some softening of the economic inequalities that are the natural outcome of voluntary interaction among economic agents with markedly unequal bargaining power.

VII

If the argument of this chapter is along the right lines, it is a mistake to suppose that resolution of the conflict between the ideals of freedom and equality is one of the standing problems of normative political theory. This must be a mistake—as I try to show in section I—because conflict between them is often logically impossible. Conflict is logically impossible whenever the ideals overlap, as they do most obviously when the freedom ideal is conceived by its sponsors as incorporating a broadly egalitarian view of the distribution of the freedoms we prize across society. And if freedom is conceived—more narrowly—as silent on questions concerning the distribution of freedom, then again (as I try to show in section II) it cannot be viewed as in direct competition with sociopolitical ideals (like equality), which derive their distinctive content from the answers they supply to such questions. A possible challenge to the "overlap" argument—namely, that the equal freedom ideal is something of a special case and that there are other versions of the equality ideal to which the "overlap" argument does not apply—can be deflected by showing, as I try to do in section III, that sponsorship of answers to the "Equality of what?" question that do not overlap with the "freedom" answer—and it is decidedly difficult to come up with plausible answers that do not—can at most generate conflicts between competing versions of the ideal of equality, which is not at all the same thing as a conflict between the equality ideal in any of these versions and the freedom ideal. There are, of course, situations in which equality-based requirements can come into conflict with (what can be represented as) claims to freedom, and I describe two examples of such situations in section IV. I argue, however, that they do no damage to the thesis of the chapter because the claims in question are not grounded in any plausible version of the ideal of freedom. Sections V and VI reinforce the conclusions reached in the earlier sections (a) by arguing against Narveson's claim that the liberty and equality ideals are flatly incompatible in the economic domain, and (b) by trying to show that the three cases of putative conflict between equality and liberty with which Dworkin works in his 1987 *Iowa Law Review* article are misdescribed if they are taken to involve a direct clash between equality and liberty.

Notes

1. The view that it is a mistake to think of freedom (or liberty) as an ideal in direct competition with the ideal of equality is expressed in a strikingly sharp way by Amartya Sen in the first chapter of *Inequality Reexamined* (Cambridge: Harvard University Press, 1992): "It is neither accurate nor helpful to think . . . in terms of 'liberty *versus* equality.' . . . Indeed, strictly speaking, posing the problem in terms of this latter contrast reflects a 'category mistake.' They are not alternatives. Liberty is among the possible *fields of application* of equality, and equality is among the possible *patterns* of distribution of liberty" (22–23).

2. D. D. Raphael, "Tensions between the Goals of Equality and Freedom," in *Equality and Freedom*, ed. Gray Dorsey (Bobbs Ferry, N.Y.: Oceana; Leiden: S. W. Sijthoff, 1977), 2:553.

3. Jan Narveson, "Equality vs. Liberty: Advantage, Liberty," *Social Philosophy and Policy* 2 (autumn 1984): 33–60. In conducting my review of Narveson's argument, I shall follow him in talking about "liberty" rather than about "freedom." Although I have decided, elsewhere in this chapter, to use the term "freedom" rather than the term "liberty," nothing of substance hinges on the decision. The terms really are interchangeable in sociopolitical contexts, or so I shall continue to assume.

4. What makes the formulation more perspicuous in the present context is that it takes more seriously the familiar point that when talk about equality as an ideal is being clarified—and everyone agrees it is in need of clarification because there is no single all-purpose account of what it amounts to that all parties to disputes about it are in a position to take for granted—one of the questions to which an answer of some sort must be returned is "Equality of what?"

5. Ronald Dworkin, "What Is Equality? Part 3: The Place of Liberty," *Iowa Law Review* 73 (October 1987): 1–54.

Chapter 6

The Compatibility of Freedom, Equality, and a Communitarian Notion of the Self

Patricia H. Werhane

Some time ago the British political philosopher Isaiah Berlin raised the following question: Is freedom, or the right to freedom, incompatible with equality?[1] By "freedom" he must have had in mind his well-known definitions of negative *and* positive liberty. *Negative liberty* means, for Berlin, that "every person has the right not to be deliberately interfered with or coerced [where] coercion implies the deliberate interference of other human beings within the area in which I could otherwise act."[2] Positive liberty, for Berlin, is more active: every person has the freedom "to be his own master" (131), or, in C. B. Macpherson's words, "the liberty to act fully as a *human* being . . . to form and follow one's own conscious choices."[3] What Berlin implies is that when everyone has the privilege, at least in principle, to exercise the right be left alone and to "form and follow one's own conscious choices," and when society defends those rights as its most important values, often the result is that those not in the position to exercise their rights equally with others end up in a disadvantageous, unfair, or unequal position relative to those capable or committed to exercising their freedoms. It may be part of the nature of rights, and in particular, freedom, that in its natural exercise inequalities are unavoidable; they develop, occur, and persist.

One response to the dilemma of the alleged incompatibility of freedom and equality is to argue that freedom is an equal moral right, claims to which entail respecting equally the rights of others. So in spite of the fact that one cannot generate the notion of egalitarianism from Berlin's notions of negative or positive freedom (although this has been attempted with positive freedom by Macpherson), one can generate real equal opportunity out of the equal right to freedom.[4] This solution, alas, does not address a deeper problem that Berlin's question raises.

Berlin's definitions of *liberty* and his questions about the incompatibility of freedom and equality come out of an Enlightenment and, in particular, neo-Kantian theory of the autonomous self as the substantive ground for one's ability to exercise one's right to be left alone, to comprehend what it means not to coerce others, and to "form and follow one's own conscious choices." Such a notion of the self, Michael Sandel and others argue, cannot be purely autonomous without being "radically disembodied" and, indeed, altogether empty. In that case the notion of freedom makes no sense because as a purely autonomous self, one is without psychological resources to form choices, to accept or reject alternatives, and deliberately to leave others alone.[5] Even if Sandel has exaggerated the consequences of postulating an autonomous self, a grounded notion of freedom, grounded in an autonomous self, if not linked in some way to other selves, not only leads to forms of atomistic radical individualism or egocentricism but also leaves us with Berlin's challenge to the compatibility of liberty and equality.

On the other hand, as a number of defenders of liberalism remind us, if the self is merely a product of and determined by a community, it is "radically situated" such that what it does is merely an outcome of the complex interrelationships in which it is continually engaged. As a result, it is not easy to explain how it is that we are self-reflective, self-critical, creative makers of history and authors of change. From a communitarian point of view, it is difficult to account for freedom in an interesting sense, and equality becomes a relative notion defined in different ways by each community. Without a notion of the substantive self, one is without a substantive notion of freedom, that is, an explanation of what appears to be one's ability to choose, change, and at least to some extent control one's life.

The debate between liberalism and communitarianism, part of which I have sketchily outlined, is well known. One masterly attempt to resolve some of these issues is exemplified in the later philosophy of Ludwig Wittgenstein. In the *Philosophical Investigations* Wittgenstein argued, in brief, that human beings are intrinsically linguistic. Language is not merely the means of communication; it is constitutive of all human experience and is the way in which we deal with whatever it is we call "reality." Wittgenstein's position on language avoids radical individualism or egocentricism of a "radically disembodied self" because, he argues, language is inherently social. Language is rule-governed, such that words and expressions are repeatable, reproducible, and thus at least in principle understandable to the community of human beings. The notion of a private language, an egocentric language created by and understood in principle only by its speaker, is impossible, indeed, a contradiction.[6]

Wittgenstein's contributions, however, are incomplete. Although he may have made inroads into what Sandel characterizes as neo-Kantian individualism (I think he did), he did not go far enough in making sense out of the notion of the self. Wittgenstein escapes radical conventionalism with his neo-Kantian notion of a rule that is constitutive of the ways in which language and, thus, human thought function or operate. But his fear of dualism, egoism, egocentricism, and solipsism blocked his ability to get at the ground of human experience *except* through language and the notion of a rule. Wittgenstein questions the notion of the first person, the self, or the ego in such a way as often to be mislabeled a behaviorist, but it is true that there is no developed notion of the self or of interrelationships between selves in his major later writing, the *Philosophical Investigations*. Indeed, Wittgenstein makes statements such as "Always try to get rid of the idea of the private object"[7] and "I is not the name of a person" (sec. 410). Thus, although he argues successfully against an egocentric starting point, he also appears to question altogether the existence of a substantive self.

There are at least two challenges to liberalism and communitarianism, as I have characterized their notions of the self, theories that, from quite different perspectives, each introduce a community-*based* notion of the self that at the same time is not purely community-*defined*. From each of these theories, out of which one derives a communitarian-based autonomous self, one can then think about differently grounded ideas of freedom and equality that are not mutually incompatible. The theories are those of Michael Walzer and Emmanuel Levinas.

In *Thick and Thin*, Walzer distinguishes a "thick" and a "thin" self. If I understand his position correctly, he accepts the position that all our experiences are perspectival and constructed. In addition, he argues, who we are as subjects is a late development from our socialization process. In that process we develop a number of interests, roles, memberships, commitments, and values such that each of us is a historical, cultural, and social product, a pluralistic bundle of overlapping spheres of foci, a "thick" self or selves. In the first instance, there is no self-as-such as a precritical, transcendental cogito, or totally ideal spectator. Self-reflection and self-criticism, what Walzer calls a "thin self," does develop, but only later out of the thick socialized self or bundle of selves. Self-reflection arises when there are inconsistencies, disagreements, or clashes between one's interests, commitments, and spheres of value, clashes that jar one into taking another point of view, a "meta" point of view that is still one's own. This meta point of view from which one judges and redirects one's interests and commitments is what Walzer calls the "thin" self. The "thin" self accounts for the unity and continuity of overlapping, changing "thick" selves; it is that aspect of oneself that "perdures" through time and change.[8] Yet, although it perdures, thus accounting for self-identify, it is nothing more than the unity of a bundle of social selves, the self-reflective locus of a vast array of experiences. The "thin" self, then, is socially derived but not merely socially determined. It explains one's ability to get a perspective on one's situation and its positive and negative features, and it accounts for one's ability to choose, manipulate, and even change events.

Paralleling his idea of a "thick" self, Walzer develops in his well-known book *Spheres of Justice* a pluralistic and relativistic theory of the good. He argues that who we are and what we value is defined in terms of social goods.[9] Social goods may overlap, but each has its own definition, "sphere" of application, values, and distributive criteria as defined by the context in which the good is valued. Different societies, different groups within a society, and different social phenomena have quite disparate social goods, so one cannot define "basic goods" or "human good" except contextually. Justice and equality, like the good, do not have simple universal definitions but are defined contextually by the particular distributive criterion defined by each social good. So, justice is relative, and equality is a complex, not a simple, notion. If any good becomes dominant across spheres, it threatens the autonomy and differentiation of each sphere and each social good. For example, in our society the sphere of political democracy is defined by equal participation of each adult citizen. Thus, buying votes tyrannizes that sphere with an inappropriate but dominant good (money). Similarly, if one takes a particular definition of equality, for example, identifying it with egalitarianism, and tries to distribute all social goods equally whatever the circumstance, then that definition of equality becomes an inappropriate and tyrannical principle in the social spheres where egalitarian forms of distribution are not fair.

An ideal society, according to Walzer, is a society in which one has a number of autonomous social goods, each with its own sphere of distribution and normative criterion of justice, and in which there is a maximum differentiation of social goods. Freedom, for Walzer, is positive freedom: the ability to participate in the determination, exchange, and distribution of various kinds of goods without the threat of tyranny either of a particular good such as commerce or of a particular narrowly defined principle such as simple equality. The result, he argues, is complex equality where no one good, even that of simple equality, dominates or monopolizes another.

In *Thick and Thin*, Walzer qualifies the relativistic notion of spheres of social goods. He maintains that running through the thickness of each sphere of social goods and, on a larger scale, through each culture is a "thin theory of the good," or what Walzer also calls "moral minimums." What Walzer is arguing is that throughout history and in different cultures there is a thin thread of coherence and agreement. The agreement is not so much on what is *good* as on some at least partial universal recognition of "bads." For example, there is wide disagreement about definitions or theories of justice, but there is mutual recognition of *injustice*. There are differing interpretations of what should count as equality, yet agreement can be reached on unjust inequalities. Although we are uncertain about the constitution of the "good life," there is widespread agreement about deficient or despicable living conditions, indecencies, violations of human rights, mistreatment, and other harms. Similarly, although we are unclear about how freedom should be defined—a positive right, coercion, or tyranny?—the absence of freedom is almost universally recognized. Berlin's negative freedom, then, is a "thin" moral minimum; positive freedom is a relative and "thick" social good. And, Walzer would argue, the incompatibility of freedom and equality occurs when there are clashes between spheres of social goods.

Interestingly, however, while developing a negative definition of freedom where coercion or tyranny is an evil, Walzer does not explore adequately how that notion relates to the thin theory of the self. He does not satisfactorily develop a metaphysical account of the derivation of the "thin" self nor account for the basis for his postulation of the ideal of complex equality. Hence, I turn to the philosophy of Emmanuel Levinas.

Levinas's unique contribution to this discussion is his argument that "morality is not a branch of philosophy, but first philosophy."[10] His objective is the "establishing of this primacy of the ethical, that is, [the primacy] of the relationship of man to man . . . a primacy of an irreducible structure upon which all other structures rest" (79). This objective, I will argue, is both the starting point for Wittgenstein's and Walzer's analysis of the self and their unstated objective as well.

How does Levinas accomplish this? He does not work his way from a starting point such as the ego, the individual, or the cogito. Nor does he begin, as Wittgenstein and Walzer do, with community, language, or convention. Nor does he start from a metaethical intuitive foundation such as Rawls's statement that "justice is the first virtue of social institutions."[11] Rather, Levinas begins with what he calls "face to face,"[12] the confrontation of two selves, a confrontation that is both irreducible and linguistic. It is as well both descriptive and normative, and who one is and thus how liberty and equality are defined become realized only in this confrontation. According to Levinas, who we are and how we define ourselves are clarified and realized only when we confront other human beings as human beings, that is, (a) when we perceive ourselves as others perceive us (as "thick" social beings), (b) when we see others as irreducible beings (in Walzer's terms, as thin selves), all of which leads to (c) the realization that we are not merely what is perceived by others and (d) that we, too, are irreducible "thin" selves.

The confrontation is linguistic because, like Wittgenstein, Levinas contends that language is constitutive of human experience. Thus, exposure to other human beings as human is both constitutive of human experience and its ground, and constitutive of language (the mode of that exposure) and its ground.[13] Unlike Wittgenstein, however, Levinas does not sacrifice what is intuitively important: a substantive notion of the self and the world of substantive but related selves. One's exposure to other human beings captures the notion of others as being ambiguous, irreducible, independent, transcendent, and not definitively defined by the community of which they are an inseparable part, nor redefinable as an object of, or for, oneself. At the end of *Totality and Infinity*, Levinas summarizes this point: "The face to face is a final and irreducible relation which no concept could cover without the thinker who thinks that concept finding himself forthwith before a new interlocutor; it makes possible the pluralism of society."[14]

In *Otherwise than Being*, Levinas implies, if I read him correctly, that this confrontation or exposure to another is the condition upon which subjectivity, the ego, the self, develops. "Face to face" confrontations involve the experience of the ambiguity of the self both as freedom, that is, as independent from the other human being one confronts, and as facticity, an object of the gaze of another—the social self, without reverting to traditional dualism or solipsism. Being "exposed to the gaze" (289) of another, a gaze that treats oneself in the first instance as an object of observation, reverts to one's own reflection on the interiority of the I, which becomes articulated as self. In this process the self is never reduced nor reducible to its facticity or to the gaze of the other, nor is any other human being reducible to an object of observation. Moreover, the self one confronts is equally inexhaustible. The self that is exposed in "face to face" confrontation develops its interiority from confrontation so that its interiority is the other side of what is observed (its facticity) and thus not dualistic. Despite the fact that the self is never fully defined nor, on the other hand, can it be, pure ego is not "disembodied" (in Sandel's sense of that term) because it depends on confrontation with another human being for its very exposure to itself as self.

According to Levinas, who each of us is cannot be discovered or defined except in a community where we confront one another. That is, we are born into, and find ourselves in a world already constituted by, language and community. A community could be as small as one other person. But a community, even a small one, is a community embedded in a Wittgensteinian world socially constructed by language. Who I am is in the first instance determined by and a reflection of that community, and it is in that context that one's thick self develops. But the community in which one finds oneself is a community of human beings who are not merely reducible to their history, culture, or practices. The irreducibility of the self (of *my* "thin" self) is discoverable, but revealed only in confrontation, and that irreducibility has no meaning except in the context of confrontation *and* community. Thus, "face to face" is a dialectical confrontation that grounds both communication with others and oneself without reducing to or being absorbed in the other. What Levinas has done is provide a descriptive analysis of (a) how it is we find ourselves in the world and in a community constructed by the conventions of symbols and language (Walzer's "thick" self or selves in a linguistically constructed world); (b) how we are in a world of others, each of whom is not merely exhaustively descriptive but is in some sense transcendent or irreducible ("thin"); and (c) how we discover ourselves as one of those complex beings. By starting with "face to face" or what Levinas sometimes calls "primary sociality" (304), one avoids the justificatory problems of constructing a community out of an individualistic perspective or, alternatively, an ego out of a conventionalist or social point of view.

Levinas is careful not to classify "face to face" as a relationship as it is ordinarily conceived. The exposure to another is neither a reciprocal relationship nor a utilitarian one. Levinas is critical of the notion of reciprocity because it implies that humans are interchangeable, that one may substitute one person for another, trade off rights for goods, justifying exploitation or worse. Because "face to face" is confrontation with another as a human being, that exposure reflects on oneself as a human self. But the other person remains that—another—she does not become absorbed in the self but remains irreducible to her usefulness and transcendent to reciprocal exchanges or duties that are sometimes defined as part of, or necessary to, human moral interactions.

Levinas articulates another sort of relationship, that of "substitution." "Substitution" describes contact with others that "is conceived as a behavior—that of substituting oneself for another."[15] This form of taking an ethical stance vis-à-vis others is to place oneself in another's place (in her shoes, so to speak), taking responsibility for another person as if one were that person. So one is responsible, morally responsible not merely *to* others but, more important, *for* others. In fact, Levinas implies that one's responsibilities for others are or should be prior to responsibilities to oneself because who I am is defined, clarified, and realized only as a result of confrontation with others.

Like Walzer, Levinas focuses on justice rather than freedom as an essential part of "face to face" and sociality, although Levinas's definition and analysis of justice is not altogether clear. In *Totality and Infinity* he writes, "Justice consists in again making possible expression, in which in non-reciprocity the person presents himself as unique. Justice is a right to speak."[16] Justice is necessary because of the multiplicity of relationships but is not meant to degrade or objectify them. "Justice remains justice only in a society where there is no distinction between those close and those far off, but in which there also remains the impossibility of passing by the closest."[17]

What I argue is that one's individual freedom is realized only as a result of confrontation with another and, as such, is prior to the notion of justice. Freedom does not arise, in the first instance, from an ego, from a decentering ideal speech situation, from a disinterested perspective behind a hypothetical veil, nor merely out of community. Rather, freedom is both the ground and normative side of sociality that is neither egocentric nor merely communitarian. The irreducibility of who I am (the "thin" self) is realized only in confrontation with another who is equally irreducible. This irreducibility is the source of the self that is not merely that which is perceived by others. It is the reflective self as chooser, critic, and self-controller. Thus, it is the source of, and identical with, freedom. At the same time, freedom has no meaning *except* in a community of others whom one confronts; it cannot be realized in solitude. Moreover, *freedom* is both a descriptive and a normative term; it defines individual irreducibility and at the same time prescribes human responsibility. This is because freedom is recognized only out of exposure to another equally irreducible (thin) self so that one has commitments to others who are distinct selves that are nonreciprocal. Freedom is inescapably part of who we are. To deny one's freedom or the freedom of others is both to bring into question one's self and to refuse responsibility for others because one's own freedom comes out of that of others.

Where does this leave us? The story of "face to face" confrontations is a dramatic exaggeration. Still, Levinas has captured an explanation of human relationships as social and linguistic encounters between people, each of whom is irreducibly independent yet inescapably in a community. Such an explanation is one interesting attempt to break the deadlock in the communitarian-individualism debate without having to sacrifice either the importance of individual freedom or the richness of the community out of which we learn about and become ourselves. This is because the selves we discover through these exchanges (both ourselves and others) are neither identical with their social "thick" selves nor independent of them.

This analysis provides a ground for Walzer's theory of the thin self, and it establishes a basis for a negative notion of freedom reminiscent of Berlin's. The irreducible self is the "thin" self; it is that about oneself that gives one the right to be left alone. The thin or transcendent self is also a thick confrontational self inextricably engaged in a community. Because each of us cannot not be engaged, we are "thick" selves as well. The thick self is the self enmeshed in social relationships, and from Levinas's (as well as Walzer's) analysis one can derive a positive notion of freedom from that thick self. Because freedom is derived from social relationships, Levinas links freedom to responsibility for others. Thus, positive freedom, "to be one's own master" or "to form and follow one's own choices" entails responsibility for others. This additional twist to the notion of freedom, the entailment of freedom and responsibility, allows one, in turn, to talk about a communitarian notion of rights, for example, the right to liberty, without succumbing to an egocentric position because freedom is defined by community and makes no sense except in the context of responsibility for others. By analogy, then, other rights claims, too, are tested on the same basis.

From Levinas's arguments one can also derive a thin theory of equality. If who one is as part of a community and as an independent ego is defined only from confrontations with others, then it is difficult to argue that one person is not equal to another because who I am even as an intentional self arises only out of the community and in confrontation with other human beings who themselves are irreducible, individual, egos. On this level of abstraction, freedom and equality are not incompatible because negative freedom comes out of the confrontation between equals, and my freedom entails, and is entailed by, yours.

It is then to Walzer we turn for his analysis of thick notions of social goods and complex equality where diversity, differentiation, and local interpretations of what is to be valued as a social good formulate context-defined notions of positive freedom and complex equality. It is on this level that communitarian relativism quantifies and qualifies what one means by the good, fleshes out the nature and scope of rights and responsibilities in particular contexts, and sets out parameters of equality. It is on this level that clashes between notions of positive freedom and ideas of equality develop, particularly when a particular social good inappropriately tyrannizes others. But running through these disagreements are the thin notions of negative freedom and equality that provide a basis for evaluating such conflicts. From Levinas and Walzer we can conclude that a community, any community, that fails to recognize persons as thin as well as thick selves with responsibilities for one another is a community that does not acknowledge Berlin's two definitions of liberty. It is a group of less-than-persons who fail to recognize the core requirements of community and who its members are as individuals.

Notes

An earlier version of the Levinas sections of this chapter originally appeared in *Ethics as First Philosophy*, ed. Adriaan Peperzak (New York: Routledge, 1995), in my chapter, "Levinas's Ethics: A Normative Perspective without Metaethical Constraints." Reprinted with permission of the publishers.

1. Isaiah Berlin, "The Hazards of Social Revolution," in *The Environment of Change*, ed. Aaron W. Warner et al. (New York: Columbia University Press, 1969), 1–27.

2. Isaiah Berlin, "Two Concepts of Liberty," *Four Essays on Liberty* (London: Oxford University Press, 1969), 122–23.

3. C. B. Macpherson, "Berlin's Division of Liberty," *Democratic Theory* (Oxford: Clarendon Press, 1973), 105, 117.

4. See Patricia H. Werhane, "The Compatibility of Freedom and Equality" in *Freedom, Equality, and Social Change*, ed. Creighton Peden and James Sterba (Lewiston, N.Y.: Mellen Press, 1989), 121–32.

5. Michael Sandel, *Liberalism and the Limits of Justice* (Cambridge: Cambridge University Press, 1983).

6. Ludwig Wittgenstein, *Philosophical Investigations*, trans. G. E. M. Anscombe (New York: Macmillan, 1953). See also Patricia H. Werhane, *Skepticism, Rules, and Private Language* (Atlantic Highlands, N.J.: Humanities Press, 1992), esp. chap. 7.

7. Wittgenstein, *Philosophical Investigations*, 2:207.

8. Michael Walzer, *Thick and Thin* (Notre Dame: Notre Dame University Press, 1994). Walzer claims to have gotten the term "perdures" from Lionel Trilling's *Sincerity and Authenticity* (Cambridge: Harvard University Press, 1972), 99.

9. Michael Walzer, *Spheres of Justice* (New York: Basic Books, 1983), esp. chaps. 1, 14.

10. Emmanuel Levinas, *Totality and Infinity*, trans. Alphonso Lingis (The Hague: Nijhoff, 1979), 304.

11. John Rawls, *A Theory of Justice* (Cambridge: Harvard University Press, 1971), 1.

12. Emmanuel Levinas, *Otherwise Than Being or Beyond Essence*, trans. Alphonso Lingis (The Hague: Nijhoff, 1981), 18.

13. Levinas, *Otherwise Than Being*, 46.

14. Levinas, *Totality and Infinity*, 291.

15. Alphonso Lingis, introduction to *Otherwise Than Being*, xxii.

16. Levinas, *Totality and Infinity*, 298.

17. Levinas, *Otherwise Than Being*, 158.

Part II

Law, Morality, and Limits on Liberty

Liberalism, Liberal Morality, and the Law

The Ciceronian dictum that we are slaves of the law in order to be free represents a view of law and freedom foreign to those of us raised in the individualist, classical liberal tradition of modern Anglo-American thought. For what we handily name "Western liberalism," law is at best a necessary evil: a convenient limitation on individual transgressions against personal liberty, while itself a great threat to that same liberty. The citizens of the United States, in particular, although apparently happy to have laws that control the undesired behavior of others, chafe madly against the rub of legal constraints on their own lives. That these citizens live with a degree of personal liberty quite unknown to prior history is a historical fact of which most are unaware. That their occasional advocacy of legal moralism and paternalism marks a departure from the heritage of liberalism, toward a conception of law and freedom more favored by Cicero than Mill, is a theoretical fact to which many are indifferent.

Yet, liberalism is, by definition, grounded in affirmation of the value of maximal equal liberty. Indeed, it seems to be *equality* of liberty that most often irks us: we require maximal liberty for ourselves and prefer something less for others. Intellectually, we may appreciate the claim that unequal liberty is not true liberty, but in practice it often proves difficult to afford the divergent choices of others the respect of equal protection under, and *from*, law. Nonetheless, most liberal theory conceives equality as a by-product of legal constraints on liberty, on the grounds that it is only as equals before the law that individuals are likely to achieve significant equality of any sort. Procedural equality (formal equality, equality of rights, and so on) is to be guaranteed by law, although substantive equality (equality of results, equal worth of rights, and so on) can never be so guaranteed. Law ensures equal treatment, not equal prospects.

Curiously, Cicero's very different conception of the role of law is premised on a similar recognition of its equality-enhancing value. He would have approved of far less personal liberty than we now demand, but he concurred in the belief that law makes citizens free *as* equals. As Benjamin Constant observed, the "liberty of the ancients" was found in equality of citizenship—of standing before law, however intrusive its reach. To be governed, at least in theory, by law and legal status rather than by the whims of rulers was the great gift of the old Roman republic, in Cicero's eyes. For him, this was the only form of equality possible; he would have thought it absurd that persons might be equal in fact or circumstance.

Thus, it is primarily with respect to liberty *as personal liberty* that Cicero would find liberal legal theory confounding. From his Natural Law perspective, the purpose of the law is to protect us from ourselves quite as much as from others. Indeed, although one might be expected to recognize and attempt self-protection from external peril, individual humans are considerably less facile at recognizing what is self-destructive in their own predilections and behavior.* Therefore, the law, as representing the acquired wisdom of an entire people, could provide not only physical but also moral and aesthetic safeguards against the individual's less rational impulses.

This contrast of ancient (conservative) and modern liberal perspectives is well rehearsed in the history of ideas. What is of special interest for our present purposes is the extent to which liberalism and persons raised in a liberal political tradition still struggle with the appeal of those ancient paradigms. Not, to be sure, that many U.S. citizens would readily submit themselves to a regime such as that of the Roman republic, with its prescriptions as to the proper number of mourners for a funeral and the maximum expense a family should devote to such occasions. Yet, as noted, we are often ready to use legal force to limit the deviance of others, and we happily accept a great deal of legal parenting.† Moreover, many inheritors of the Western liberal tradition rest uneasy with the fact of substantive in-

*This flaw in individual perception was appreciated by no less a liberal theorist than J. S. Mill. But Mill's pessimism concerning the collective wisdom of social groups facilitated his conclusion that individuals should be allowed to go to hell in handbaskets of their own devising.

†Perhaps this simply evidences the extent to which most human adults remain childish: at once independent and contemptuous of authority and, yet, eager to benefit from nurturing and care when we so please.

equalities and with the theoretical distinction between such equality and purely formal or procedural equality.

In this second respect, liberalism seems discomfitted even by the one premise it fully accepted from the older tradition: that substantive equality is either an impossible goal or one inappropriate to law. Despite that premise, we have often found formal equality of rights and standing to be inadequate to our sense of justice. Even when that substantive complaint has not been at issue, the notion of purely formal equality before law has frequently appeared to be something less than the pellucid and discrete concept we had imagined.

Nowhere are these difficulties more evident than in contemporary efforts to deal with concrete legal questions that strain our theoretical commitments. The five chapters in Part II require us to confront those stress points in liberalism as *praxis*, as producing law we must live with and under. Those from Natalie Dandekar and Robert Moffat situate problems of liberty and equality in the inescapably immediate and contextual sphere of medical practice and patients' rights. Wade Robison's and Deirdre Golash's chapters raise conceptual issues of true weight for practice in, respectively, civil law protection of privacy and the criminal law institution of punishment. And Kenneth Henley brings into question the very distinction between equal rights and equal worth of rights through his argument that concern for equality under law warrants publicly financed policies aimed at redressing substantive inequities.

We can explore the individual chapters in greater depth by considering some of their common themes and conundra. Although the reader may well discover several such recurrent concerns, what follows will focus on notions of equality and, in particular, on the ways in which sameness and difference are relevant to the ideal and the realization of equal liberty. This approach also illuminates competing understandings of liberty, of its relation to other types of freedom, and of its importance in our lives. Readers might also take note of two features of the contributions in this part: first, that all assume the compatibility of, at least, specific forms of liberty and equality; second, that liberty rights are often referenced in support of equality claims, and vice versa.

Equality as Sameness, in Difference, and of Liberty

One of the more striking features of the chapters by Dandekar and Moffat is their revelation of highly concrete ways in which purportedly equal treatment leads to substantively, and tragically, inequitable outcomes. By affording the same treatment to individuals in materially different conditions or situations, medical practitioners and the law overlook vital disparities that, in the opinions of our authors, ought to be accounted for in medicolegal policy and decision making.

Moffat's powerful advocacy piece, informed by intimate experience with treatment practices concerning the terminally ill, discloses ways in which applying identical policies to the cases of physically able and physically limited persons can lead to a substantive denial of equal liberty for the latter. Granted the individual's moral and legal right to determine the manner and time of her own death, Moffat observes that concrete differences in ability to end one's life mean that the disabled patient cannot exercise this right whereas the physically able patient (or nonhospitalized person) can. Insofar as assisted suicide is forbidden by medical and legal policies, Moffat argues, the result is an effective denial of equal liberty to those who are "most in need"—in need of help, in need of respite from suffering, in need of the very right that they are unable to exercise without assistance from others.

A particularly bitter irony is suggested by further contrasting the situation of psychically incompetent (nonautonomous) patients with that of psychically competent but physically disabled patients. For although medicolegal practice allows a third party to serve as substitute decision maker for a nonautonomous patient in choosing to discontinue life-sustaining treatment, it does not permit the autonomous patient to obtain practical assistance in giving effect to his own choice to die. In this way, greater respect is afforded to the lost or unrealized autonomy of incompetent patients than to the liberty (the effective realization of autonomy) of competent patients. And yet, both types of patients are claimed to "have" precisely the same autonomy-right of choosing to end their lives.

The omission/commission distinction, as pertinent to the distinction between passive and active means of ending life, raises its hoary head when we compare the cases of nonautonomous and autonomous but physically limited patients. As Moffat observes, the latter are likely to prefer active means to end their lives because passive means necessarily portend extended suffering. Of course, the physically able and psychically competent person may legally commit suicide (unassisted) by active or passive means, that choice being as much hers as was the original choice to end her life. Yet, this more complete freedom is denied to the physically disabled, autonomous patient only by virtue of her inability to effect her choices without aid from others.

Perhaps it may be argued that to end another's life by active means is wrong, whereas to end one's own life by active means or to end another's through passive means is not wrongful. A direct response to this set of moral proposals would require considerable discussion. Rather than enter into the omission/commission debate, let us respond on Moffat's behalf with an analogy. The current state of medicolegal policy regarding assisted suicide, as contrasted with unassisted suicide and passive euthanasia, might be likened to an imaginary moral-legal view that acknowledges the right of persons to eat food, allows third parties to determine whether incompetent persons would wish to be fed, but prohibits anyone from assisting a person who desires to eat but cannot obtain the food or is unable to consume it in normal fashion. Under such a view, law and custom would permit anyone with the material and personal means to purchase and consume food while forbidding any provision of aid to the poor or the physically disabled.*

It is possible that Moffat, himself, might prefer to argue against the passive/active means distinction from the disparity in suffering that policies based on the distinction would produce. But the analogy captures the absurd inequities of respect and status that may follow from a superficially equal treatment and that his presentation so affectingly illuminates.†

Dandekar, too, reveals paradoxes of liberty and equality in her examination of neonatal care practices. The argument begins with recognition of every patient's equal right to determine her/his treatment in the face of contrary determinations by medical practitioners. On this basis, noncompetent patients, including neonates, are properly afforded representation through the "substituted judgment" of others, preferably of family members who are both most likely to know the wishes of formerly competent patients

*It could be argued that the analogy is unsuccessful because persons normally want to live but do not normally want to die; thus, it is proper to deny aid to those who choose death but not to those who choose life. But then, of course, we must reassess the claimed respect for autonomy, which grounds the right to die. Perhaps we respect more fully autonomous choices of whose content we approve than we respect those with whose content we are uncomfortable.

†And, to this extent, I believe it provides a response to advocates of nonconsequentialist views more in keeping with their intuitions than does a response based entirely on the comparative suffering of individuals.

and most likely to bear the financial and emotional burdens of treatment decisions for any noncompetent patient.

As Dandekar's analysis shows, substituted judgment is most familiar as a device to ensure the rights of patients to refuse unwanted treatments that would be paternalistically imposed by medical care providers. But in some cases, notably those of neonates being represented by their parents, the substitute determination may be in favor of continuing care or obtaining additional forms of care, against medical advocacy that treatment be discontinued or that new treatments not be undertaken. Here, in other words, the patient is represented as demanding access to care rather than as refusing care. Presumably, whether the medical practitioners' motivations in such cases are aptly described as paternalistic turns on the specifics of the case and on the rationale for discontinuing or denying treatment. If they believe that the treatments in question are unlikely to advance the best interests of the patient, their view may be described as paternalistic. But, often, the recommendation that treatment be abandoned or forgone incorporates consideration of the justice interests of other patients who need the same treatment but who cannot be afforded access if the "first" patient receives it.

Such conflicts of equal access claims arise frequently where scarce and expensive technologies are among the treatments at issue—and this is commonly the case in the context of neonatal care. If equal access is understood abstractly, we might conclude that the neonate who first obtains the desired technology should have access to it for as long as her representatives insist upon it. So too, we might hold that if a technology is available it should be provided to those who first demand it, not withheld on the grounds that others may come along who will need it more or who could derive greater benefit from it. But, as Dandekar observes, such an understanding would deprive "later" neonatal claimants of substantive equality by effectively blocking their meaningful access to care.

In sum, the highly partial instincts of parents representing their own newborn must be balanced by some substantive assessment of the reasonableness of treatment in each individual case and by impartial concern for the substantive equality claims of other neonates. When, as Dandekar claims, practitioners as well as parents insist upon using scarce technologies out of partiality for the patient ("this is *my* patient") and without regard for the interests and claims of other patients, equality concerns are heightened. The result, in either situation, may be a tragic waste of available resources and, so, a tragic loss of lives that could have been saved. Here, indeed, substantive equality demands its due against more formally conceived rights to equality and to personal freedom.

Next, Golash and Robison ask us to consider the meaning of equality in the context of criminal law and civil law constraints on liberty. For Golash, the question is whether we can claim to regard criminals as equal moral persons while subjecting them to punishments not, or not effectively, aimed at communicating with them *as* moral agents. For Robison, the question is whether we overlook a privacy interest equally serious and equally worthy of tort protection as some currently so protected because we fail to recognize that other persons are exercising their liberty in a harmful manner.

Arguing that punishment, as imposition of suffering, cannot serve as a mode of cognitive communication, Golash aims to undercut any theoretical justification of punishment as an agent-respectful attempt to convey social messages to deviant individuals. Through analysis of the intended (ideal) function of punishment of children by parents, she depicts all punishment—as distinguished from discursive techniques—as intended to shape emotions and responses rather than to inform or present competing views. Moreover, she contends, punishment can function only in this way: as a form of training suited to dealing with companion animals and young children, neither of which we perceive as moral agents equal to ourselves. Indeed, as Golash observes, it is precisely because we do not recognize the equal moral agency of nonhuman animals or of children that we resort to punishment in our dealings with them.

Now, this may be derided as an idealized characterization of most instances when adult humans punish children or nonhuman animals. Unhappily, we know that anger, not any intelligent effort at training, is often the immediate cause of punishing actions. Still, even punishment occasioned by anger can be interpreted as illustrating Golash's argument. For we may ask why punishing a child or nonhuman animal is considered acceptable, to any degree, whereas striking another adult under similar circumstances would not be. Is it merely a matter of might making right? Or is it that our anger is itself a manifestation of our inability to address children and nonhuman animals as equal moral agents? Our frustration in dealing with children and companion animals may be unwisely *expressed* by punishing them, but the feeling of frustration—of being thwarted by the incapacities of the other with whom we must deal—is both familiar and, at the least, excusable (within certain limits).

A critic sympathetic to Golash's argument might suggest that criminals, for practical reasons, must be restrained in order for communication to begin, somewhat as children must sometimes be controlled before they will accept instruction. This preserves the communicative model by justifying punishment as the necessary means to the independently defensible end. But Golash could respond that holding our *equals* prisoner is not a standardly justifiable approach to communicative dialogue, notwithstanding that most adults have sometimes been tempted to "force" another adult to "at least listen." Here, again, what is justifiable, if unpleasant, in our relations with children is not justifiable in our relations with equal moral persons.

A less sympathetic critic might dispute Golash's analysis of communication as cognitive rather than emotive in function. To this she could respond by observing that discourse ordinarily is understood as an appeal to reason and to the rationality of others. Certainly, a justification of punishment based on the claim of communicating with the criminal as a moral equal could not accept a blurring of the lines between communication and indoctrination.* Indeed, the extent to which emotional suasion substitutes for rationality marks the extent to which honest and respectful discourse has given way to manipulation. Even instruction of those considered equal as moral persons but, perhaps, less experienced or less thoughtful than their would-be instructors can be distinguished from the techniques of management. And, Golash is surely correct that the latter are methods suited to handling nonagents, not methods we employ in a spirit of equal respect for other moral persons.

Turning to private law, Robison directs our attention to constraints on those who violate the privacy interests of others. Through examination of the ways in which false rumors can damage the individual who is their unfortunate and unwilling subject, he reveals how a misguided notion of equality as sameness of conceptual categories is the source of unequal protection. To be the victim of calumny, particularly if one is unaware of it, Robison argues, is to be harmed in ways different from but equally injurious to those associated with legally acknowledged invasions of privacy.

By a skillful blending of philosophical analysis and social psychology, Robison takes us through the possibilities of injury to the victim of "false

*And so, the critic unsympathetic to Golash's theory of communication presumably is one unsympathetic to the punishment theories at which her critique is aimed.

light." Many of these are, as he says, harms external to the victim. That is, they may include harms to the victim's professional, social, and financial interests—harms contingent upon the response of other persons who believe what is falsely claimed about the victim. Yet, this orthodox understanding of false light overlooks the harms to privacy interests that are inextricably bound up with the very nature of a false depiction of the *person*. The narrative power of a rumor is no less for the rumor's being false. Indeed, as Robison's discussion evidences, the falseness of such a "story line" can misaffect all the victim's normal behavior and interactions with others.

Furthermore, the effects of the false light may impinge directly on the victim's interior life in a number of ways. She may begin to reassess her own self-image in view of others' apparent perceptions of her. If she discovers the false light in which she has been placed, her efforts to rectify the situation may easily be misinterpreted by others. She may become painfully inhibited and self-conscious in her relations with others. She may even, in a nasty paradox, feel compelled to reveal the true details of her private life in order to counter the false narrative. Thus, her own autonomy and liberty are compromised by lies circulated by another.

That these effects constitute significant harms to privacy interests seems clear. The knowing calumniation of an unsuspecting victim is a misuse of one's own liberty and, thus, a prima facie wrongful violation of the liberty of others. Although liberalism would forbid a (merely) moralistically motivated proscription of lying, as such, Robison's revelation of the serious internal harms that may befall a victim of false light advances the case in favor of civil recourse. That the harms of false light are not reducible to the harms entailed in recognized privacy torts is, Robison contends, beside the point. Or, rather, it is the point: false light is a special affront to privacy interests because it entails a unique pattern of significant harms. As such, it merits legal redress as surely as do established privacy torts, although it harms the victim in distinctive ways.

Robison concludes that theoretical desire for conceptual simplicity has obscured the very real damage done by conduct that does not fit within existing, favored categories of privacy wrongs. But he shows that in the case of false light, as in the case of different forms of privacy wrongs, the genuinely equal protection of the liberty and autonomy of all persons necessitates special legal constraints on abuses of liberty by some.

Finally, we come to Henley's article on equality of rights under law. Critics of liberalism have long held that the distinction between formal equality and material equality is either morally obtuse, theoretically unstable, arbitrarily manufactured, or some combination of these. Many liberals, as well, have been dissatisfied with the distinction, and many hearken to the leftist claim that formal equality of rights is at best a nominal good where material inequalities make for unequal *worth* of rights. Henley takes up the dispute with the contention that entrenched ("transgenerational") material inequality leads to state-administered deprivations of procedural equality. In this, he echoes Jeffrey Reiman's now-famous dictum "The rich get richer and the poor get prison."

But Henley further argues that the state's involvement justifies the use of progressive taxation to support specific policies aimed at (re)establishing equality of rights. The crux of Henley's argument is that the state's role nullifies, so to speak, the private character of the origins of material inequalities that develop into established *class* differences. His argument thus remains within liberal boundaries regarding private sphere material concerns and public sphere procedural ones. It is the effects of entrenched class differences ("transgenerational poverty") on the administration of law that bridge the distinction between equality of rights and equal worth of rights, according to Henley. And that, he claims, is a bridging that liberalism, by its own lights, cannot overlook.

Thus, Henley advocates admittedly redistributive policies intended to remedy unequal treatment under law—rather than policies that might more directly address the material inequities which are, in some sense, the source of those procedural problems. More equitable police protection for poor neighborhoods, provision of high-quality legal representation to those who cannot afford private counsel, assistance for those in need of bail or other supports during the legal process, training for legal officials to counter the probable attitudinal effects of class stereotyping—all this and more Henley suggests as needed to ensure that the perfectly ordinary workings of the law do not work to undermine the rights of all citizens to equality before the law. Additionally, he contends, progressive taxation to finance these efforts is both equitable and a reasonable intrusion on the liberty of more advantaged citizens.

Henley's chapter is highly nuanced, and much of his position turns on sophisticated disputation within the literature of liberal theory. But its practical import cannot be underestimated, for he discloses the profound interconnection of "theory" and "practice"—much as he reveals the profound connectedness of the public and the private. His analysis of what we might term the substance of procedural equality evinces the dynamic of theory and practice.

We do not simply "apply" theory to practice. As all the contributions to Part II teach us, theory and practice inform each other. At least, this is so where both the theory and the practice are intelligent and humane.

—Christine Sistare

Chapter 7

Liberty and Equality in Neonatal Intensive Care

Natalie Dandekar

Medically scarce technologies force hard choices. Life and death situations in neonatal intensive care units (NICU) complicate choices in ways that can force us to extend our understanding of the meaning of liberty and equality within just institutions.

Consider the situation of a parent whose newborn is fortunate enough to be using a technological intervention, extracorporeal membrane oxygenation (ECMO). Without this intervention, the neonate would have died. With the intervention, the infant, now some weeks old, continues to survive. But the medical team offers the information that this baby has not derived the hoped-for benefit. Although most similarly circumstanced babies would have been capable of independent survival after this length of treatment, this baby cannot survive without continued use of ECMO.

Another newborn needs this equipment and will die without it. Yet removal means one's own child will die. Should a parent hang onto hope and insist that her infant be permitted to remain on this equipment or should she be open to thinking about what such insistence means for that other equally needy infant?

In such a tragic case, the parent stands in for her infant offspring. The infant, as a patient, has the liberty to give informed consent to treatment decisions—to demand or refuse treatment. Because the infant cannot consent, the parent must exercise substituted judgment, providing for the best interests of the patient, choosing what the patient would choose if the patient could choose. But questions arise: Why should this be the responsibility of the parent? What values is she to call upon? Should she assume her child would choose continued life without regard to any other value? Would her child, as a citizen and member of the community within which medicine is practiced, choose to consider the moral demands of justice? How should these potentially conflicting values be weighted? What value system should the parent ascribe to this child whose interests she is duty-bound to represent?

Within the NICU, the medical team has a fiduciary responsibility to care for an infant whom it is already treating. But it also has an obligation to promote the moral demands of just medical practice. In this chapter, I sort out some of the impacts of the moral requirement of impartiality (or fairness) on just medical practice within the NICU to provide insights into the relationship of liberty and equality.

Substituted Judgment and Meaningful Protection: Personal Liberty within the NICU

Personal liberty defined as the autonomy of patients is currently regarded as one of four major values constraining just medical practice. Long-standing traditions promote nonmaleficence and beneficence as the primary day-to-day values of medicine. Beneficence is interpreted as the responsibility to preserve life, restore health, and relieve suffering. Nonmaleficence requires that the physician obey the injunction to do no harm. These values require that medical interventions promote the patient's good. They do not guarantee that the physician determine what it is that the patient sees as her own good as distinct from the good the medical caregiver sees as worthwhile. Thus, beneficence and nonmaleficence are compatible with what is now called medical paternalism. The principles of autonomy and justice counter the pull of medical paternalism by institutionalizing a social culture in which patients as abstractly equal individuals are guaranteed rights against the fiduciary but paternalistic interventions of medical-care providers. Justice as applied to medical care supports rights claims in accordance with relevant equality among individuals. A just medical system assumes that those with equally urgent medical needs have, on that basis, equal rights to medical resources.

Within the social culture of medical practice the principle of autonomy guarantees a wide range of patient rights such as the right to privacy, to be treated with respect, and so on. Autonomy also protects the rightful liberty of those who function within the institution of medicine as care providers. In this chapter, however, I focus on respect for patient autonomy as a functional barrier that prevents the imposition of paternalistic medical decisions on a patient who is not a competent decision maker, one who is incapable of giving informed consent.

Heidi Malm, following Joel Feinberg's usage, notes that *autonomy* is a complex term in that it refers sometimes to an ideal, at other times to a right, or a capacity, or a de facto possession. Malm further points out that autonomy "as a capacity . . . to evaluate and choose among one's options in light of one's long-term goals and values is most relevant to discussions about the grounding of dignity and respect for persons qua persons. But the right of autonomy, . . . the right to choose and pursue one's own ends in life provided that one does not interfere with the similar rights of others is invoked in responses to paternalism."[1] This means that the sense of autonomy that is relevant in medical practice need not meet the narrow Kantian criterion of ideally universalizable rational choice. It is enough that a patient be competent to judge for herself among ends that do not interfere with the rights of others. But even given this softer, broader notion of autonomy, the requirement that another act to protect the autonomy of a neonate is puzzling and needs explication.

As formulated in the popular press, the central meaning of autonomy as the right to choose and pursue one's own ends in life becomes, through the device of substituted judgment, compatible with heteronomy, its normative contrary. The autonomy principle thus extended is taken to include "being free to make decisions involving one's own *or a family member's* health and well-being."[2] Through the mechanism of substituted judgment a competent decision maker appointed to represent the noncompetent patient is supposed to exercise choice on another's behalf. Whereas the doctor's choice is, however benevolent, liable to be seen as a paternalistic invasion of a patient's liberty, the choice made by the patient's representative is held to represent the patient's own autonomy.

Substituted judgment as protecting personal liberty may possibly derive from the same logic that supports the claims of political officials to represent the citizens whether or not those citizens voted for the elected official. As all citizens are held to "own" the political choices made by their government, so too a noncompetent patient is provided with a representative whose choice on the issues requiring patient consent are then held to be owned by the patient. Nor is it essential that the political representative be the person for whom a citizen has voted. In the Unites States, for example, government representatives are generally elected by a small minority of the citizens. Yet, it is presumed that the actions of such officials obligate citizens in ways that are compatible with the liberty of a populace.[3] A modest extension of that logic permits the personal representation of a noncompetent patient by a competent decision maker charged with the duty of exercising substituted judgment to do so in a way that is compatible with the liberty of the noncompetent patient.

Any more direct route to justification of substituted judgment as compatible with the autonomy principle is blocked by the simple fact that one's family is not oneself. Though the courts have tried to define criteria for allowing proxies to act as decision-making surrogates in order to protect a noncompetent patient's autonomy rights, they generally must rely on the patient's life history as a source of relevant cues to the patient's "own" current wishes. Thus, with *Quinlan*[4] the New Jersey Supreme Court provided a precedent for parents to act as proxies for a patient in a persistent vegetative state. In the absence of any legally binding document designating their right to that role, Quinlan's parents represented her by providing convincing evidence that the choice they were making was compatible with the previously long-held values of their daughter.

Substituted judgment was further amplified during the following years. Justice Armstrong[5] wrote that the Saikewicz case held substantive rights of the competent and the incompetent person are the same in regard to the right to decline potentially life-prolonging treatment. The conceptual mechanism by which the incompetent person has the right to refuse medical treatment is "substituted judgment," meaning the judgment the incompetent person would himself make in the circumstances if he were competent to do so (82). From this reasoning, it is clear that although substituted judgment is a conceptual mechanism used to protect liberty, the rationale for substituted judgment derives from the force of the principle of equality. Inasmuch as the competent and the incompetent are equally medical patients, the right "to decline treatment" should be available to both.

In 1979, Massachusetts relied upon another counterfactual locution to broaden further the courts' understanding of substituted judgment: "It . . . would be the ward's wish, if competent. . . . But because the ward is an incompetent person the law intervenes . . . to protect the rights of the incompetent person by determining what . . . [both his close family] and the attending physician [recommend when they consider] . . . the best interests of the patient and which they feel he would choose" (84–85).

In a review of the ways in which the courts have sought to adjust the limits of substituted judgment, Sanders and Raffin list *Eichner v. Dillon*, a 1981 case in which the director of a Catholic order was permitted to exercise substituted judgment to withdraw a ventilator from a colleague in a persistent vegetative state. Past actions of the patient were brought forward to show that when competent, the patient had indicated such wishes. In addition, the attending physicians considered continued intervention medically futile.[6]

According to Sanders and Raffin, prior to 1988, the courts had also accepted substituted judgment in a case where family members demanded withdrawal of any type of life support subject to the fulfillment of an expressed wish by the patient, or an implied wish substantiated by the patient's values and lifestyle, or the probability that the expected net burden of posttreatment life outweighs the expected benefits (177). However, by 1988 court decisions began to pull back from providing such extensive decision-making rights to family on behalf of a mentally incompetent patient. In *Cruzan* the courts imposed a high standard of clear and convincing evidence for withdrawal of life-supporting treatment.[7] Nevertheless, the doctrine of substituted judgment seems to represent an effort to counter the presumed weight of medical paternalism by providing alternative representation of the wishes the patient would have if the patient were, counterfactually, capable of owning wishes.

The rationale for substituted judgment combines the principles of equality and liberty in that it is based on the perceived need to promote an approximate equality of liberty among patients of equivalent medical neediness. In this respect "medical neediness" presumably offers a clear, though limited, response to what may be termed Narveson's challenge (this volume), for in the case of seeking substituted judgment, the advocate of an equality principle insists that patients of equivalent medical neediness should have equal opportunity to pursue their own interests, rather than be the pawn of medical paternalism. Where substituted judgment provides the noncompetent with a representative who speaks for the patient's own interests, it serves to provide the noncompetent with rights equal to those available to competent decision makers.

Past actions and the implied wishes these actions suggest offer one basis on which substitute judgment may rest. But for the parents of a neonate, no such basis can exist. Kenneth Kipnis and Gailynn Williamson argue that an alternative basis might be derived from what they call a "thank you test." This is "comparable to the justification parents sometimes employ when imposing unwanted . . . lessons: 'You will thank us for this when you grow up.'"[8] The thank-you test provides a prospective route by which the patient's representative can exercise substitute judgment in such a way as to provide for the equal liberty of competent and noncompetent patients. It rules out the appropriateness of interventions that would leave the child so severely impaired as to be unable to conceive of saying thank-you for giving me this opportunity. It supports the request of interventions for which thanks might eventually be in order.

Where an intervention is likely to promote a life marked by severe cognitive impairments, Kipnis and Williamson's thank-you test provides reasons against presuming that the patient's representative is making a choice in the patient's own interests. In the Baby L case, for example, the parents demanded and obtained life support against the advice of physicians. The infant is said to survive with impairments so severe that death could be considered preferable.[9]

Nevertheless, there still seems one compelling reason for relying on a family member to serve as the noncompetent neonatal patient's representative. This follows not from any argument based on the sanctity of the family but from the principle Jaggar enunciates as a basic liberty right of democratic societies, "that decisions should be made by those, and only by those, who are importantly affected by them."[10] Because in our society the mother of a child generally finds her life chances most affected by the requirement of child care, the substitute decision maker within the NICU is, and ought to be, the one who will be responsible for the care and upbringing of the infant.

However, as Sistare has pointed out, this decision has at least one troubling consequence.[11] Assume that those who bear the responsibility for parenting this infant into the future have to exercise substitute judgment to make a choice either to refuse or demand some treatment, whether or not that choice accords with the advice of the attending physician. Where this is the case, then we have to acknowledge that faced with what these parents regard as the prospective burdens of choice (whether these be constituted in monetary, emotional, or moral terms), they may agree to a course of action that to an impartial spectator seems different from the choice the self-interested patient would have made for herself. As Jaggar admits, in other circumstances reliance on this principle is no guarantee against making the wrong decision.

Where Jaggar argues that the pregnant woman's right to make a choice derives from her prospective responsibility, I argue that the parent's duty to make this choice likewise rests on her prospective responsibility. In each case, the right and the duty derive from the contingent fact that as this society is now constituted, no other party is as likely to bear the responsibility of providing the child with the necessary conditions of a full human life.

No other party has the right to impose this kind of weight of prospective responsibility on the one who will bear the burden without that individual's consent.

Drawing the line in this way has problems that even the best counseling can only help to alleviate. I take it these problems help us discover the limits to which substituted judgment can protect the equality of liberty among patients only some of whom are competent decision makers.

In sum, even for neonates, the task of protecting personal liberty is meaningful. Yet, protecting the autonomy of neonates poses two special problems with respect to substituted judgment. First, the neonatal patient's representative has less of a basis upon which to derive clues to the desire the neonate would hold if a neonate could communicate choices. Lacking the record of past behavior or expressed wishes, the Kipnis-Williamson thank-you test offers a more abstract basis for approximation. Second, because of the contingent facts as our society is now constructed, the parent whose life will be overwhelmingly affected by these choices has both the right and the duty to make these choices using the strongest version of substituted judgment of which she is capable. Despite these difficulties, substituted judgment demonstrates a commitment to provide all patients with equal liberty, regardless of their competence as decision makers.

Substantive Equality within the NICU

Though the liberty of the noncompetent patient is premised upon treating patients equally, the exercise of substituted judgment may conflict with other requirements of equality. As Sanders and Raffin noted, when doctors informed the Wanglie family that the continued use of technological supports to prolong Mrs. Wanglie's life was both futile and costly, Mr. Wanglie exercised substituted judgment to insist on continuing his wife's medical care. Although the Wanglie's insurance policy covered the $800,000 per year costs involved, the medical community saw this elevation of the principle of patient autonomy as overcoming the combined weight of all three of the other principles of ethical medical practice. The elevation of patient autonomy prevented the medical community from imposing a paternalistic decision, but it also prevented the medical community from applying "notions of distributive justice to limit autonomous decision making."[12] Very likely, there are parallel situations in which a family's economic situation permits some parents willfully to demand the provision of costly treatment to a neonate who is unlikely to derive much benefit. Here, too, medical professionals will be correct in perceiving the liberty rights of some as impeding the attempt to afford medical care in terms of a more substantive understanding of equality rights.

However, other troubling cases within the NICU afford an additional perspective on the ethical difficulties adherent to claims about distributive justice when these come into conflict with liberty rights afforded to substitute decision makers. Robert Truog has described ethical difficulties surrounding the use of extracorporeal membrane oxygenation (ECMO).[13] As Truog describes it, ECMO—a high-cost, labor-intensive, and knowledge-intensive form of cardiopulmonary bypass—is available at only a few centers around the nation. Neonates with respiratory failures can be supported with this technology for more than a month, but as of 1989 data from the national ECMO registry indicates that more than 99 percent of newborns who will survive ECMO therapy need this support for less than two weeks (13).

Truog reports that despite the statistical indices, some parents and caregivers believe that as long as there is one chance in a million, they ought to keep a needy infant on this form of life support despite the poor prognosis. Truog notes that this is a potentially wasteful use of an expensive resource but emphasizes that he is concerned because "this practice can (and does) adversely affect the health and survival of other ill newborns. Infants who require ECMO frequently die if they cannot gain access to the therapy within several hours, and many are too ill to . . . transport to an alternate ECMO center" (13). Truog's observation makes it imperative to rethink the validity of some assumptions that currently enter into decisions about the allocation of scarce resources between patients with similar needs. Those assumptions, which permit, or require, such disturbing outcomes, include three that themselves make a prima facie claim to be accepted formulations of fairness in just medical institutions. These assumptions therefore constitute subjects in need of special scrutiny:

1. That the fiduciary relationship between physician and patient requires the physician to be exclusively committed to act as that patient's advocate, against the apparent interests of any other physician's patient.
2. That because all patients with similar needs have an a priori equal right to the use of scarce resources, the maxim "first come, first served" provides at least a rough justice in allocation.
3. That even where there is justification for limiting access to treatment, unless patients and their families have been advised in advance that

therapy may be discontinued under specific conditions, withdrawing treatment would be wrongful taking.

Murphy proposes that nonphysicians defer to the practice of physicians in order to resolve injustices of medical allocation.[14] Ethical outsiders might best help by suggesting ways to structure the problem as accessible to the autonomy of physicians. From this perspective, too, relevant questions seem to focus on the three assumptions mentioned above.

First, is a physician's fiduciary relationship to each patient necessarily single-minded, as suggested in the first stated assumption? Truog reminds us the fiduciary relationship between physician and patient is routinely understood to permit putting off a scheduled procedure for a day or two because another (physician's) patient needs the procedure more urgently. Such postponement is regarded as a professional courtesy.

It remains to be explored whether such courtesy can or should undermine the force of fiduciary responsibility to the extent that a physician willingly removes a patient from a life-sustaining treatment with the consequence that the patient dies. Because provision of ECMO means the difference between life and death, in the case where two babies need ECMO, both can be said to need the treatment with equal urgency.

Carl Wellman suggests that the fiduciary relationship between doctor and patient in cases of life and death needs should be likened to that which holds between patient and doctor during the kidney transplantation procedure.[15] In these cases, where an initial transplantation fails, that particular patient needs a second operation. Even though other patients on the waiting list are urgently in need of a first operation, Wellman points out that an initial failure to effect a cure seems to strengthen the single-mindedness of the fiduciary relationship between medical team and postoperative patient. If anything, the team members are now committed to providing this patient with a second, even a third, kidney in hopes of achieving success. Though they know that other needy patients await a chance at a first kidney transplant, they believe that in providing the first treatment they acquired a special obligation to save *this* patient—an intensification of the initial fiduciary relationship. Only if further transplantations also fail is the medical team likely to be willing to dissolve the initial fiduciary relationship on a basis of fairness to others.

Some notion of "you've had your chance" seems appropriate to the use of ECMO in the NICU. But consideration of the practice in organ transplantation suggests that it is also a good thing for a medical team to increase its commitment in the face of an initial setback. A distinction can, however, be drawn in the following way: second efforts at organ transplantation may provide a cure. But if additional time on ECMO cannot provide the benefit of a cure, then the cases are in that important way not parallel. The physician's commitment to act as advocate for a specific patient should realistically include helping the patient and the patient's family to recognize the limits of the benefits to be derived, and to take a position in which fairness to others is also a factor.

Two other assumptions remain to be discussed. Turning to these, we may ask, to what extent does prior possession establish continued claim? I have already introduced the idea that ECMO offers different levels of benefit over different durations of use. Robert Weir has pointed out that within medical terminology a beneficial treatment may accomplish any of six goals:[16]

1. Make the medical management of the patient easier for the health care providers involved.
2. Provide short-term relief without long-term benefit.
3. Improve conditions without being curative.
4. Cure a pathological condition.
5. Maintain the status quo condition of the patient for an extended period of time.
6. Add to scientific understanding of the medical process.

The statistics cited by Truog suggest that after two weeks the ECMO treatment provides benefits only in senses 2, 5, and possibly 6. The first neonate benefits only in the minimal senses of 2 and 5. So long as the first neonate remains attached to ECMO, the second, equally needy, neonate has no chance for treatment. But the circumstances of the first infant have changed over the weeks. Where initially the first infant had a chance to derive benefits of type 3, the probability is now that the first infant no longer can expect to derive benefits of type 3. Unless the second infant is given access to ECMO, the second infant has not had such a chance. Moreover, so far as the medical staff can predict, the second might well benefit in sense 3. Because benefits of correction are medically more desirable than benefits that only offer short-term relief or maintain the status quo, the question of withdrawing care from the first infant to afford a chance to the second is not merely one of utilitarian calculation about maximizing benefits across a generalized population.

Should this be seen as a question of fairness among equals? Is a baby who can no longer derive sense-3 benefit from a treatment to be seen as equal to one who can derive such benefits?[17] If they are initially equal, except for the fact that one has had temporal priority, why should distribution of this scarce medical resource be governed only by the right that Hobbes called *First Seizure*[18] rather than by an alternative agreement that appeals to some more obviously moral criteria of fair distribution?

It is morally troubling that the maxim of playground fairness, "You've had a chance, now give someone else a turn," cannot be invoked after the beginning of treatment. If the chance at ECMO is regarded as a contract between NICU and needy neonate, perhaps it should be described either as time-limited or benefit-dependent or both.

Truog's argument suggests that equality must reflect both the urgency of the need (without this treatment either baby will die) and the likelihood that the intervention will provide equivalent medical benefit (equality of outcome) to either. As Kipnis has pointed out, this approach would be compatible with, and perhaps merely derive from, the medically accepted practice of triage.[19] But in addition, a focus on fairness requires some criterion that is impartial between parties and yet sensitive to the different benefits each may derive. The presumption that possessions belong to the firstcomer must in this case be pitted against the presumption that the secondcomer also deserves a chance.

When should possession be subject to withdrawal? ECMO is an external, mechanical intervention. It is in this respect unlike medical interventions that provide palliation, comfort, and caring to a patient. It is also relevantly unlike the organ that once transplanted comes to be part of the person's bodily self. In accordance with the day-to-day values of medicine, both beneficence and nonmaleficence require that palliation, comfort, and other dimensions of caring must not be subject to withdrawal at all. A patient who can no longer expect cure remains deeply in need of this human dimension of care. Nor is the provision of comfort to one a denial of comfort to another because these are not, in the normal course, scarce resources. Just medical practice must continue to make these dimensions of caring available to all equally and without partiality.

Nor, as Malm points out, will a just medical practice countenance removing a patient's transplanted gallbladder on the grounds that it is not fully curing this patient and may well provide maximal benefits to another. Once the organ is implanted, it becomes part of the bodily person and is thus governed by a different and more stringent set of protections aimed at insulating personal integrity.[20]

Provision of a life support such as ECMO differs from the provision of palliatives because scarce resources differ from those in plentiful supply. It differs from the transplanted organ in remaining externally connected to the person of the patient and thus not coming within the insulating effect of privacy protections. Thus, it seems that we, as a society, must decide between permitting use of ECMO-type interventions to be governed by what Hobbes has called the right of first seizure or by some other principle. If we were to ask what principle would people choose if they were denied knowledge of the kind that would enable them to rig the principles in their own favor, I believe that the case for "a fair chance for each" would be selected over the right of first seizure because the latter seems to take temporal priority as a power advantage and therefore to build morality on a basis of might rather than a basis of fairness.

Conclusion: Liberty and Equality in the NICU

Modern principles of autonomy and justice function as limiting principles to the traditional values of medical paternalism. Yet, the discussion to this point has shown that within the NICU, both concepts need to be extended in order to function across a wide range of medical decisions. Autonomy is extended by means of substituted judgment. Justice, narrowly construed to refer to the economic aspects of distributive justice, needs to be extended to take in two ethical aspects of equality relevant to medical practice.

The tragic choices that need to be made when two infants urgently need the same limited medical resource illustrate the potential conflicts between liberty and equality. The liberty protection available through substituted judgment conflicts with the obligation to treat equally urgent cases justly in terms including fairness of opportunity.

In this last section, I describe how the foregoing discussion sheds light upon the relationship of liberty and equality. First, it seems that Malm is correct in holding that the liberty protected against medical paternalism consists in "the right to choose and pursue one's own ends in life provided that one does not interfere with the similar rights of others."[21] In that case, as I have shown in the first section, liberty is intrinsically tied to equality protections. As social persons for whom the practice of rights is established in our institutionalized interactions, we participate in constructing a world in which it is a prima facie good for persons to have and be in a position to act upon and satisfy their interests, desires, objectives, and purposes. The mechanism of substituted judgment derives from the effort to secure the same rights (against medical paternalism) to noncompetent decision makers as have been secured by competent decision makers.

Where the noncompetent were previously competent, or lived long enough so that those appointed to make the substitute judgment can understand the significance of their response as indicative of preference, the substitute is morally bound to represent the patient's wishes faithfully. Neonates, by definition, are so young that no representative can have grounds to feel certain about what these babies would want. Here, substituted judgment, on the principle of representation, requires that those choosing on behalf of the neonate act to protect the personal liberty of these infants to the extent that these are constructed as legitimate.

Legitimacy, in turn, rests on the perception of fairness. With respect to a scarce neonatal resource such as ECMO, both liberty and equality bear a complicated relationship to fairness, for on the one hand it would be unfair, in our society, to ask anyone but the parent to serve as the neonate's representative. Yet, the basis for holding the parent thus duty bound to exercise substituted judgment on the infant's behalf is that any decision about treatment for the newborn will most profoundly affect the parent's own life. Thus, the basis for holding the parent responsible for providing informed consent on the infant's behalf is the grounds for fearing that the parent's judgment will be distorted by a conflict of interest.

Here, where the mechanism of substituted judgment is most strained, the need to reflect on what constitutes relevant aspects of fairness becomes most important. The neonatal intensive care unit (NICU) should be seen as a moral space within which liberty and equality pertain to the rights derived from the relevant equality of technology-dependent newborns. In this context, liberty cannot be simply understood by reference to autonomy. Instead, understanding liberty requires moral analysis of two relationships. The more obvious is that between individual autonomy and substitute judgment. But equally important is the relationship that liberty has to the need to sustain equality among those whose circumstances are, in the medically significant respects, alike. However, the concept of equality cannot simply be understood by reference to economic justice. Nor can it be encompassed by reliance on the maxims of first seizure, such as "first come, first served" and "possession is nine-tenths of the law." Instead, I argue for the adoption of a morally appropriate understanding of equality of access as an operational concept of just medical practice. Where liberty protections conflict with fairness, objections to special pleading—a fallacious effort to make one exception to a rule that one wishes to have hold for other cases—carry special weight. Discussion of the potential conflict over the use of scarce resources such as ECMO thus offers strong confirmation of Sterba's claim (this volume) that the conflict of equality and liberty can be viewed as a conflict of liberties. Where the haves derive only a minimal benefit from use of ECMO, they may be seen as akin to the rich who seek to retain the liberty to use their surplus for luxury. Where relevantly similar have-nots might derive a maximal benefit, they may be seen as the poor who seek the right to use those goods for basic needs. In the neonatal intensive care unit, where the conflict is one between the equality of needy neonates and the liberty to use ECMO, this discussion supports the claim that those who may derive a maximal benefit have a morally preferable liberty right. But I also contend that this liberty right should be spelled out as a part of the initial understanding on which access to ECMO is premised. To achieve fairness in the distribution of scarce medical resources to needy neonates requires a practice of use in accordance with some principle of time-limited shares. Once a period of maximal benefit is established, then that sets the time period. A firstcomer has a fair chance during that first time period, but if, after that period has expired, another neonate needs access, then the right of first seizure should give way to the right to fair opportunity. One who might maximally benefit should be seen as having precedence over the one who can expect only minimal benefits from continuance. I think, with respect to socially constructed scarce goods, this principle is more fair than the appeal to power implicit in rights adherent to prior possession.

Insofar as liberty derives from a social commitment to the basic fairness of equality, liberty protections must necessarily be subsumed by the requirements of fairness. Where liberty does conflict with fairness, the need for medical practice to be and to be perceived as fair is overriding.

Notes

I want to thank Millie Solomon, Principal Investigator for Decisions Near the End of Life, for permitting me to use the library of EDC during the summer of 1994, and for her helpful comments on the resulting chapter. I have also benefited by the discussion of this chapter at the AMINTAPHIL meeting, November 1994; by further discussion with

Ken Kipnis, who kindly permitted me to read a draft of his research paper on a related topic; and by the comments of the editors of this volume.

Because it promotes grammatical simplicity, I refer to the parent as singular and female. I do this without intending any prejudice to cases in which only a male parent serves as the representative decision maker or in which two parents must agree on a decision.

1. H. M. Malm, "On Respecting Autonomy or Personal Preferences in Medical Practice: A Reply to Dandekar" (AMINTAPHIL Response Paper, Charleston, S.C., 1994), 2.

2. Kathy A. Fackelmann, "DNA Dilemmas, Readers and 'Experts' Weigh in on Biomedical Ethics," *Science News*, December 17, 1994, 408, italics added.

3. The theory of political representation is riddled with conceptual difficulties; however, social contract theories have legitimated the acceptability of the claim that representative government expresses the will of a free people.

4. *In re Quinlan*, 70 N.J. 10, 355 A 2d. 647, 79 ALR 3d 205 (1976).

5. Christopher J. Armstrong, "Opinion in the Matter of Earle N. Spring," in *Social Ethics*, ed. Thomas A. Mappes and Jane S. Zembaty, 3d ed. (New York: McGraw Hill, 1987), 81–85.

6. L. M. Sanders and T. A. Raffin,"The Ethics of Withholding and Withdrawing Critical Care," *Cambridge Quarterly of Healthcare Ethics* 2 (1993): 175–84.

7. *Cruzan v. Director, Missouri Dept. of Health*, 110 S.Ct. 2841 (1990).

8. Kenneth Kipnis and Gailynn M. Williamson, "Nontreatment Decisions for Severely Compromised Newborns," *Ethics* 95 (October 1984): 90–111.

9. John J. Paris, Robert K. Crone, and Frank Reardon, "Physicians' Refusal of Requested Treatment: The Case of Baby L," *New England Journal of Medicine* 322, no. 14 (1990): 1012–15.

10. Alison M. Jaggar, "Abortion and a Woman's Right to Decide," in *Living with Contradictions: Controversies in Feminist Social Ethics*, ed. Alison M. Jaggar (Boulder: Westview Press), 282.

11. Christine Sistare, editorial observation.

12. Sanders and Raffin, "The Ethics of Withholding and Withdrawing Critical Care," 179.

13. Robert D. Truog, "Triage in the ICU," *Hastings Center Report*, May-June 1992, 13–17.

14. Cornelius Murphy, point raised during AMINTAPHIL discussion, November 1994.

15. Carl Wellman, point raised during AMINTAPHIL discussion, November 1994.

16. Robert F. Weir, *Abating Treatment with Critically Ill Patients: Ethical and Legal Limits to the Prolongation of Life* (New York: Oxford University Press, 1989).

17. This question rests on both an empirical and an ethical footing. If the data gathered from the national ECMO registry are not sufficient to support the apparent generalization, then removing the somewhat slow to respond first baby in order to help the second baby on the assumption that they are no longer medically equally capable of

benefiting from the treatment may truly wrong the former. To establish that the two babies are no longer medically equal, one must be certain that the statistical claim is reliable. But suppose that the statistical data are reliable. Then the ethical question we have been discussing applies with full force.

18. Thomas Hobbes, *Leviathan*, ed. with an introduction by Edwin Curley (Indianapolis: Hackett, 1994), chap. 15, p. 98.

19. Kenneth Kipnis, point raised during AMINTAPHIL discussion, November 1994.

20. Natalie Dandekar. "Privacy: A Concept for Embodied Persons," *Philosophical Forum* 24 (summer 1993): 331–48.

21. See discussion above.

Chapter 8

Liberty, Equality, Eternity: The Case for Assisted Suicide

Robert C. L. Moffat

When matters of life and death are addressed, philosophers tend to focus analysis on such complex decisions as treatment of neonates and allocation of scarce resources in situations such as the intensive care unit. In those settings, they may argue, the common meanings given to freedom and equality are inadequate for analysis. Although such challenging issues are without question quite philosophically interesting, they arise relatively rarely in comparison with more routine questions, such as the exercise of autonomy as to when to die. Recent court decisions have made significant strides in bringing law closer to being in step with relatively settled moral philosophy.[1] In the process, those court decisions demonstrate that conventional understandings of the meaning of liberty and equality can still carry important weight.

Letting Die

The current state of the law is exemplified by a leading Florida case arising from Mrs. Estelle Browning's wish to die in peace.[2] The Florida Supreme Court held that she had the right to refuse medical treatment including even food and water, in order that she be allowed to die. Withholding food and water will eventually have the effect of bringing about death. Hospice workers, for example, are able to tell us, within a reasonable degree of certainty, how many days it takes to die without water, how many days it takes without food. However, doctors will note that doing without hydration is rather uncomfortable. Therefore, they would recommend just cutting off the nutrition, in which case death will follow somewhere in the vicinity of seventeen days. Clearly, that is not exactly quick and easy. Of course, if individuals happen to be in a permanent vegetative state, as Mrs. Browning was, then (so far as we know) they would not be aware of the discomfort of starving to death. However, we do not know what kinds of dreams one might have during that process. To sum up, under the *Browning* case, one has the constitutional right to have passive measures that allow one to die by refusing medical treatment including even food and water.

That right to refuse all medical treatment is founded both on the right of privacy protected by the Florida state constitution and on the more limited privacy right recognized under the U.S. Constitution in the *Cruzan* case.[3] At the same time, the court in *Browning* is quite explicit about not endorsing active measures. There is no right to command a doctor: "I'm ready to go; give me the pills." Under these decisions, one has no legal alternative to the three weeks of starvation. The reasoning behind such decisions is exemplified by the treatment of the decision to have an abortion in *Casey v. Planned Parenthood.* There, the Court stated that the decision to have an abortion "involves the most intimate and personal choices a person may make in a lifetime" and constitutes a "choice central to personal dignity and autonomy."[4] In *Cruzan*, the Court viewed the decision of a terminally ill person to end his or her life as involving similar intimate and personal choices. The focus of all these constitutional privacy decisions is on autonomy protected by the right to liberty under the Fifth and Fourteenth Amendments.

At the same time, some of the leading state cases, such as the *Browning* case, make clear that the right to privacy is sufficiently encompassing that one need not be in a terminal state in order to exercise the right to refuse medical treatment. Of course, one who is not a patient would not need permission to stop eating. Anyone who had a mind to do so could starve herself to death. At some point that person might be discovered and hauled off for medical care. Such an individual might find herself in the situation of the teen in Miami who decided that it was no longer worth it to him to take the antirejection drugs for his transplanted liver. The authorities attempted to intervene, but the courts made them respect the young man's autonomy.[5] In any event, the *Browning* case makes it very clear both that being terminal has nothing to do with having the privacy right to refuse medical treatment and that being able to refuse medical treatment includes refusing nutrition and hydration. The court is also quite adamant that such measures are not assisted suicide because they are only passive. Thus, *Browning* takes passive measures as far as they can be stretched. Up until May 1994, that was as much help as the law would provide in assisting someone to die. After cases like *Browning*, the only way in which aid to the dying could be further expanded was by legal intervention that would permit the use of active measures.

Assisting Suicide

That next step occurred for the first time in a federal case in the District Court for the Western District of Washington in Seattle challenging Washington state law. On May 3, 1994, in *Compassion in Dying v. Washington*, Chief Judge Barbara Rothstein endorsed active measures.[6] Compassion in Dying is a charitable organization that seeks to aid terminally ill patients who have expressed a wish to die. In this instance, it helped three such patients present their claims for assistance to the court. The organization was able to vouch for the seriousness of their wish to die because the patients had met its criteria for assistance. Its standards require that a patient make three separate requests to die, and that the last request be at least forty-eight hours after the second request. In addition, the standards require that a physician review the medical file to make certain that the patient is actually terminal. They also require a medical examination to make certain that the motivation is not ineffective pain management that could be improved, and to reaffirm that the person really does desire to die. One important fact that was different in this case was that none of the plaintiffs were being supported by artificial nutrition and hydration; therefore, they could not ask for passive assistance, such as the right that Mrs. Browning exercised to have the feeding tubes disconnected.[7] To win support for active measures, they had to offer new arguments. The remainder of this chapter examines those arguments.

Liberty Arguments

The main argument upon which the court relied was that autonomy is a protected liberty interest under the Fourteenth Amendment. The court analogized the right to decide to die to the decision to have an abortion upheld in *Planned Parenthood v. Casey*. The court found that the decision to opt for active euthanasia "involves the most intimate and personal choices a person may make in a lifetime" and constituted a "choice central to personal dignity and autonomy."[8] In summary, the court found that the liberty interest recognized in *Casey* to choose an abortion was equally applicable to the right of the terminally ill patient to exercise liberty in making an autonomous decision to die.

The court proceeded to discuss the standard recognized in *Cruzan* of the right to refuse life-saving hydration and nutrition and concluded that the next logical step was to recognize the right of the individual to choose active measures rather than such passive measures: "The question for this court is whether the choice to commit physician-assisted suicide falls within [the] realm [of privacy protected by the constitution]" (at 1461). The court continued: "Based on the reasoning set forth in *Casey* and *Cruzan*, the court concludes that a competent, terminally ill adult has a constitutionally guaranteed right under the Fourteenth Amendment to commit physician-assisted suicide" (at 1462). The court observed that twenty-eight states make it a crime to assist suicide; twenty-one do not. No state makes suicide or its attempt a crime (at 1464 n. 9). Hence, the only potential criminal liability is for a doctor or someone else who assists a suicide. In the state of Washington assisting a suicide is a class C felony potentially punishable by up to five years in prison (at 1459). In Florida, which is more typical, assisting a suicide is one form of manslaughter and carries possible imprisonment of up to fifteen years.[9] Clearly, such punishment is likely to pose a significant deterrent to any doctor who might otherwise be inclined to dispense mercy.[10]

What course might medical assistance take? Prescribing the fatal drugs and telling the patient how to take them would be the most common method of assisting a suicide. Even physicians disposed to help tend to be rather contemptuous of Dr. Kevorkian's machine.[11] They see his contraption as a lot of showmanship; they would more likely prescribe an overdose of barbiturates. Even now, some physicians may provide a prescription for drugs that, in an overdose, would be likely to produce death but that would be perfectly appropriate for pain relief when used according to directions. In many terminal cancer cases, the dose of morphine prescribed for pain relief is eventually increased to a fatal point. However, that action tends not to bother the physicians who routinely deal with terminal illnesses, so long as the motive of the action remains ambiguous. If they can claim that they are seeking pain relief, then they seem not to worry that the side effects of the pain relief might be fatal.[12] Other physicians, not used to treating terminal illnesses, may indulge quite silly worries, not only that the increased morphine could quicken the death of the terminal patient but even that the terminal patient might become addicted to the pain-killing drugs.[13] But physicians experienced in treating terminal patients do not concern themselves about prosecution in such quite typical cases because the ambiguity of adequate pain relief would make it virtually impossible for even the most determined prosecutor to gather sufficient evidence of a crime.

In any event, ambiguous measures are not satisfactory to those who seek effective aid in dying. They are only partial because ambiguous measures must remain ambiguous. They are unreliable because they may not be available, depending upon the attitude of one's physician. They are inconsistent because they may not be immediately effective and because how well they work varies, depending upon factors such as the ability of the terminal patient's body to metabolize the drugs used. Thus, the plaintiffs in the Washington case sought more effective measures. In place of the present partial and unsatisfactory patchwork approach, they requested that their physicians be able not only to prescribe unambiguously lethal drugs but also to instruct and assist the patients in using them. Moreover, they wished that their physicians might be able to go ahead and prescribe lethal drugs so that they could terminate their lives when they chose to do so.[14] The court granted them that right as a matter of constitutionally protected liberty.

Equality Arguments

Because there were no nutrition and hydration tubes to disconnect, the passive-measures approach of the *Browning* case provided no help for the patients in the Washington case. If they were to die, they needed lethal drugs to help them. Hence, they not only claimed the right to assistance as a matter of constitutionally protected liberty but also claimed a denial of equal protection in light of the fact that Washington state law permitted terminal patients to have nutrition and hydration disconnected. Their argument was that because they were just as terminal as patients dependent on artificial nutrition and hydration, the state law denied them equal protection when it failed to provide them with equivalent means to an early exit (1466).[15] The court accepted this argument as a ground of decision, although those patients could have starved themselves to death simply by stopping eating without any intervention by the court. The court may have ignored that possibility because such a course of conduct would presumably be rather more difficult for terminal patients to carry out than discontinuing artificial nutrition and hydration. Nonetheless, Washington state law does allow both classes of terminal patient to starve themselves to death.

However, even though that equality argument is not especially strong, there is a better equal protection argument not addressed by the court. The more serious category problem on this issue is between persons who have the present ability to commit suicide without help and those who are unable to do so. Some patients may be unable to act because they have lost their mental control. Others may lack the physical ability to swallow the lethal drugs. Still others may lack the physical strength to put the drugs in their mouths. In some patients, ingestion is no longer possible. If everything for a patient has to be intravenous, that person is seriously disadvantaged in comparison with people who have the ability to act for themselves. Such differing abilities may be the source of a serious contrast in treatment. Failure to allow for the difference in capacities that otherwise similar individuals have to exercise liberty can be an effective denial of that liberty. By the same token, such failure can result in what the courts refer to as disparate treatment, even though the treatment is technically identical.[16] Moreover, such a failure to provide equal treatment is particularly damaging because precisely those people who are most likely to want to commit suicide are the very ones who are less likely to be able to do so without assistance. Moreover, an effect of that discrimination against those who are unable to commit suicide on their own is that they may be tempted to go ahead sooner. Indeed, some ethical observers have criticized some of the cases that Dr. Kevorkian has taken on the grounds that it was too soon.[17] Such results are far more likely when patients have to choose between proceeding now while they have the present mental or physical power to act or waiting, with the risk that no one will be able to help them when life or pain becomes unbearable.[18]

Patients may also wish to act while they are certain that they have their mental faculties because they fear—and their fears are well-founded—that if they wait they may lose all opportunity to act. At present, they are not guaranteed that they can have someone else act for them.[19] Although advance directives, known to the public as living wills, are very important and extremely helpful, they are limited by the scope of the law. Thus, an advance directive is effective in permitting the discontinuation of nutrition and hydration. But because of the laws prohibiting assisted suicide, an advance directive, no matter how sensible, that instructed one's physician to provide an easy death under certain conditions would be ineffective because the physician is requested to act in a manner that is still criminal under existing law.[20] Only a repeal of the legislation or a case such as *Com-*

passion in Dying that strikes down the law on constitutional grounds will allow people to have physicians or others assist them with active measures to terminate life. To deprive those most in need of assistance in dying the same right that others have to commit suicide is to visit upon them a serious lack of equal treatment.

Conclusion

Assistance to those who wish to die in peace is not a philosophically complex issue. That power has been sustained in the Washington case on the basis that to refuse such a request for humanitarian treatment would interfere intolerably with the liberty of those patients. Although the case also found a denial of equal protection based on these patients having no feeding tubes to disconnect, a better ground of equal treatment is available in the fact that those patients who are most in need of help are denied it, and those not in need of assistance are legally free to exit as they please. In this case, then, liberty and equality arguments reinforce each other. Although neither liberty nor equality arguments are difficult or complex in this setting, we should not make the mistake of assuming that autonomy is unimportant. As long as 80 percent of Americans die in hospitals,[21] and as long as millions in nursing homes are denied this fundamental right of human dignity, we must continue to reaffirm the importance of this particular expression of the values of liberty and equality.

Notes

This chapter is dedicated to the memory of my late wife Janette Leslie Moffat. In life, she was my teacher in many things, but especially on this issue. In her death, we must learn from her example. She believed passionately in the need for assisted dying, based on her experiences in witnessing the suffering of the terminally ill while nursing at the Royal Prince Alfred Hospital at the University of Sydney, Australia. That same belief sustained her when her own time came, much too prematurely. I believe that the grace, beauty, and good humor with which she met the end of this life was due in extensive measure to her expectation of compassionate assistance in the leaving of it, even though that expectation was disappointed at the end. Perhaps, the moral of her story is that as long as we lack the moral courage to provide compassionate assistance in dying, we should at least have the grace to lie by assuring those we love that they will be spared unnecessary suffering.

1. E.g., Tom L. Beauchamp, "Suicide," and James Rachels, "Euthanasia," both in *Matters of Life and Death: New Introductory Essays in Moral Philosophy*, 3d ed., ed. Tom Regan (New York: Random House, 1993).

2. *In re Guardianship of Estelle M. Browning*, 568 So. 2d 4 (Fla. 1990).

3. *Cruzan v. Director of the Missouri Dept. of Health*, 110 S.Ct. 2841 (1990).

4. *Planned Parenthood v. Casey*, 112 S.Ct. 2791, 2807 (1992).

5. "Teen Can Stop Taking Medicine," *Gainesville Sun*, June 12, 1994, 5A; "Boy Forced into Hospital Gets Apology," *Gainesville Sun*, June 14, 1994, 4B; "Boy Who Refused Medication Dies," *Gainesville Sun*, August 21, 1994, 3B.

6. *Compassion in Dying v. Washington*, 850 F. Supp. 1454 (W.D. Wash. 1994). The decision was overturned 2-1 in a decision by John Noonan, who, prior to his appointment to the bench, was the best-known American scholar of Roman Catholic canon law. He characterized the issue as whether there is a "constitutional right to aid in killing oneself." 49 F. 3d 586, 591 (9th Cir. 1995). That decision was reversed 8-3 on the ground that the terminal patient's liberty interest in hastening death outweighed the state's interest in protecting life. 79 F. 3d 790, 836–37 (9th Cir. 1996)(en banc), cert. granted sub nom. *Washington v. Glucksburg*, 117 S.Ct. 37 (1996).

7. The Washington case is limited to terminal patients. Although that appears to be important for public relations purposes, the fact is that the case presented only the petitions of terminal patients. Hence, it would have been improper for the court to address any issue other than terminal patients. However, the reasoning of the court could be applied to nonterminal patients as well.

8. *Compassion in Dying v. Washington*, 1460.

9. Fla. Stat. 782.08 (assisting self-murder). For representative penalties, see the list in *People v. Campbell*, 335 NW 2d 27 (Mich.App. 1983).

10. It is true that prosecutions of doctors for such assistance are highly unusual. However, the mere threat of prosecution is normally a powerful deterrent. And it remains powerful, even when the prosecutorial policy may be (as it often is) to take such cases before the grand jury for what amounts to an advisory opinion on whether to proceed with prosecution.

11. This conclusion is based on conversations with physicians in the College of Medicine at the University of Florida who deal with terminal patients in their medical practice.

12. A current example is provided by Francis D. Moore in his memoir *A Miracle and a Privilege: Recounting a Half Century of Surgical Advance* (Washington, D.C.: Joseph Henry Press, 1995). The book is excerpted in "Prolonging Life, Permitting Life to End," *Harvard Magazine*, July-August 1995. He states: "I can remember many patients in pain, sometimes in coma or delirious, with late, hopeless cancer. For many of them we wrote an order for heavy medication to be given regularly by the nurses. Morphine by the clock. We were assisting with a softer exit from this world. Nurses helped willingly. This was not talked about openly and little was written about it. It was essential, not controversial" (46). See also 51.

13. A new report urges general practitioners not to be wary of the overuse of pain-killing drugs in terminal patients. Nathan Cherny and Russell Portenoy, "The Management of Cancer Pain," CA—*A Cancer Journal for Clinicians* 44 (1994): 262. See also American Pain Society Quality of Care Committee Consensus Statement, "Quality Improvement Guidelines for the Treatment of Acute Pain and Cancer Pain," *Journal of the American Medical Association* 274 (1995): 1874.

14. *Compassion in Dying v. Washington*, 1459.

15. On review, the court found it unnecessary to reach the equal protection argument (79 F. 3d 790 at 838). However, a challenge to a similar provision of the New York statutes was found to violate the guarantee of equal protection because New York did "not treat equally all competent persons who are in the final stages of fatal illness and wish to hasten their deaths [and] the distinctions made by New York law with regard to such persons do not further any legitimate state purpose; and accordingly, . . . the statutes lack any rational basis and are violative of the Equal Protection Clause." *Quill v. Vacco*, 80 F. 3d 716, 727 (2d Cir. 1996).

16. E.g., *Compassion in Dying v. Washington*, 1467.

17. See Beauchamp, "Suicide," 106–7 (section titled "A Case of Unjustified Assisted Suicide").

18. See Robert C. L. Moffat, "'First Do No Harm': Mixed Signals in Our Thinking about Life and Death," in *Spaces and Significations*, ed. Barbara Kevelson (New York: Peter Lang, 1996), 109–34.

19. Physicians may be evolving new attitudes on that score. Francis Moore states: "It is my credo that assisting people to leave the dwelling place of their body when it is no longer habitable is becoming an obligation of the medical profession." Moore, *A Miracle and a Privilege*, 47; see also 51: "The doctor should do his duty, which is to give the patient the best possible chance for good minutes, hours, days, but avoid prolonging agony."

20. In anticipation of possible legal change, however, I have modified my own living will. Note the italicized portions in the excerpt that follows:

> If at any time I have a terminal condition or *am diagnosed as being in a vegetative state* and if my attending or treating physician and another consulting physician have determined that there is no medical probability of my recovery from such condition, I direct that life-prolonging procedures be withheld or withdrawn when the application of such procedures would serve only to prolong artificially the process of dying or *of noncommunicative existence*, and that I be permitted to die naturally with only the administration of medication or the performance of any medical procedure deemed necessary to provide me with comfort care or alleviate pain. *To the full extent allowed by law, I also direct that my dying be aided by the most expeditious active measures available*.

21. Sherwin Nuland, *How We Die* (New York: Knopf, 1993), 255.

Chapter 9

Punishment, Family, and State

Deirdre Golash

Moral equality is perhaps the form of equality most readily regarded as consistent with liberty. Respect for others as moral equals requires that we respect their liberty. Yet, it is often argued that in one specific context—that of criminal punishment—respect for others as moral equals actually requires that we deprive them of a significant part of their liberty. Herbert Morris, for example, has argued for purely retributive punishment on the basis that the right to be treated as a person entails a right to be punished. More recently, however, a number of writers (including Morris) have argued that our respect for others as moral equals requires that we punish them in an effort to improve their moral characters.[1] R. A. Duff suggests that "punishment . . . expresses our concern . . . for the criminal's own good as a rational moral agent and a member of a moral community."[2] Similar arguments have also been made by Jean Hampton and Robert Nozick.

The moral reform theory derives a substantial part of its credibility from the analogy—implicit or explicit—with parental punishment. Its advocates seek to demonstrate that such punishment reflects a deep concern for the good of the offender, similar to the concern of parents who discipline their children. Both Hampton and Morris make explicit use of this analogy. I shall argue that parental punishment is specifically justified by the lack of moral equality between parent and child (in the case of young children) or is crucially dependent on the emotional bond between parent and child (in the case of older children). Moreover, as soon as we come to regard our children as our moral equals, punishment ceases to be appropriate. Thus, our intuitions regarding the justifiability of parental punishment should not form the basis for a derivative intuition that state punishment for the purpose of moral reform is likewise justified.

What Justifies Parental Punishment?

The paradigm case of justified punishment is punishment inflicted by a loving parent on a child for a wrong done by the child, where the punishment is intended to show the child that her behavior is wrong and to reduce the likelihood that it will be repeated. Doubts that such punishment is justified arise only to the extent that there are doubts about whether it is necessary to achieve these goals. Because most of us were punished as children, and feel that we would be worse off had we not been, we are inclined to regard state punishment of criminal offenders as likewise appropriate and justified. To evaluate the validity of this intuition, we need to examine with some care the justification of parental punishment.

The disciplining of children, of which punishment is often a part, is an integral part of the parent's effort to promote the overall good of the child. Parental punishment can be understood as an effort to promote the long-term good of the child through the teaching of socially acceptable behavior[3] and the development of good moral character. Seeking the child's good in these respects is not merely a desire of the parents but a duty of parenthood. A parent who is indifferent to the behavior or moral good of the child is failing in one of his most central tasks.

Punishment and Behavior

Children become capable of harming themselves or others before they become capable of appreciating the consequences of their actions. For this reason, the parent-toddler relationship is characterized in large measure by the parent's efforts to control the choices made by the child. This the parent typically accomplishes through either coercion or manipulation. Physical constraints are often used to keep children in an environment where they cannot injure themselves or others. Psychological manipulation may be used to obtain the child's acquiescence in peaceful cooperation with playmates. Often, this may be accomplished simply by focusing the child's attention on a range of choices acceptable to the parent. Inevitably, however, the child will be faced with situations in which she perceives a choice, has sufficient physical freedom to act on it, and yet is tempted to make a choice that is morally wrong. For the child too young to understand a rational explanation of moral principles, punishment provides a prudential reason for compliance. At this early stage of moral development, as noted by

Kohlberg, the child has no grasp of morality beyond that of "forbidden" and "not forbidden."[4] Thus we make rules (which can seem only arbitrary to the child) and insist on compliance. We punish the child for running into the street *because* the child *cannot* understand the consequences of doing so. We punish her for tearing up our books or papers because we can't explain why they are important to us. We punish her for hitting her baby brother because she doesn't care if he is hurt. At this stage punishment is merely a substitute for rational explanation.

We train the child in the same way that we would train a dog: through simple conditioning. Whatever method we use—physical constraint, psychological manipulation, or punishment—to gain the child's compliance with rules she does not understand or agree with, we fail on the simplest level to address the child as a moral agent: either we do not allow her to choose or we supply nonmoral reasons for compliance. This is acceptable precisely to the extent that the child indeed is not a full moral agent. At this stage, the actions of parents who seek to teach their children how to behave are justified by the fact that, morally, they "know better" than the child, and by the related fact that the child is not a full moral agent.

Parental Punishment as Promoting Development of Good Moral Character

Continuing to punish on the behavioral level becomes increasingly problematic as the child develops moral agency. In practical terms, the child with an appropriately developed sense of self will increasingly chafe at the subordination of her will to that of her parent, so that parental control can be maintained only at the cost of a significant escalation in the scale of sanctions. At the same time, the practicality of physical constraint and psychological manipulation decreases. As the child moves closer to full moral agency, the justification for imposition of the parent's will also becomes progressively weaker. The parent is then subject to both a practical and a moral necessity to allow the child to make her own choices in an increasingly broad sphere.

To assure that these choices are not morally disastrous, the parents must seek to mold her moral character rather than simply her behavior. Here again, parents have a number of methods at their disposal: they may teach by example, by discussion, or by punishment. To understand the role of parental punishment in promoting the child's moral good at this stage, we must first have an account of good moral character, toward which punishment aims. I shall argue that moral character has both a cognitive and an emotional component, and that punishment (beyond the behavioral stage) is primarily directed toward shaping the emotional component of moral character. Specifically, I shall argue that the central function of parental punishment is to mold the child's attachments to (moral and other) values.

What Is Good Moral Character?

A person having a good moral character has a defensible view of what is morally right, is disposed to act in accordance with that view, and is morally autonomous, that is, she has the ability to make her own independent evaluation of what is morally right.[5] Moral development thus has both a cognitive and an emotional component. The cognitive component consists of the development of appropriate moral beliefs and the ability to apply them to new situations. The emotional component consists of the development of a disposition to act in accordance with those beliefs—that is, the development of a set of emotional attachments to values. Change or development of moral character involves cognitive moral learning, the development of new attachments, or a conflict of attachments resulting in a change in the structure of attachments to values. If punishment contributes to moral development, then, it must be either through imparting cognitive learning or through changing attachments to values.

Punishment as Imparting Cognitive Learning

Can punishment impart cognitive understanding? Cognitive moral learning takes place on two levels: learning the content of moral rules, and understanding the principles that underlie these rules so that one can apply morality to unfamiliar situations. There is no qualitative difference between such learning and other forms of cognitive learning, like the learning of mathematical formulas and principles. This type of instruction is directed toward the understanding. At one time it was fashionable to teach arithmetic by rapping the knuckles of students who got wrong answers, but it is now generally recognized that such methods are not optimal for learning. Similarly, to the extent that moral learning is seen as a cognitive task, it does not make sense to impart it through pain or deprivation. The infliction of pain is obviously not addressed to the cognition of the offender, whether child or adult.

Even if punishment were a desirable method of enhancing learning, it could not convey the appropriate concepts. Suppose, for example, that a child believes (falsely) that one's moral duties to others vary according to ethnic groups. It is evident that punishment cannot teach *that* such beliefs are wrong, any more than a rap on the knuckles can teach the concept of mathematical equality. At most, punishment (in itself) can convey that a specific act is wrong in the eyes of the parent (as a specific answer is wrong in the eyes of the teacher); through inductive reasoning, one might eventually deduce the underlying principle. Punishment can convey that a specific act is prohibited (in the sense that it incurs negative social consequences), but the understanding of why the act is prohibited must be provided apart from the punishment itself.

Punishment as Changing Attachments to Values

In the appropriate circumstances, however, punishment can serve to develop concern for others and attachment to the values of the parent. One way that we can come to be concerned about those to whom we were previously indifferent is through the concern for them of others we care about. For example, we may be concerned about the welfare of a friend's lover, whom we have never met, because we know his welfare affects our friend. Still, we do not become as concerned about his welfare as our friend is, or as concerned as we are about the welfare of our friend. It is a secondary kind of concern; if that person's welfare ceased to affect our friend, it would cease to concern us.

A different kind of transferring of values occurs, however, when we share or may come to share the reasons our friends have for being concerned about someone. For example, we may adopt as our own the friends of our friends, not just because the original friendship provides the occasion for spending time with them but also because we are disposed to look for and to appreciate the qualities our friend values in them. The same holds for the lower level of interest and concern those close to us display in the affairs of broader groups of people. We are more open to the persuasion of the friend than of a stranger. The stranger can rely only on rational arguments; the friend appeals to our predisposition to believe that the things he values will also have value for us, as well as to our desire to retain and to deserve his respect for the qualities that form the basis of the friendship. The parent who has an appropriate concern for the interests of all others is similarly in a strong position to transfer that concern to the child, who shares the parent's reasons for that concern, and who is predisposed to believe that the things the parent values will also have value for her.

In a well-known essay, W. V. O. Quine postulates that our (cognitive) beliefs are (more or less) coherently structured, with some beliefs being more central to the entire system than others.[6] Faced with a choice, we will give up less-central beliefs rather than more-central ones, but even the most-central ones (mathematical truths, for example) are subject to correction, given a sufficient threat to other parts of the belief structure. The structure of our attachments to values is similar. Like our beliefs, some of our values are ones to which we are deeply attached; to others, we may have only a mild degree of attachment. When multiple attachments can no longer be simultaneously sustained, we will typically choose to sacrifice the one to which we are less firmly attached.[7] If my favorite food turns out to be cancer-causing, I am likely either to discount its delights or to minimize my fear of cancer. If I discover that my religion conflicts with my sexual preferences, one or the other will have to be changed.

Just as beliefs about logic and coherence have the function of adjudicating among conflicting beliefs, our most-central values have the function of adjudicating among conflicting values. For example, I value my own material well-being; I also value the well-being of others. Sometimes (if not constantly) the two conflict. Sometimes it is possible for me to sacrifice my well-being for that of others with little or no sense of loss; that is when my attachment to some third value, such as fairness, tells me that it is my own well-being that must give way. When we say that fairness *demands* that I pay my debts, it is a psychological as well as an ethical demand of which we speak. The degree of my attachment to ethical values such as fairness can be measured by the extent to which I will in practice sacrifice other values (which need not be limited to my own well-being) to adhere to them.

Although values and beliefs are strongly interactive, they are not identical. At the extreme, I may hold ethical beliefs in the same way that I hold beliefs about theorems of geometry; it would take a lot to convince me that they are not true, but I do not really care about them very much. (I have no attachment to the good.) I may believe strongly (i.e., fairly centrally) that discrimination against some group is wrong (giving up this belief would seriously disrupt my belief system) yet fail to be disturbed by instances of such discrimination: I simply judge them wrong, but they don't bother me. A person of good moral character has a structure of moral beliefs that is defensible on a cognitive level and a structure of attachments to values that is appropriate to their place in that belief structure. Such a person not only believes strongly that slavery is wrong but also has a high degree of emotional aversion to slavery. In fact, a person who fails to have a defensible set of moral beliefs but who yet is attached to values in the same way will in one sense have a better moral character than the person who does have a defensible set of moral beliefs but who is excessively attached to his own well-being on an emotional level. We can imagine, for example, a professor of moral philosophy who has developed a sophisticated moral theory of which he is justifiably proud, and to which he of course subscribes, but who miserably fails to put this theory into practice. Similarly, we can imagine a person who believes, on a cognitive level, in the relevance of many indefensible distinctions among persons but who is yet, on an emotional level, given to an indiscriminate compassion that in practice leads him to ignore those distinctions. Each fails to give effect to his cognitive moral beliefs—itself a moral failing—but the second is a morally better person than the first, in the sense that more of his actions will be morally defensible.

A person's moral character, then, consists in part of the complex of values to which he is attached and the strength of these attachments. Attachments to the welfare of particular persons and to religious and cultural values are necessarily, if messily, mixed in with attachments to ethical values. I say "necessarily" because these attachments can conflict across category boundaries, and the ways in which such conflicts are resolved reflect directly on moral character. The conflict is often both a conflict of beliefs on the cognitive level and a conflict of attachments on the emotional level, but may involve emotional attachments without corresponding beliefs. The degree of a person's attachment to the value of fairness, for example, is best measured in relation to the lengths to which he will go to discount his attachments to particular persons. (Note that this is not a conflict between fairness and loyalty; loyalty is, to some degree at least, independent of the felt degree of attachment.) Similarly, cultural values, such as the preservation of historical materials, may directly conflict with ethical values, as may at least a subset of religious values, such as prohibitions on the use of certain materials. I make here no substantive claim, either that ethical values must always be primary, or the contrary; I simply point out that all of these values occupy to some extent the same domain, in that the areas in which they influence behavior overlap to a significant degree.

When beliefs are shown to be inconsistent, I must either give up one of the beliefs or give up my belief in consistency. Similarly, when there is a continuing conflict in my attachments, I must give up one of the attachments or find some way to accommodate both. The disciplining of children is necessary to bridge the gap between the natural attachments of children and the attachments their parents wish them to develop. Children learn that (some of) their natural attachments conflict with their attachment to the parents, not merely when there is a direct conflict of interest but also when they act contrary to the parents' values. For example, the child naturally attached to her own self-interest realizes that she cannot continue to be selfish, even in private, and retain the genuine love and approval of the parent. Thus, it is crucial that her attachment to the parent be sufficiently strong to overcome the competing tug of self-interest. A weaker attachment may well result in the child's devaluing the relationship rather than compromise her natural attachment to herself (just as adults may accept a cooling of relations with friends rather than reconsider their most central values).[8]

For the child who is strongly attached to the parents, it will not be enough to gain their outward approval. Such a child who acts against the parents' values behind their backs will feel false and undeserving when praised for her good behavior. In Haim Ginott's telling example, a child praised by his parents for his good behavior on a car trip responded by deliberately upsetting the car's ashtray, filling the car with choking dust. It later turned out that he had been quietly wishing for (and constructing in detail) an accident in which his baby brother would be killed but he and his parents would survive. The parents' praise at this moment created such a sense of guilt and falsity that he felt the need to reveal what he saw as his "real self."[9]

The significance of the child's attachment to the parents in promoting moral development can be seen by comparing our reactions as adults to situations in which we simply desire someone's approval instrumentally to our reactions in situations where there is a genuine relationship. It is common for us to desire to gain the approval (or to avoid the disapproval) of most of those we have dealings with; such approval in general makes life more pleasant and smooths the path to our goals. But in many of these situations, the approval serves to a greater or lesser extent a purely instrumental purpose. To take an extreme example, a prisoner of war will benefit from avoiding the disapproval of his guards, who have a great deal of power over him.

Thus, he may make an outward show of compliance and even respect. Nevertheless, he will not hesitate, as soon as a guard's back is turned, to drop all semblance of compliance. His desire for the guard's approval is purely instrumental, and the guard's possession and exercise of power fails utterly to reach his inner character. At the other end of the spectrum is the effect on us of those people we deeply love and respect. We ordinarily do not find it satisfactory simply to gain the outward approval of our friends; instead, we wish to be loved for our real qualities. We also want our friends' approval to be an expression of their genuine feelings for the qualities we really possess; what we seek is a connection between true selves. Such relationships are deeply satisfying. In contrast, should I obtain requital of my love of another through lies, deceit, and a false display of the qualities I know they value, my initial satisfaction will prove hollow: it is not I but only my false representation that is loved.

The child, then, seeks the genuine approval of the parents. Punishment can play a role in expressing strong parental disapproval both by serving as a simple expression of anger and as evidence of what the parent is willing to do to prevent the behavior. There is thus a direct tie between the parent's initial deterrent intentions and the effect on character Here, the contrast between the parent's usual behavior and the punishment is significant, because the child knows that the parent finds it difficult to impose deprivation on her, and so knows that the parent's desire to stop the behavior is strong.

Limits of Parental Punishment

The possibility of using punishment as a means of transferring values to the child does not by itself justify punishment. Values may also be transferred through other experiences that appeal to the emotions, such as literature and drama. Children also learn values from the example set by their parents and others, and from the reactions of their peers.The older child may be as moved by the parent's verbal expression of how he feels about the behavior as she would be by punishment designed to stop it; if this is to be effective, however, parent and child must share an understanding that the words are indeed adequate to change the behavior. Similarly, the older child may be stopped from dangerous behavior by a verbal explanation of its consequences.

There is no necessary connection between punishment and any particular form or degree of transgression. We can easily imagine a parent reacting to a child's theft of money from another family member by first scolding, then by increasing the allowance of the guilty child; or to a child's striking her baby brother by reassuring her of the parent's love. The appropriateness of punishment, in the family context, is entirely dependent on the degree to which it is in fact necessary to the child's moral development.

Punishment is justified only when it is the only way, or at a minimum, a more effective way, of teaching the child (or some specific child) the limits of acceptable behavior. A parent may be justified in imposing punishment in preference to other methods of instruction because she does not have the patience or the resources to make other methods work effectively, or because she does not believe other methods are as effective. But a parent who has the resources, and who has had success in using other methods, would require some further justification for reverting to punishment. Punishment always involves deprivation for the child, and such deprivation must not be imposed gratuitously. Thus, punishment is justified only where it is (reasonably believed to be) a necessary means of achieving moral development.

In sum, then, parental punishment is justified where

1. Its purpose is to promote the long-term good of the child, and either
2. It is directed at changing the behavior of a child, where
   (a) the child is not a full moral agent,
   (b) the desired change in behavior is morally defensible, and
   (c) the punishment is (reasonably believed to be) necessary to change the child's behavior; or
3. It is directed at improving the child's moral character, where
   (a) the child is sufficiently attached to the parent to wish not merely to gain the parent's overt approval but also to deserve that approval,
   (b) the desired change in the child's attachments to values is morally defensible, and
   (c) the punishment is (reasonably believed to be) necessary to express the extent of the parent's disapproval, and thus to change the child's value attachments.

There is some oddness in speaking of the parents' actions as "justified" or "unjustified." We are hesitant to criticize the actions of parents in disciplining their children except in extreme cases. This stems from two sources. The parents are of course not in a position of omniscience; thus their actions must be justified relative to what they perceive. The level of effort they ought to make to improve their knowledge must be evaluated relative to the other tasks that fill their lives, not to mention the incompleteness of the available wisdom. And mere knowledge is often insufficient to change a pattern of interaction that has developed over time. Thus, we hesitate to criticize parents not because their actions are outside the realm of justification but because we appreciate the difficulty of their task. More important, though, we recognize the significance of the parent's intimate knowledge of the child's character, previous behavior, and responsiveness to punishment. Any parent of more than one child knows that a punishment that will leave one child scornful and unrepentant may be deeply wounding to another, more sensitive child. In leaving the punishment of children up to the parents, we rely in more than one way on the closeness and the loving nature of the relationship.

Parental Punishment and Moral Inequality

When, and why, do we stop punishing our children? Obviously, we don't wait for them to become morally perfect. To some degree, of course, we simply lose our power over them. But most parents still retain, and some parents still exercise, some power even over their adult children. We tend to stop punishing our children when they become our moral equals. This does not mean that they share all of our values or even that we judge them to be morally good. Rather, it means that they have adult rational and emotional capacities, so that we judge them capable of making their own moral decisions. Even if we think we still can effectively punish them, we refrain from doing so out of respect for their moral autonomy.

Notice this does not have to mean that the parent becomes entirely indulgent or gives up on changing the child's behavior. Rather, there is a shift away from punishment and toward other kinds of negative consequences—the kinds of consequences we impose on our peers.

As Roger Wertheimer notes:

> Wrongdoing can justify denying the wrongdoer claims and entitlements—to protection against injury during the wrongdoing, to the profits of wrongdoing, to goods needed to compensate victims of the wrongdoing. Further, we may properly deny loyalty to the disloyal, deny equal opportunity to the treacherous, and deny to the disaffecting title to a claim on our affections. We may justly deny a wrongdoer any claim to our generosity, benevolence, esteem, trust, and virtually any of our goods. We may desert those who desert us, abandon them to a desert of their own making,

> a lifeless, desolate wasteland bereft of the benefits of our community and society. . . . Wrongdoing can justify feelings of resentment indignation, outrage, remorse, guilt, and the like.[10]

Interestingly, none of the possibilities listed here (necessarily) constitutes punishment, though all are painful and most are (or can be) intentionally imposed on wrongdoers. Instead, they are more plausibly seen as the natural consequences of the wrongful act itself or the disapproval of others that it incurs. Consider that we do not typically seek to punish our friends; indeed, the idea that we take an action *to punish* a friend for wrongful behavior is at odds with the equality that the relationship implies. Yet, there is no such peculiarity in the idea that we may require our friends to bear the consequences of their transgressions, which may range from temporary discomfort caused by sharp words to the permanent loss of some part of our esteem. As our children become our moral equals, the consequences we impose on them also take on this quality.

The State

Parental punishment, then, may be justified either as a way of changing the behavior of the young child or as a way of promoting the moral development of the older child. Criminal offenders, unlike young children, are full moral agents; thus, it is immediately apparent that this part of the justification of punishment in the parental context is not transferrable to state punishment. (Of course, there are also a number of other compelling arguments against justifying criminal punishment on the basis that it changes behavior.)[11] My primary concern, however, is with the use of the parental analogy to support state punishment on the basis that it promotes the moral development of the offender.

As noted above, several writers have proposed that state punishment might instead be justified not by its effect on behavior but, rather, by its effect on the moral character of the offender. Theories proposing to justify punishment on the ground of "moral reform" or "moral education" of offenders suggest that punishment for these purposes is consistent with a deep concern for the well-being and autonomy of the offender.

There are several different versions of moral reform theory that differ in important respects. All of them, however, share the following three central tenets:

1. The source of wrongful behavior is the failure of the offender to appreciate the wrongfulness of his conduct.
2. This failure is a defect of moral character (and as such, harmful to its possessor).
3. Hard treatment is necessary to communicate to the offender the wrongfulness of his conduct. (It does not necessarily follow that the hard treatment will cure the character defect; the offender may reject the message.)

In contrast to traditional rehabilitative theory, moral reform theory is intimately tied to respect for persons in the Kantian sense. Such respect forms the ground for the assumption that the offender's moral character is subject to positive change and also entails strict limits on the means that may be used (they must respect the autonomy of the offender, not coerce his will). The offender is to be shown why his act was wrong and to be given moral reasons to change his behavior, but he is not to be forced to change. Because moral improvement is in the offender's own interest, the attempt to effect it does not involve treating him as a mere means to society's ends.

Proponents of moral reform theory emphasize that it is not a teleological theory, justifying punishment by its efficacy in producing better moral character.[12] Rather, it is the addressing of the offender as a moral agent, to which punishment is said to stand in a logical rather than contingent relationship, that forms the essential purpose and justification of punishment. On this view, it does not matter whether the offender "receives" the message sent by punishment; the sending of the message is self-justifying as an appropriate response to wrongdoing by a moral agent. The message is justified because it is true, important, and directed at the moral good of the offender; the form in which it is sent (hard treatment) is justified because it is the only form in which the appropriate message can be delivered. Thus, the punishing of even the hardened offender unlikely to repent is justified by the attempt to make this communication. Duff, for example, argues that ideally we should impose hard treatment on all serious offenders, even those unlikely ever to repent, on the ground that we have no right to assume of anyone that he cannot achieve moral redemption. For such a course of action to be justified, we would have to think that of all the options available, punishment has the best chance of working, even though we set that chance at near zero. Perhaps more significant, we would also have to believe that punishment presents an even more negligible chance of *retarding* moral development than it does of advancing it.

The justification for sending the message cannot be entirely separated from its intended effect on the recipient's character. The message is not "directed at" the offender's moral good if it cannot reasonably be expected to promote that good. The language of communication suggests that the message thus sought to be imparted is a cognitive one. As we have seen, though, punishment is not the best (much less the only) method of communicating on a cognitive level. Instead, punishment, at least insofar as it can further moral development rather than simply behavioral change, operates on the emotional level—the level of attachments to values.

When the state seeks to mold moral character, not only does it fail to address the offender's cognition but the emotional bond—the mechanism through which the punisher's disapproval can have an effect on the offender's character—is missing. Just as the guard in the prisoner-of-war camp cannot expect to affect the characters of his charges, the state cannot expect to affect the characters of its prisoners. For the state's strong expression of disapproval to have an effect comparable to the expression of disapproval by the parent, the person punished must desire not merely to win the state's approval but also to deserve that approval. It is only the exceptional criminal offender, in our society, who stands in this relationship to the state.

Moral reform theories of criminal punishment describe the offender as (like a child) in need of moral instruction yet seek to respect the moral autonomy of the adult. The tension between these two ideas is palpable. We must have great confidence in the correctness of our moral ideas in order to punish anyone in their name; yet we are enjoined from imposing those views on the offender, who (we know from his actions) does not agree with these ideas. But there is no escaping the contradiction: why are we sure enough of our ideas to punish at all, if we are not sure enough of them to extract agreement at any price? The two poles are simply presenting our ideas on the cognitive level (all persons are morally equal) and, at the other extreme, coercion of the offender's will, breaking of his spirit, until he agrees with us. Punishment is simply a point between the two. It exerts some emotional pressure on the offender, short of the amount needed to guarantee agreement, but it is still an emotional pressure that makes agreement more likely than taking the exclusively cognitive route.

Some individuals may indeed undergo an improvement in moral character *during* incarceration; this is not to be confused with change *effected* by punishment. The source of change may come from the forming of personal relationships with counselors, fellow inmates, or others. Change may also come as a result of introspection; however, such change is not likely to constitute a change of character, in the sense of a change in the values adhered to; instead, like reflection on one's own beliefs, it is likely to reduce internal inconsistency and conflict. Just as reflection on one's own beliefs is unlikely to produce a radically different set of beliefs, moral introspection is unlikely to change one's values. Such introspection is most likely to produce positive change for those who have unthinkingly acted on values contravening their most central values; that is, for those who already have, at the deepest level, a good moral character (and thus are the least in need of reform).

Conclusion

I have sought to draw attention to important differences between family and state punishment, in the hope that the institution of criminal punishment will not continue to benefit from its surface similarity to the quite different practice of parental punishment. Although I have not shown conclusively that change in behavior or moral character cannot be a justifying purpose of criminal punishment, I have argued that, if so, it must be on a basis quite different from those that make these purposes legitimate in the family context.

Notes

This chapter was originally presented as a paper at the AMINTAPHIL conference in Charleston, S. C., November 10–12, 1994. This version reflects improvements suggested by Burton Leiser and Jeffrie Murphy in their formal comments on that occasion. I am also indebted to Brian Forst, Paul Leighton, James Lynch, Julianne Nelson, Joshua Rider, and Laurence Thomas, all of whom read and commented on this chapter in various earlier incarnations.

1. Herbert Morris, "A Paternalistic Theory of Punishment," *American Philosophical Quarterly* 18 (1981): 263; Robert Nozick, *Philosophical Explanations* (Cambridge: Harvard University Press, 1981), chap. 4, "Retributive Punishment"; Jean Hampton, "The Moral Education Theory of Punishment," *Philosophy and Public Affairs* 13 (1984): 208; R. A. Duff, *Trials and Punishments* (Cambridge: Cambridge University Press, 1986).

2. Duff, *Trials and Punishments*, 234–35.

3. Of course, the parent may choose to teach the child to behave in ways that are not acceptable to broader social groups. For example, a parent may teach a child to dress

differently from others for religious reasons or not to salute the flag at school. But the behavior taught is always that which is acceptable to the parent, and with rare exceptions, to some social subgroup.

4. Lawrence Kohlberg, *Philosophy of Moral Development: Moral Stages and the Idea of Justice* (San Francisco: Harper & Row, 1981).

5. I am indebted here to Laurence Thomas's account of good moral character in *Living Morally* (Philadelphia: Temple University Press, 1983), 3–25.

6. W. V. O. Quine, "Two Dogmas of Empiricism," *From a Logical Point of View*, 2d ed. (New York: Harper & Row, 1963), 20–46.

7. This is not the same as sacrificing one value in a particular situation. I might, for example, have to choose between going to work today and staying home with my family; my choice of one does not mean I give up my attachment to the other. Rather, attachments are (painfully) sacrificed when they cannot be sustained, for example, to preserve my self-esteem, I assign less weight to my professional ambitions; to protect myself from the ongoing pain of separation, I reduce the level of my attachment to an absent friend. This is typically not a matter of conscious decision.

8. Although self-interest provides the most obvious example, the point does not depend on the rather controversial proposition that children are naturally attached to their own self-interest. As long as the natural attachments of the child vary from the attachments the parents wish her to have, the transferring of values will occur in the same way.

9. Haim G. Ginott, *Between Parent and Child: New Solutions to Old Problems* (New York: Macmillan, 1965).

10. Roger Wertheimer, "Understanding Retribution," *Criminal Justice Ethics* (summer-fall 1983): 22–23.

11. In traditional utilitarian terms, the infliction of pain or deprivation on an offender can be justified if it is for the greatest good of the greatest number—in particular, if it makes either the offender or society ultimately better off. The problems with this justification for punishment may be briefly summarized as follows. First, it places no weight on the guilt of the offender, so that it would theoretically justify "rehabilitation" of innocents if that would improve the general welfare. Second, it treats the offender as a mere means to the improvement of society; his own autonomy is not valued, and indeed may be significantly trammeled by techniques that are effective in changing his desires or personality structure. Third, there is no logical connection between the gravity of the crime and the deprivation to be imposed; the amount of deprivation is tied to the prospects for improvement and the social benefits to be gained thereby.

12. Parental punishment, in contrast, is easily justified on teleological grounds. The typical objections to these grounds have little force in the family context. If the aim of parental punishment is repentance, there is indeed no need to punish the already repentant child, and no one will find reason to deplore this. If, on the other hand, repentance can be made significant and lasting only through punishment, the parents should punish the

repentant child. If punishing the child for a particular offense will result in defiance rather than deterrence, it is better not to punish but to look for some other path to the child's understanding. Often, the punishment will be proportional to the gravity of the offense, but if it is less severe and yet serves the goal of moral development, there is nothing to criticize. In short, if whatever system of punishment (or nonpunishment), with whatever system of exceptions and idiosyncrasies, results in the production of an adult of sound moral character, without causing unnecessary pain to the developing child, then that system is fully justified.

Chapter 10

False Light

Wade L. Robison

We harm each other in countless ways—in revenge and indifference, in gratuitous teasing, and in intentional torture. We harm each other individually and we institutionalize harms—in entrenching social inequities and so denying fair equality of opportunity, in marking persons by generic features that degrade.

Compared to these harms, saying false things about a person's private life seems absolutely benign.[1] It is directed at an individual or individuals, and any harm is confined in that way. Besides, if what is said is false,[2] nothing private has been revealed. So, we may ask, what harm is done? We all know the falsity of our childhood retort "Sticks and stones can break my bones, but words can never hurt me!" Words can hurt, but it may seem, when the words are false, they can no more touch one's core than reveal it. One ought to be able to go on, as we tried to do as children, as though nothing had happened.

Of course, part of what we feared as children was that others would believe what they were told, and, it may be thought, harm can come only if people believe one's private life has been revealed. It is the false light that creates and carries the harm, on this reading, and one's privacy, not being disclosed, is not invaded. It has been said of Richard Nixon that he had no conjugal relations with his wife after his defeat in the California gubernatorial election in 1962. If we assume this is an example of false light, the harm cannot be that the Nixons' private life was revealed, for, *ex hypothesi*, it was not. Parents or others may be harmed when falsely accused, long after the fact, of molesting children,[3] but, on this view, their inner selves are untouched. The harm, it is claimed, is thus not a distinctive kind of harm to any privacy interest, certainly not worth the category it has in tort law.[4] Yet, this understanding of false light is fundamentally misconceived. To see how this is so, we need to look more closely at it and its implications.

The Harm as Essentially Extrinsic

Suppose I tell you that a former secretary of state has a tattoo of a tiger on his tush. If we assume this statement about a private matter false, it raises the most obvious and yet puzzling aspect of false light, for the statement is not *about* the former secretary in any way that invades his privacy any more than is the claim about the Nixons. Neither discloses anything because both, we presume, are false.[5] So why suppose false light an invasion of privacy, occupying a slot, along with intrusion, disclosure, and appropriation, among the four standard ways of invading one's privacy?

It is certainly to be distinguished from intrusion and appropriation. Intrusion requires intruding—by reading someone's diary without permission, by walking in on a couple making love, by opening a stall door in a toilet when the stall is occupied. Putting someone in a false light requires only saying something about a person's private life that puts the person in a false light. If we thereby intrude, it is only in a metaphorical sense.

Appropriation requires the taking without permission of some part of someone else's identity for one's personal benefit—by using Caruso's name on one's cigars without asking or paying him,[6] by pretending to be a famous male fashion photographer to convince beautiful women to pose for you,[7] by selling a cellulose-reduction firm a photograph of a fat friend and her child standing nude in a stream, facing the other direction. But putting someone in a false light does not take anything from that person and need not be done for any benefit.

If we concentrate on the failure of false light to connect with its purported object, it looks like a bungled disclosure. A leading case of disclosure is that of *The Red Kimono*, a movie of a woman who had lived a high life of prostitution and been a defendant in a sensational murder trial. She moved to relative respectability in a small midwestern town where her history was unknown to anyone, including her husband. She was exposed when the movie appeared.[8]

Suppose the wrong person is pointed out as the reformed prostitute. This woman would be bathed in a false light. A provocateur tried to disclose, but failed. The harm here would not be like shooting a cow instead of a deer, which is a success of sorts. That could occur if the provocateur, by accident, lit upon someone with a similar past. But if the target is innocent, a harm occurs, of a sort that needs to be discouraged, but one parasitic on disclosure.

Yet, whether the provocateur made a mistake or carefully calculated the false light to look like disclosure, false light does not disclose. Whatever the provocateur's intentions, that is, false light, on this view, does not invade anyone's privacy. It appears to but fails—just as any false empirical proposition fails to assert something about the world.

False light is thus not, on this reading, a distinctive kind of invasion of privacy but a failed disclosure that cannot cause harm by invading anyone's privacy. Any harm that may come from false light is external, its extent and even existence dependent upon the truth or falsity of further contingent propositions about the effects of the falsehood on the beliefs of others and the effects of those beliefs. One must assess the harm by asking, "Am I harmed when people believe these false things about me?"—a question whose answer is not obvious, with the kinds and degrees of harm a function of perhaps some complex formula relating the likelihood of others believing what is said, the perversity of what is said, the prior character of the person bathed in false light, and so on.

Indeed, false light may cause no harm at all on this reading. Think again of that former secretary of state and the supposed tattoo of a tiger on his tush. I may put him in a false light, but real harm can occur, on this reading, only if a provocateur gets the right falsehood, one that is both believable *and* damaging. If someone believes that having a tattoo of a tiger on one's tush is a sign of a joie de vie that makes the former secretary less bland than he may sometimes appear, then he may be benefited, at least in that way. No necessary connection exists between casting false light on someone and causing that person harm.

On this analysis, false light is similar to mock intrusion. By vigorously rattling door knobs on toilet stalls, or curling our fingers over the top of the door and standing on tiptoe as though we were going to lift ourselves up, we may cause nervousness if the person within thinks we are about to intrude, and so we may harm—or thrill—the person, but we would not have intruded and so not have invaded anyone's privacy. Just so, on this view, false light does not invade one's privacy and so cannot harm in that way, and it may be false that people believe the falsehood or, if they believe it, that the belief causes harm to the individual. We have no more need for false light among the privacy torts on this analysis than we have for mock intrusion: each may cause harm but not through an invasion of privacy.

A Distinctive Harm

Yet, the harms of false light are not properly appreciated and understood if thought to be wholly external. The statement that the former secretary has a tattoo of a tiger on his tush may bemuse us. The accusation that Nixon did not sleep with his wife (and notice that he is the unwilling party by this story) may cause us to smile, saying, to ourselves, "Well, that would explain it!"—his uptight way of moving through our world. Yet, we ought to be uncomfortable with that smile and those thoughts. There is something at least mildly offensive about poking at their private lives.[9] It seems at least prima facie wrong, that is, not just contingently so, knowingly to say something false about someone's private life: it may be justifiable, but it is wrong unless it is justifiable.[10]

This response is backed by another aspect of the standard view of false light. We can imagine cases where a false proposition about someone's public life is both more believable and more damaging than one about the person's private life. If the existence of the harm depends upon others believing the claim and upon the effects of those beliefs, then whether the claim is about a private or a public matter is only contingently relevant. A provocateur would consider whether people are more likely to believe a claim about a person's private life, or one about the person's public life, or a mixture of the two, and then speak accordingly.

If any harm in false light rests upon what is believed and damaging, what it lights is irrelevant except for the tactical decision as to what sort of statement about one's life is most believable and damaging. The standard view of false light thus makes it irrelevant that the statements are about private matters. Yet, saying something about something private presents itself, at least initially, as having a status different from saying, for instance, that Nixon never wore shorts in public.

We can get a better sense of the different status by asking ourselves how Nixon, or Pat, might respond to the one-liner about their private lives, given that the worm of doubt has been planted. Unlike claims about their public lives, the one-liner is unverifiable without the complicity of Nixon or his wife or intrusive invasions of their privacy. So if we are not to invade their privacy to assess the one-liner, its falsity can be ascertained only by Nixon or his wife revealing something true about their sexual relations.

A distinctive, and ironic, harm created by false light is thus that it may force the person to disclose—to become a public confessor, a demeaning role. The person whose private life has not been revealed by the false light may need to reveal it to avoid the harms produced by a believable false light. In the hands of a clever provocateur, false light can thus be a diabolical way to invade someone's privacy. It can put us in a position where we can avoid the implications of the false light only by *our* lighting up our core to public view.

Yet, to deepen our understanding of the ways false light can invade someone's privacy and touch one's core, even without revealing it, we need to up the ante from one-liners, like the Nixon anecdote, to a sustained story. More important, we need to flip our perspective from the proposition that is the source of the false light to the person or persons bathed in that light so we can comprehend how the false light affects their lives. We have been looking at the false light itself, but if we look at false light from the perspective of the person bathed in it, we shall see the harms it causes more clearly.

So, let us presume someone who is innocent but with a rough enough personality for false light to fasten upon.[11] We need to imagine a person with the sorts of imperfections we all have, and to let some contingent events, combined with those imperfections, provide a firm foothold for the false light. It will help to pick a fault that will heighten people's emotions and cause them, even as they wonder at the accusation, to back away; a charge, perhaps, of sexual misconduct of some sort. If that is the charge, it will help as well to suppose that the person has continual access to innocents in confidential settings. My aim is to sort out and track the relevant harms.

A False Light

You hear it at lunch. One woman is telling another about a local doctor, and you are sitting where you cannot help but hear.[12] She heard that he has been taking advantage of attractive women who come to see him.[13] Nothing overt at first, just a quiet recognition that they are attractive. One feels, well, flattered, and yet uncomfortable, by that look. If there is a response, she says, he responds, but always in measured terms, always following the woman's lead. So he has had affairs with patients, and no one has ever complained. "That's not all," she adds. She has heard that he has taken advantage of some after sedating them. "You know!" she says, when pressed for details. "He tells them he needs to give them a shot of something to make sure everything is all right, and then he makes love to them while they are not really *with* it, while they are manageable, but don't know what they are doing."[14] "And," she adds, "he did the same things where he was before he came here. That's why he had to leave."

They talk on. You know the physician, have met him socially, in fact, have never seen anything suspicious, and wonder about the story. It sounds sleazy. He is supposed not only to make sexual advances but, when they are not successful, to use his position as a physician to get what he cannot get by his advances. Worse, she is not talking about a single incident but a history—not a single act but a character flaw confirmed by his having been caught once and continuing.

Because, *ex hypothesi,* the judgment is false, *we* know that he has done nothing of the sort, but you, listening to that conversation, do not know that. What do you do?[15] You pay more attention the next time you see him, for one thing. Does he act normal? Is there anything about his manner that betrays a deeper—or an odd—interest? Does he seem on edge? You do not cultivate him. You are acquaintances, and you keep it that way. The stories may not be true, but you do not invite him for drinks or go out of your way to meet up with him at social events. You keep him where he was. And you are careful when you meet him. You do not ask him how his practice is shaping up. You do not give him a handle for an embarrassing response—in case the story is true and he knows that others know and wants to confide, or bluster—and you do not say anything that could give him a clue that you know.

If your spouse has come not to like your family physician and wants to try that "Dr. So-and-so, you know, the one we've met," what do you do? You tell what you heard and recommend someone else. Your friends? The new couple across the street who ask you to recommend a physician? If you recommend him, and the stories are true, it would be as though you were an accomplice.

When, along with the other members of the board of the charitable organization to which you belong, you are trying to find someone in the community to help represent your organization, do you choose him? Even though he is bright, personable, and interested? Or do you find someone else?

Multiply your own reaction by those of all who have heard the story, repeated at lunch, over the phone, by friends and acquaintances, with variations and hyperbole. Count in the number of his patients who have heard the story and decided that though they personally have not been treated that way—"He could tell right away, I think, that he wouldn't be able to get away with any of that with me!"—they do not want such a sleazy person for their physician—"if he *is* sleazy, but why take a chance?"

What will be the consequences? The physician will find the number of his patients dropping, that far from succeeding, he is losing ground. Even some of his old friends may fade, and there is little of that change in one's relations that one expects, none of that variation as some of one's acquaintances become friends. He finds himself not quite "accepted" in town. The organizations and groups he thinks himself suited for do not find him suitable. His practice diminishes and his social life stagnates.

We have been supposing the physician without a clue. Not being guilty of anything, he cannot know, without a hint, what is being said about him. Those who believe it do not tell him because, after all, he already knows. Besides, one hesitates to say anything in such a situation. What is the point? He would deny it, of course, and where would one be?

Yet, we need only imagine that some of those who have heard are not as discreet and self-controlled as you and that when they see him, they are embarrassed, or angry, and show by their manner that *something* is not right. Some people react to him in ways that make him feel as though he were an offensive object—which puzzles him very much. Even those he knows fairly well seem somehow constrained with him, as though they were careful *not* to be at ease. He vaguely feels that something is wrong but is at a loss to grasp what.

"Maybe I just cannot sustain a relationship," he thinks, "and maybe I cannot sustain a practice for the same reason. My patients don't like me after they find out what I'm like. Have I changed somehow," he wonders, "or am I just imagining those reactions and so discomfort others, and they show it?" Not quite clueless, but with no idea of the rumor, he turns, as is natural, to wonder if something is wrong with *him*.

Let us suppose now that he hears the story—officially, when a partner writes to ask him to leave because all are suffering because of what he is doing, writes to say that if they had known why he had left his previous practice, they never would have taken him on and that it would just be best for all concerned, himself included, if he leaves quietly.

He is stunned—as one would be who had done nothing and knew nothing. The shock is like that he sees in his worried but hopeful patients when he tells them they have cancer. They do not hear much of what he says for several days, at least, and he must check back over the next few weeks to be sure they comprehend the details. Just so with him.

As he emerges from that shock, he must come to see, quickly, the enormity of it all. His life has been altered by these falsehoods the way the flow of a stream is disrupted by a submerged boulder. When his life passed over that boulder he has no idea, but the consequences cannot be undone. The truth of the matter is irrelevant as far as the damage is concerned. That is brought home starkly to him by the official letter. A simple confidential call to his old partners would have removed so much suspicion, he thinks,[16] but the rumor is so pervasive, and so believable, that he has been judged and sentenced without a hearing by those who are best positioned, and ought to be most concerned, to ferret out the truth.

The External Harms of False Light

In law it is helpful to think of a person as a set of legal relations, having one legal right that this person not trespass and another that that person not, having this legal power and that, and so on.[17] Just so, it is helpful to conceive of a person as a unique set of interests that change but that can be grouped together in a narrative that embodies a person and the way that person relates to others as he or she goes through life.[18] A person is at least a bundle of interests, to borrow a phrase from Hume, and this bundle marks the person's position in the world. One will associate with some people rather than others because of those interests, prefer to work at some jobs rather than others, and so on.

False light throws into this set of interests a new variable, altering the set, like a new planet distorting the orbits of the old by its gravitational pull or, in the analogy used before, like a boulder put into the stream of one's life, changing the narrative flow in ways both abrupt and subtle, throwing up new currents and eddies and bubbles. The effects on the narrative stream may be few. I suspect the lives of the Nixons were changed not at all by that one-liner. But the new variable may profoundly influence the narrative of one's life. Just as one had no control over the dropping of that boulder, so one has no control over the effects. One's interests are changed, and so one's life is changed, no matter what. Indeed, the metaphor of the boulder may mislead because the eddies it creates disappear once the main currents reassert themselves. But a false light may drop into one's life, as it were, over and over again, as the rumor is repeated, and so the narrative flow of one's life is distorted, again and again, with or without one's knowledge.

There is no doubt at all that the good doctor's interests were substantially harmed—whatever the long-term effects of the false light. Each of us occupies what I call a social position, marked out primarily by the intersection of economic, cultural, and social lines of force. How much income and wealth we have, what sort of social standing we have, among other relevant variables, make differences to our lives—not just in what we can do but in how we are treated by others and thus to how we can relate to them. Jokes about used car salesmen and lawyers turn on this notion of a social position.

When one is put in a false light, one's social position can be harmed. A physician loses clients, and income decreases. Moving to start a practice again somewhere else brings all the economic losses attendant upon registering in a new state, in selling one's house at a time not of one's choosing, in moving one's goods. One has all the social losses accrued in taking one's children out of school, in disrupting the career of one's spouse, in finding, if possible, a new circle of friends. These sorts of losses affect the physician we have been describing, and the harms done to him are substantial. He has no guarantee, for instance, that the story will not follow wherever he may go and disrupt his life once again.

But I want to put these harms aside. These are the harms that come from people believing what is falsely said of him. They are, in that way, external to him and seem not to touch his core. In saying that I do not mean to mark them as any less significant than the harms to one's privacy I shall emphasize. Indeed, a person's life can be ruined by what others believe because of a false light. It is not that the usual story of what goes wrong when one is bathed in false light is wholly mistaken, but that it is not the whole story. It understates the extent of the harm and misrepresents its nature, for it ignores what is peculiarly harmful about false light.

The Privacy Harms

You may be ignorant forever of a false light that radically altered your life, so socially inept that no inkling of a difference ever penetrated. So what is the harm to your privacy—given, *ex hypothesi,* that what is said about you is false?

One harm is that others think they know something private about you that you did not reveal. You are thus, for one thing, not on an equal footing with others. They think they are privy to your life in a way you do not think you are privy to theirs. So they have a status like voyeurs vis-à-vis you.

They will thus be looking for things about you that they never would have been looking for otherwise, for some things you do that are innocent will be seen as grounds for suspicion because of the false light. Suppose the good doctor meets a female patient at a lunch counter; she asks him to join her; he accepts. The meeting is innocent enough except that in the context of the false light, it invites suspicion for those who think they are in the know and see the two sitting together and wonder whether the woman is in the know and whether, on the chance she is not, they should say something to her.[19]

The false light creates a story line and so has narrative power, creating a way of looking at events such that an innocent event can look malevolent in a false light. The *status* of the doctor's acts and omissions has changed because of the false light. He is now *under suspicion*, and so, with that story line, what would have been innocent is seen as confirming his bad character. He is thus denied the normal presumption of innocence. Indeed, that presumption has been flipped because the narrative power of the false light means that acts that *are* innocent are taken as further evidence of depravity. The presumption of equality that normally marks our relations with others has been radically altered. That is one set of harms.

But he has also lost control over his public image. It is not for nothing that you find it an invasion of privacy when someone reads your private letter and then tells the world. You have lost the power to control that information and so lost the power to modulate what is known and not known by others about yourself—lost the power to control your public image, to your intimate friends, your acquaintances, and the world.[20]

Worse, it is not just that others think they know something about your private life. The false light can be so garish and so public, and provide so powerful a narrative for your acts as effectively to prevent you from *being* yourself. You will have lost not just the capacity to control what others know, or think they know, about your private life; you will have lost the capacity to be believed and the power even to express yourself. Every attempt to be natural and spontaneous will be viewed in the false light. "Wouldn't you try to act natural too if you had worn a red kimono?" Far from being an individualized act of harm—a single false thing said and a single harm to the individual—the harm becomes institutionalized for that person, the person accused being systematically marked out from others and degraded.

Even though you do not know of the false light, you will have lost your capacity for free expression. Whatever you say or do will be construed in terms of the false light. The comforting hand on the shoulder of a patient, the innocent one-liners you let fly, the glances at others—all these will be construed in ways quite different from those you intend. So your freedom is constrained. Even though you think you are expressing yourself freely, everything you say and do will be construed by those who think they are in the know in ways far different than they would be were you not under a false light.

Indeed, the situation is worse than that: others will presume that you know. "How could he of all persons not know that he is taking advantage of his patients?" So it will not be just that you are prevented from being yourself but that your every expression will be taken as an attempt to manipulate how you are perceived. Because you (are presumed to) know that others see you in this (false) light, you will be presumed self-conscious in your actions. You will be perceived as not just under suspicion but also as *in there*, trying to act in ways that belie the suspicion. Having lost your capacity for innocence, your every expression will be taken as a sign of an inner hidden core manipulating a public image for supposedly good effect.

These harms will occur to you even if you do not know you are being bathed in false light. And if you come to know? At least two stages must be distinguished here. You may come to sense that something is wrong, have the sense of bewilderment and subsequent hesitation that come from feeling that things are not quite right because of how others are responding and not responding to you. You may come to sense yourself as an *object* of some sort but not know why. So you may come to have the self-questioning and critical attitude toward yourself that comes from wondering whether those vague feelings represent something truly there. You will feel the disdain and distrust and repugnance—each one, and all, sufficient to make your self-confidence tremble, your image and your sense of yourself unsure.

And if you come not just to sense but to know? You must wonder who knows and who does not. Your spouse? Your children—old enough to understand the rumors but not old enough—who is?—to bear what taints them by association? Your friends? Your associates? It would be too dramatic to imagine your meeting people being like those condemned in Japan and waiting for breakfast: not informed of the day of execution ahead of time, they hear each morning's footsteps with dread. Yet, there is dread and more. Unlike those condemned, who learn each day what the footsteps bring, you may never come to know who thinks they are in the know and who is not, who is dissimulating and who is not.

That people had heard and yet treated you normally itself carries losses. You can no longer trust them or trust your own sense of when people are honest and when not. You must now approach the world more cautiously, with more circumspection and less trust. After all, you have been taken, and you do not know how often or by whom.

How long has this been going on? How much of your present life has been configured by the false light? The person you met whom you felt comfortable with and yet who did not respond to those overtures of friendship? The little odd things that you have ignored, as so much of the chaff of life, sent up as results of this false light like riffles in a stream?

What can you do? Because whatever you now do will be perceived in a false light, not much you can do can make much of a difference. It might help to find out, if you can, the supposed basis of the rumors. To the extent you assume good intentions, you must ask whether it was something misunderstood—an ambiguous expression uttered and missed, a Freudian slip that slipped right past you? Is it vindictive? Did someone plant the story and fan it, adding details to urge it along?[21] Have you been mistaken for someone else? If the rumor was just a rumor without a name, did someone say, "Oh, I know who it is. That's Dr. So-and-so. He's the only one who's come to town recently."

In any event, whatever you find out, you are in a position others are not in. As we saw, being put in a false light can have the odd effect of making a confession preferable to letting happen whatever happens. As one of your partners might put it, "There can be no privacy in a matter like this!"[22] Those with whom you are associated, professionally or personally, will demand all relevant information because they must protect their interests and the interests of innocents. The doctor's partners in practice have to be sure that patients are not harmed; your spouse must protect herself and the children.

Not knowing whether the false light has a basis, you may be at a loss to know what to say, but perhaps you were tempted with a patient, just as the patient was tempted with you, and perhaps that is somehow the source. So you tell but point out that it was only a temptation, not an act, and certainly not part of any "history of making sexual advances." It is ironic, you might add, given the rumors, that you and she did not succumb precisely because you are a doctor and she your patient.

Your motives for telling are no doubt mixed—a concern that you be believed by *someone*, a desire that those you love are immunized, if possible, against the story, a sense that the depression this has put you in is best served by being open, a concern that those tainted by association with you have the option of disassociation, the claims that others, like your partners, have on you because of the damage to them, a concern to stop the rumors from spreading. These motives all conspire to confession of whatever might be relevant, and a diabolical provocateur could so cleverly fashion the false light that you had little choice but to confess. One irony of false light is thus that it can force you to shed light on what you otherwise would have kept private.

Another set of ironies comes because the more morally sensitive you are, the more extensive the harms to you when you come to know that you have been bathed in a false light. The capacities to distance yourself from your own interests and to have an empathetic understanding of the interests of others are essential for you to make acceptable moral judgments. So the more you are capable of seeing the harm to others caught up in the rays of the false light directed at you—your spouse, your children—the more you will suffer. Were you unconcerned about the interests of others, you would suffer less the harm to those innocents. That is one irony.

A second is that to the extent that you are moral, you must probe yourself and try to comprehend how this could have happened, forcing yourself to that bitter look at yourself we all would prefer to forgo. "Do I have such temptations? Is there something about the way I relate to people that makes the false light plausible?" The believability of the false light means that others see footholds on your character for such a conception, and if you are self-conscious enough to wonder what it is about you that might allow for such a belief, by so many, and if you are concerned enough about your character to try to sort through what it is that makes the belief sustainable, you will find yourself like that "poor Mr. Crawley," the clergyman in Trollope's *The Last Chronicle of Barset.*[23] He was accused of taking a check for twenty pounds, and though he began sure that he did not do it and could not have done it, his self-assurance at his uprightness began to crumble as the evidence seemed to become firmer and more and more people around him treated him as a known thief. He had begun thinking himself the most upright of clergymen, having chosen a poor ministry over certain wealth, convinced of the harms of money and the obligations of those who choose to be clergy. But in the end he realized that, indeed, he *could* have done what he was accused of doing and wondered how he could have been so blind to his character defects. He became so convinced that he could have done it that he doubted his clear memory that he had not (794) and decided to give up his living.

Beset with self-doubt, and knowing how so many who knew him believed such a falsity, one that cut to his very understanding of who he was, he could only have wondered whether something about the way he presented himself made it seem that his exterior was a shell, that he was in there peering out, assessing—devious, manipulative. And so he might ask, "If that is how they see me, why should they believe anything I say?" In that he is like our good physician, who must ask, "What is the gain of painful revelation if it will seem like so much manipulation?" False light can force a painful and deeply ironic dilemma, between confession that is not believable and silence that will be taken as acquiescence.

Privacy

The issue I am concerned about is not what harms can accrue to persons because they are put in a false light but whether any of those harms are sufficient to account for our marking out false light as a distinctive way of invading someone's privacy. I think they are.

First, when others know about the false light but you do not, you have lost the capacity to control your public image. One of the reasons we have for sustaining a right to privacy is that it provides individuals with control over information about themselves, information they can give others or not as they see fit. So private diaries are private just because no one else is to see them and so know whatever it is that the author is thinking. Intimate friends are presumably intimate in part because we have let them in on matters we would not want the world to know. One harm that comes from disclosing a private diary is that, as we saw, you will have lost control over information about yourself that you can use to regulate how others see you and respond to you. Putting someone in a false light harms the same interest. That person will be perceived in the false light and so will have lost the power to control how he or she is perceived.

Second, when you find out about the false light, your chances of controlling its effects are diminished by just how believable it is. Whatever you say and do may well be seen in the light shed by the falsity, and you will be seen as manipulative. But, independently of that, you may be forced by circumstance into telling something about your private life that you otherwise would not have told. Whether you feel compelled to disclose will depend upon contingent factors that you have little control over—the nature of the falsity, whether others in a relation to you are so harmed they must ask what you have done, and so on. False light can thus be a peculiarly diabolical way to invade someone's privacy. Someone's saying something false about your private life may put you in a position where not revealing something private may cause more harm than revealing. So you may be forced to reveal what you otherwise would never have made public.

Third, when you turn upon yourself the query of what it is about you that may have made the false light believable, you will find that your very sense of yourself has been appropriated. The most damaging form of appropriation occurs not when someone takes your picture and makes commercial use of it. The most damaging form occurs when the *person* is appropriated. The man who pretended to be a well-known fashion photographer in order to seduce women made it difficult, if not impossible, for the actual fashion photographer, Richard Avedon, to approach any woman whose face might have intrigued him to see if she would be willing to be photographed. His freedom was constrained by what someone else had done in his name. He could no longer just be himself but had to take into consideration how what he did would be viewed by others who were aware of what the imposter had done. Suppose that Avedon would never consider approaching a woman in such a situation and thus that he would view what the imposter had done with distaste—as offensive behavior. In that case, he would have to realize that others might now think of him as the sort of person who would do something he considers offensive, and, to that extent, his public image would have been appropriated. Just so, one harm of false light is that your sense of yourself will be fashioned by that light. You will not be able to be yourself. One harm of false light can be intrinsic, that is, since it puts into question, as with Mr. Crawley, who you are.[24]

All this suggests that false light is a particularly interesting kind of invasion of privacy, not reducible to a single harm but fully understandable only in terms of the variety of ways in which it may harm one's privacy interests. In discussions of privacy, commentators have taken as their organizing principle Prosser's analysis of privacy into four torts. Each except false light has had its advocate as the real meaning of privacy. Fried has defined privacy in terms of disclosure; Gerety in terms of intrusion; and Judith Jarvis Thomson in terms of appropriation, which she considers a property right. False light has been shunted to one side, either without argument or as an uninteresting variant of disclosure.

When we examine it, I suggest, we find just those harms commentators have thought constitutive of the other privacy torts as well as some unique harms of its own. Disclosure? A clever provocateur, with a well-designed false light, can force you to *self*-disclosure, demeaning you by putting you in a position where you have to invade your own privacy, as it were. Appropriation? A provocateur can construct such a powerful narrative for those around you that you are unable to express yourself, your every attempt to be who you are taken as so much evidence that you are trying to manipulate public opinion. Intrusion? If the rationale for what is harmful about the tort of intrusion is that it denies the liberty of those intruded upon to control information about their lives, then false light is as much a tort, for a powerful narrative not only can force you to reveal what you would otherwise have been kept private but will necessarily change the way others perceive you, taking from you what power you have to control and modulate your relations with them. And what is unique about it? That it produces such a *set* of harms, I suggest, and that it perversely implicates you in the production.

All this suggests that the general concept of privacy is complex, not reducible to a single kind of harm, but that is a question I shall not pursue here. However the concept is analyzed, it will have to handle a form of harm that prima facie looks not to be an invasion of privacy at all but yet *can* touch a person's core and, it appears, is harmful in each of the variety of ways that other commentators have tried to elevate to the essential single meaning of privacy.[25] It is another question whether putting someone in a false light should bear a price and, if so, what the price should be.[26]

Notes

1. The concept of privacy is a complex one, with a complicated legal and philosophical history. One feature of that history is the attempt to find some common core to the various uses of the concept, an attempt that is manifested in a variety of endeavors to reduce all invasions of privacy to one kind of harm. It has been construed, for instance, as an invasion of property, rendering all the privacy torts of intrusion, disclosure, false light, and appropriation reducible, on this view, to the tort of appropriation. See in this regard Judith Jarvis Thomson, "The Right to Privacy," *Philosophy and Public Affairs* 4 (1975). Tom Gerety attempts to reduce all invasions of privacy to intrusion so that disclosure, for example, becomes a way of intruding upon someone's privacy. See "Redefining Privacy," *Harvard Civil Rights–Civil Liberties Law Review* 12 (spring 1977): 247–48. Charles Fried reduces all invasions of privacy to disclosure; for him intrusion becomes a form of disclosure. See "Privacy," *Yale Law Journal* 77 (1968): 475.

One of the aims of this chapter is to ask whether false light is a distinctive way of invading privacy. If it is, then at least one way we can invade a person's privacy is not reducible to any of the others, and we will thus be in a position to lay out the anatomies of the various forms of invasion and determine what distinct interests, or set of interests, are involved in each case, without having as our goal a final reduction.

2. We may put someone in a false light by saying something true about the person that, in a particular context, might be expected to be taken amiss. Yet, it seems the essence of false light that even if what is said is, strictly speaking, true, what is understood is false. In any event, causing harm to a person's privacy interests by saying something false about those interests seems the most counterintuitive. If we can explain how saying something false about a person's private life is an invasion of privacy, we can later handle whatever variations are introduced when false light is thrown by saying something true.

3. The accusation against Cardinal Bernardin of Chicago may serve as an example here. He was accused of molesting a seventeen-year-old boy seventeen years ago. A $10 million civil suit was later dropped because, it has been claimed, the accusations against the cardinal "were false memories" ("Was It Real or Memories?" *Newsweek*, March 14, 1994, 54). The cardinal said, "My life will never be the same because of this" (ibid.).

4. Gerety thus says that "the injuries pleaded [by false light] are . . . to the public and not the private self." He thinks that "public identity stands in need of legal protections that defamation will not allow and privacy will not justify" but claims that "false light, in both its remedies and its rationale, belongs with defamation as its unacknowledged but not illegitimate offspring" ("Redefining Privacy," 258).

5. It may, however, be true that a former secretary of state has a tattoo of a tiger on his tush. We will presume it false for our purposes here.

6. For a long list of such cases, with differing harms and benefits, see William L. Prosser, "Privacy," *California Law Review* 48, no. 3 (1960), esp. 401ff.

7. A man impersonated Richard Avedon, conning his victims out of money and sex. See "The Phony Photographer," *Newsweek*, September 19, 1977, 43. The con man sometimes got money from his victims, but usually, it seems, he was after sexual favors. This is thus a good example of how appropriation may be for nonmonetary benefits.

8. *Melvin v. Reid*, 112 Cal. App. 285, 297 Pac. 91 (1931). See Prosser, "Privacy," 392–93.

9. I want to add, "in just that sort of way." After all, Nixon is a public figure, and, at least in the United States, much that is private among ordinary citizens is not presumed immune from public scrutiny among politicians. But whether Nixon and his wife slept together has no obvious relevance to his capacity to serve in public office and to do so honorably and morally. That is why I want to add a restricting clause: it is an invasion with no redeeming social or moral values that seems at least mildly offensive. I am claiming that it *seems* mildly offensive; that is how the matter initially presents itself. The suggestion is that we ought not to preempt the possibility of that response by adopt-

ing without further ado an analysis that comes from concentrating upon the falseness of false light.

10. I put to one side the issues raised by unknowingly putting someone in a false light.

11. Choosing an example is never philosophically innocent. At the worst, one's example may just mirror the essential features of one's theory, and, at best, one's example will accentuate some features of the complex set of harms and depress others. The Nixon anecdote illustrates this second point well. After all, would you believe Nixon whatever he might say? Or is there that residual of doubt? "Old tricky Dicky," one says to oneself. "If I cannot trust him about public matters, why should I trust him about private ones?" What we know about Nixon's character may prevent any revelation from working. "Where there's smoke, there's fire," we think, forgetting about smoke bombs. So we smirk at the one-liner because it confirms a public view of him rather than altering our relation to him. We need an example that does not confirm a person's character. Yet in fastening on another example, we should not lose sight of one implication of false light accentuated in the Nixon case. The right worm of doubt can become a serpent, swallowing alive the person, who is unable to convince anyone, by any disclosure whatever.

12. Of course, it is an interesting question whether you are invading their privacy by not moving or letting them know that you can hear. Are you intruding? Are they talking too loudly for where they are? Are the tables bunched so closely together it is not possible to sit next to anyone and not hear what it going on at the next table? What these questions begin to illustrate is how very complicated it can be to determine whether there has been intrusion, for instance.

13. It is impossible to sustain a believable story without specifying sex when the accusation concerns the person's gaining sexual favors. But though I write old-style here, with masculine pronouns, one could tell the same story using a female as the protagonist—a college professor accused of seducing male students, for instance. I have also assumed heterosexual sex, but, again, that is not essential.

14. With apologies to John Cheever, from whom the idea for this story is drawn, with appropriate changes, and to Daniel DeFoe, to whom I owe some of the plot's details.

In Cheever's story, a woman enters a physician's examination room, at loose ends. The doctor touched her, "she thought, with a gentleness that was not clinical," though she recognizes that her perceptions may be "distorted by lewd dreams, drunkenness and a near sleepless night." By touching him, she tacitly invites him to make love to her—or so he thinks and she comes to think. See John Cheever, *The Wapshot Scandal* (New York: Harper & Row, 1964), 232.

DeFoe uses a judicious combination of defamation and false light in *Moll Flanders*. A woman has failed to win the declaration of a man who asks her about her estate and decides she has not enough. Moll suggests that the they spread the story that the woman is rich and he is poor, and Moll later adds that he is about to be discharged from his position, has several wives, and is "debauched in his morals." His other prospects become uninterested, and he decides he has mistaken the financial state of this otherwise attractive woman. So he asks for her hand in marriage, even though he cannot now ask her how much money she has and she can ask him—because of the rumors she and Moll have spread. The professed motive for spreading such falsities about him, and her, is not revenge but justice. Defoe argues that the practices of courtship are heavily biased against a woman because they allow a man to ask questions a woman is not permitted to ask, and the only way to rectify the inequities of the social practice is to put the man into a false position. See Defoe, *Moll Flanders* (New York: Washington Square Press, 1968), 69–76.

15. I mean the description to follow to be a perfectly *normal* response to what a person has heard. That is not to say that we would not fault someone for responding in these ways but only to say that such responses—and hence the harms they engender—are to be expected.

16. It is unlikely that any such call would settle matters for the partners of this physician. It is too common for those from whom we ask recommendations to respond falsely when there is something to hide, especially when the truth may provoke a lawsuit.

17. I do not refer to *kinds* of relationships here but to that entire set of individual relations that make up a person's legal repertoire. I thus have a right that you not hit me and distinct rights that each and every person in the world not hit me. I may give up one right without giving up all, that is, allow you to hit me without opening myself to being pulverized by the masses.

18. This set is only contingently unique because there is nothing necessary about the truth that only one person will have a particular sets of interests, Leibniz to the contrary, but the likelihood of that occurring is minuscule because interests are in part determined by one's position in the world and, so, one's viewpoint. My aim is Leibniz's, namely, to secure the particularity of individuals, but I do not think it can be argued that that particularity is anything but contingent.

19. It invites suspicion of the patient too, of course. The harm is not confined to the physician but infects innocents as well.

20. This is Fried's view. See note 1, supra.

21. DeFoe has Moll Flanders do this very cleverly. When someone asks about the rumors, she adds to them that the young man has another wife, or two, in some of the Indies, though that is common enough for such like, and that he is deeply in debt to the owners of his ship and about to be turned out as captain. The combination of publicly verifiable information that no one is likely to verify and additional (false) details is deadly.

22. In some positions, the demands of privacy and confidentiality will override any demand for information. A psychiatrist is thus in a moral box if accused of making sexual advances on a patient by the patient. He has an obligation not to reveal what he knows from therapy, but that information may be just what would explain why this patient has accused him. This may be a moral dilemma with no obvious solution.

23. Anthony Trollope, *The Last Chronicle of Barset*, ed. Stephen Gill (Oxford: Oxford University Press, 1980), 104.

24. Again, this will be a contingent question, whether your very understanding of who you are is put into question. In distinguishing between the extrinsic and intrinsic harms of false light, I am not distinguishing between kinds of propositions but between kinds of harms—those that affect only one's external relations and those that touch one's core.

25. The concept of appropriation has been generally misdescribed. That privacy tort arose out of cases in which what seemed to be at issue was compensation for the use of one's name or visage, and so it is perhaps understandable that the concept of appropriation has been presumed to be a form of denial of a property right. But as the Avedon case makes clear, someone can appropriate one's identity as well. These forms of appropriation are likely to become more prevalent as more and more extensive data banks of personal information become available and individuals appropriate them for their own purposes.

26. I have not argued explicitly that false light is conceptually distinct from defamation, though, I would argue, the implication of my analysis is that they are quite distinct. The complications of proving this deserve separate consideration, however. But it should not be thought that there is no difference because lawyers make so little use of the tort of false light, opting instead for defamation. Lawyers may choose to rest a case on defamation rather than false light for a variety of reasons having nothing to do with their legal status and everything to do with such other features as, for instance, its being easier to prove defamation. Or, as the argument of this paper suggests, they may wish to avoid the sort of public disclosure on the part of their client that false light so perversely encourages.

Chapter 11

Poverty, Equality, and Taxation under the Rule of Law: A Tension within Classical Liberalism

Kenneth Henley

The classical-liberal reconciliation between the political ideal of liberty and the political ideal of equality is achieved through the overarching ideal of the rule of law: each individual is entitled only to that liberty delineated within the rule of law to protect the liberties of all, and all are entitled to equality only as to their treatment by the state in the application of law. As F. A. Hayek wrote, "The great aim of the struggle for liberty has been equality before the law."[1] So far this account might appear consistent with a redistributive regime that aims at lessening substantial inequalities of wealth (for instance, through significantly progressive taxation of income and high inheritance taxes); the laws to be equally applied—and thus the liberties to be protected—might have a content requiring a large measure of redistribution. But there is an essential element remaining in the classical-liberal account: law must set apart and protect private spheres of action and property.[2] These private spheres constitute the liberties that are reconciled with equality within the rule of law, for if all aspects of an individual's life were open to command by the state there would be no individual liberty at all, except on sufferance. Equality before the law is a classical-liberal ideal only on a particular substantive understanding of law.[3] And so on this account equal treatment by the state cannot be used as an argumentative wedge to introduce the aim of redistribution of wealth because most wealth will be produced within the private sphere. Furthermore, any attempt based on an independent normative argument to use the coercive power of the state to lessen substantial inequality of wealth must be at least challengeable from this perspective, for it may itself trespass into a protected sphere of individual liberty. And the classical-liberal view is that although some very modest reduction of material inequality might be legitimately managed, substantial material inequality is necessary within a regime of equality before the law (87–88).

This classical-liberal challenge to redistribution at first seems well-founded, given its framework. Clearly, a government with the authority to command within all aspects of life must be tyrannous, and (less clearly, even denied by some outside classical liberalism) there must be a great deal of private economic life if the state is to be limited enough in its claims of authority to protect the individual from ever-increasing state control. But despite this initial plausibility, I think the classical-liberal objection to all redistribution results from a kind of myopia, looking only at the particular threat to liberty and the rule of law posed by state-coerced redistribution itself. Looking further even within a classical-liberal framework, an argument can be made for some degree of redistribution of wealth for the sake of the rule of law and the equal protection of individual liberty. The outcome for a clear-sighted classical liberal will then depend upon a balancing of the argument against redistribution as a dangerous encroachment by the state upon a private sphere of liberty, and the argument for some redistribution in order to maintain equality under the rule of law for all economic classes and social groups.

The general functioning of the law is undermined by extreme concentrations of poverty, especially when these are strongly transgenerational and identifiable by race or ethnicity.[4] Impoverished groups do not have the same allegiance to law, nor can they be expected to—they have less of a stake in the structure of property the law in part exists to protect. When poverty is combined with a sense of separateness based on race or ethnicity and a history of oppression, general antagonism to the legal system and its officers seems natural. The much greater likelihood of being punished by the legal system[5] leads to a questioning of the reality of equality under the rule of law, creating the sense that the law protects the wealthy and is aimed at oppressing impoverished groups. This sense persists despite the fact that members of impoverished groups are disproportionately also the victims of crime, for it is obvious that fewer resources are devoted to protecting the poor against victimization than to protecting the less threatened wealthy. Poor victims and potential victims are not accorded full equality before the law any more than are poor suspects and defendants. It might be insisted that the perception of oppression of poor suspects alternating with indifference toward poor victims is irrelevant, and all that matters is that the legal system, with all its human imperfections, seeks equally to protect the poor and in the process poor suspects and defendants will inevitably feel the force of the law. But if the rule of law is to be affirmed and strengthened, the perception itself matters a great deal.

And the perception is not entirely out of touch with reality. Although much law enforcement aims to offer the same protection to the poor as to the rich in life, limb, and property, there are nonetheless differences in the relation of law to the poor and to the rich or the middle class. Some of these real differences support a sense of oppression on the part of the poor when coming under the scrutiny of law enforcement, as well as a sense that the poor are provided less protection by law enforcement from crime.

The distinction between equality of rights and the unequal worth of rights[6] might be invoked by a classical liberal to deny that concentrations of poverty pose a difficulty for equality under the rule of law. This response asserts that the law recognizes, for instance, an equal right of all to be protected in their property rights; although this protection is admittedly more valuable for those with more property to be protected, this is the result of differences in the private sphere rather than unequal treatment by the state. So it is admitted that in general the rule of law is of more worth for the wealthy and the respected than for members of impoverished groups, but still there is equality under the rule of law. But despite the clever distinction between rights and their worth, there is a point to Anatole France's gibe that the law in all its majesty forbids both the poor and the rich to sleep under bridges. And despite the classical-liberal tendency to resist seeing this point,[7] I believe that it is particularly crucial for those concerned with equality before the law.

The distinction between a right and the worth of the right cannot be used successfully to defuse the issue of actual or perceived oppression of the poor by those entrusted with maintaining and applying the law, for the actions of enforcing the law are paradigmatic cases of state rather than private action. The problem posed for equality under the rule of law is that concentrations of poverty lead to inequalities in the administration of law. These inequalities of treatment by representatives of the state may be occasioned by differences generated in the private sphere, but nevertheless there is in the end inequality of treatment by the state in its enforcement and application of law.

It might be argued that except in cases of misconduct by representatives of the state, there is no inequality of treatment here: the equal application of law requires different treatment of the burglar and the law-abiding citizen. The individual not currently subject to legal sanction is equally under the law, for he too is subject to sanction if he breaks the law. Like many clear truths, this point derives its truth from a limited range of cases—namely, those in which it is true! There are surely many cases in which the law is no respecter of persons, and the wealthy and respected person who breaks the law is treated exactly as would be the poor and despised. But it is not only in cases of official misconduct that the poor and despised are more likely than an equally guilty respected person to come under the heavy hand of law enforcement, more likely to suffer incarceration and the disruption of life during the legal process, more likely to be convicted, and more likely to suffer severe punishment.[8] And at each stage the perpetrator of the more severe harm is the state itself.

Here the difference between equality under the rule of law and various other rights can be seen clearly: when Smith's equal right to express his political views is limited in worth by his limited wealth, there is no intervening state action inflicting the consequences of his lesser wealth upon him; he is simply unable, for instance, to purchase space in a newspaper or to purchase a chain of newspapers to control their editorial outlook. All of this occurs in the private sphere. The equality of the liberty to express political views consists simply in equal noninterference by the state; the distinction between the equality of the right and the unequal worth of the right to various individuals can be used successfully to defuse the appearance of inequality of rights in such cases. But when Pitt's equal right to counsel is limited in worth by his limited wealth, there is intervening state action inflicting the consequences of his lesser wealth upon him. If Pitt's inability to buy expensive legal talent is crucial in his feeling forced into a painful plea bargain, or in his being convicted, or his suffering a particularly severe penalty, it is the state itself that treats him less well than he would have been treated if wealthy.

The problem of unequal treatment by officials of the state is not confined to the various stiff penalties exacted by the state for the failure to hire expensive lawyers.[9] Outside the class of actual misconduct, there is a quite inevitable difference in police, prosecutorial, and judicial attitude and action toward those who are not respected members of the community as a whole. Not being respected in the whole community is correlated with poverty, but it is not the same thing. There are some people who have a place in the community conferring respect despite their relative poverty, but even they may initially be treated with heightened suspicion by officials of the law if their immediately evident characteristics (such as the combination of race or ethnicity and mode of dress) class them together at first impression with those lacking respectability.

It might be claimed that what I am describing *is* a form of official misconduct. But though such discriminatory attitudes sometimes do lead to actual misconduct, it would be demanding too much of human beings within such a class-divided society as ours to expect no significant difference in attitude and action toward those perceived to be a more likely threat. (And at various points of the process, such as the question of bail and to some extent in sentencing, the person's general relationship to the community is even formally relevant.) Official perceptions and attitudes toward those outside respectability have the same ambiguous status as the perception by the poor that the law protects the rich: the perception is exaggerated and a source of great trouble, but it is not without foundation. Yet, there is this great distinction: official perceptions lead directly to actions using the coercive powers of the state, and the perceptions of the poor do not.

The other side of the failure to accord equality before the law to the poor is also clearly state action that cannot be set aside using the distinction between rights and their worth: the legal system fails to provide protection from crime to the poor similar to that provided for the rich (and the middle class). There is an immense unmet need for law enforcement in areas of concentrated poverty. Yet, local political boundaries and their differing tax bases often produce quite different levels of funding for law enforcement. This inequality of funding depending upon political boundaries raises issues similar to those regarding unequal funding of public schools, and clearly reveals the obstacle of concentrated poverty to even the classical-liberal goal of equality before the law. And even within the same municipality, disproportional resources are often devoted to prevent and respond to crime against the wealthy (or the famous) and the solid middle class.

If it is granted that even within a classical-liberal framework extreme concentrations of poverty are an obstacle to equality under the rule of law, it of course does not follow that there are permissible means of removing that obstacle within classical liberalism. If there are not, then the classical liberal must confront the result that under our social conditions there is neither full equality under law nor the prospect of advancing toward that goal without sacrificing liberty: the classical reconciliation of liberty and equality will be closed off. But are there really no permissible means within classical liberalism of providing greater resources to promote equality before the law or even resources to lessen concentrations of poverty?

I will not discuss the dispute whether sufficient individual liberty in personal life can be protected if the state has full command of economic life, for not only is such economic control inconsistent with classical liberalism, it seems that entirely separate grounds of economic inefficiency and low productivity condemn such a command economy. However, the question of lessening substantial inequalities of wealth through significantly progressive taxation and high inheritance taxes is quite different, in two respects. There is divided opinion whether such taxation creates disincentives to economic productivity;[10] even if there were a point at which such effects were significant, a modest amount of redistribution might be obtainable at a less steep level of progressivity. And second, taxation can be so structured that it does not involve state decision making favoring or disfavoring particular enterprises or requiring particular actions of service or production.

This second characteristic of taxation undermines attempts like Robert Nozick's to portray taxation as a kind of forced labor.[11] Not only is there a huge difference between coercing an individual to perform brain surgery and taxing the income from such work, the difference is precisely the kind that a classical liberal should attend to because it is the difference between being at liberty in choice of occupation and not being at liberty. Forcing someone to give up some of his earnings from performing brain surgery, if it is wrongful, is a kind of theft rather than the quite different wrong of enslaving someone and commanding his labor.

Unlike Nozick, F. A. Hayek does not assimilate taxation to forced labor,[12] nor does he consider taxation as such wrongful even when it is used to provide benefits that go well beyond the minimal state.[13] Hayek's account of legitimate taxation and his general account of liberty and equality under the rule of law seem to me the best within the classical-liberal perspective, so I will explore reducing the threat of concentrated poverty to the rule of law within a basic Hayekian framework—though with a quite different conclusion.

Hayek's rejection of the minimal state is possible because he distinguishes between the levying of taxes, backed by the coercive power of the state, and the use of the tax money to provide services and benefits,[14] with neither coercion nor state monopoly (except in the cases of providing a legal system, protecting legal rights, and providing a military).[15] In Hayek's view, the coercion used to collect taxes does not in itself infect the providing of services and benefits with coerciveness: it is a separate question whether the state is using coercion when it provides, for instance, public schools or some form of insurance.

I think that Hayek in effect reintroduces the minimal state within this more limited justificatory question: is the state justified in exercising a coercive monopoly over a particular kind of service or benefit? This reintroduction is much more plausible than a utopian minimalism such as Nozick's. If the state simply provides a service or benefit without claiming exclusivity, the burden of justification is entirely different in kind, merely a matter of whether the tax money is available, given the level of taxation consented to by the people, and whether it could be used better in some other way. Although important questions, these are not as fundamental as whether the state has any right to use its coercive power to raise tax money for purposes beyond those of the utopian minimal state. The Hayekian minimally coercive state is free to offer services and benefits to people just as a private corporation is free to do so, and this freedom does not become a coercive monopoly simply by virtue of the use of coercion to collect taxes paying for the offered services.

Despite his admiration for structures evolved through trial and error, Hayek argues against all redistribution, even when it has the stamp of an evolutionary origin as does significantly progressive taxation. Although there are many other questions raised by Hayek and others concerning the effectiveness and desirability of redistributive taxation, I will address only Hayek's argument that redistributive taxation violates one of the requirements of the rule of law on the classical-liberal conception of this ideal. If this claim of Hayek's were justified, the rule of law itself would place severe limits upon state action to redress inequality before the law occasioned by concentrated poverty, although some other very limited means of redress might remain open.

Hayek allows that some progressivity in income tax rates may be needed to correct for the regressivity of other taxes,[16] and even allows for a very slight, incidental progressivity of total taxes (323). But Hayek opposes any real use of taxation to redistribute wealth.[17] The rule-of-law argument against redistributive taxation depends upon Hayek's view that generality is fundamental to the rule of law: "When we obey laws, in the sense of general abstract rules laid down irrespective of their application to us, we are not subject to another man's will and are therefore free."[18] In a regime that uses taxation to redistribute wealth, the rich minority is under the domination of the will of the less wealthy majority, and this is inconsistent with the rule of general, abstract law: "Even if progressive taxation does not name the individuals to be taxed at a higher rate, it discriminates by introducing a distinction which aims at shifting the burden from those who determine the rates onto others. In no sense can a progressive scale of taxation be regarded as a general rule applicable equally to all (314).

Even though in his view flat-rate proportional taxation can be legitimately used to help those in need, Hayek seems to see redistributive taxation as robbery of the rich by the poor under the color of law. I view Hayek as reversing Anatole France's gibe. It is as if Hayek ridiculed redistributive tax law by saying, "The law with all of its concern for equality exacts higher rates from the rich and the poor alike, as long as their income is well above the norm." But Hayek's argument is not convincing, for it ignores the reality that the wealthy wield great political power in a system of representative democracy with constitutional safeguards of political participation. The rule-of-law argument against redistributive taxation works only if the wealthy can be seen as dominated by the forces establishing redistributive taxation. If progressive taxation reached a confiscatory level, this might be a perception with some underlying basis (like the present perception of impoverished groups that they are dominated by law enforcement). But moderate progressivity cannot create such a sense of domination, for the rich will after all retain sufficient wealth to maintain disproportionate power in the legislative process. The force of Anatole France's gibe depends upon our realistic sense that "the law" is the creature of the rich, at least in respect to prohibiting vagrancy. For the reverse gibe to have such force, we must be convinced that redistributive taxation results from a class victory over the rich. Although such a situation is imaginable, it bears little relation to present realities. Moderate redistributive taxation might be instituted or increased in order to lessen the concentrated transgenerational poverty that threatens the rule of law itself, rather than to deprive the rich of wealth that the powerful poor want. The wealthy themselves ought to accept such a policy, for they benefit disproportionately from the rule of law and the social stability it brings. This would not then be the domination by the majority of the rich minority.

My point that the rich ought to accept some redistribution to further equality before the law must be understood in relation to my argument that the state inevitably often wrongs, for instance, indigent defendants by directly harming them in ways they would likely escape if rich. The obligation of the rich to redress these wrongs must not be confused with the motivation of fear. Richard Epstein criticizes the use of "an uneasy union of police power and implicit in-kind compensation" in arguments justifying redistributive taxation as involving the "compensation to the rich . . . that they are spared the violence that would overcome them if the poor were shut out from the social gains." This is, he says, "little more than a strategic bribe," and he rightly points out the defect of such justifications:

"The police power does not routinely justify penalties upon legitimate acts as an indirect means to control illegitimate ones."[19]

My point, however, is a different one. Rather than fear and prudence, I urge duty as a justification. Those who benefit disproportionately have an especially stringent obligation to prevent any wrongdoings on the part of the very system that benefits them. When the poor are not treated with equal concern and respect by police, prosecutors, judges, and other officials, there is a genuine rights-based claim for correcting these failures to deliver on the promise of equality under the law. Though it is not always considered wrong to motivate people to redress wrongs by pointing out how prudent such justice is, on this topic I doubt the motivational force of such seeming realism—for the rich are in fact very successful in this society at insulating themselves from the violence and other ills arising from concentrated poverty, and surely this is a crucial part of the political failure to break the grip of social pathology upon the truly disadvantaged.

Hayek's rule-of-law argument against redistribution also fails for another reason besides the fact of the great political power of the wealthy. Hayek must portray the wealthy as a closed class of nameable (though not named) individuals in order to argue that redistributive taxation proceeds without a truly general law, equally applicable to all. But later in the same attack on redistributive taxation, Hayek claims that steeply progressive tax rates have the undesirable effect of blocking entry to the ranks of the rich. Until progressive taxation, "the rich were not a closed group" and this was "the most important compensation for that inequality which is inevitable in a free-enterprise society."[20] Then on Hayek's own admission, in a free-enterprise society the rich are not a separate, nameable class—not a nameable minority that might be victims of discrimination by the kind of failure of generality of law that Hayek earlier claims to identify. I think the lesson should be that progressive taxation must not be allowed to become so steep as to block the formation of new fortunes, so that the top of the economic structure remains open. But our present concern surely needs to be elsewhere. Concentrated transgenerational poverty, especially when closely identified with race or ethnicity, does produce a relatively closed group of the truly disadvantaged (nameable though not named), and here is the real place for concern over equality before the law and the generality of law.

So there is some justification within classical liberalism for extra money to be taken from the wealthy, upon the legislative decision of those disproportionately representing the wealthy, in order to diminish deprivations by the state of equality before the law for the poor. How ought this extra money to be spent? There are two very different approaches, and it might seem reasonable to try both. The direct approach would use the extra money to fund specific interventions proximate to the likely failures to accord equal concern and respect to the poor in the application and enforcement of the law: more money for public defenders, for training police to treat all equally, and for more such equality-trained police and other personnel in impoverished areas. Here it is crucial to focus on the need for equal resources of law enforcement for poor victims (and to protect the poor from victimization) as well as for poor suspects and defendants. Equality before the law should mean that a particular kind of crime will receive roughly the same attention and resources whether the victim is wealthy or poor. The tendency of the rich to depend upon private security measures and to distance themselves from impoverished neighborhoods has increased the difference between rich and poor in the resources available for protection, while also undercutting support for the large increases in spending needed to provide the rule of law for all, not just the rich. We are becoming a society that approaches an extremist individualist fantasy of private law enforcement, and the redistributive taxation justified by my argument could be directed against this tendency that promises an end to the rule of law.

The second way to spend the extra money is indirect in its relation to the deprivations of equality before the law grounding the justification. The redistributive taxes could be used to attempt to break the grip of concentrated, transgenerational poverty. Because I have argued that there are inevitable official failures of equality before the law, given such poverty, there seems some justification for using the extra money to decrease the incidence of the underlying social pathology. Of course, particular attempts to redress the difficulties for the rule of law might be ineffective or even counterproductive. For instance, some aspects of welfare programs immediately aiding the poor might in the long run encourage dependency and unwise decisions to bear children, thus further entrenching an identifiable underclass with even worse consequences for the rule of law. But the failure of particular programs should not be used as a general point against all efforts to lessen the transgenerational concentrations of poverty so inimical to equality under the rule of law. Perhaps private economic development in areas of concentrated poverty could be capitalized with tax money (or encouraged through tax incentives, with the lost revenue recouped by higher inheritance taxes and more steeply progressive income taxes, for instance). If the classical-liberal economists are correct, perhaps the most effective way to lessen concentrations of poverty would be to use the redistributive tax money to lower the borrowing needs of government, thus freeing capital for economic growth that will lift all boats.

I do not claim to know how to lessen the extreme concentrations of poverty found in our society. My argument is only that such poverty undermines equality under the rule of law, and that within a Hayekian framework of classical liberalism there is conceptual room for some redistributive taxation in order to further the goal of equal liberty under law. The argument seems even stronger for direct use of redistributive taxes to provide for more resources of law enforcement to protect the poor from victimization and to protect the rights of poor suspects and defendants. It seems unfortunate to me that classical liberals, including Hayek, have come to the opposite conclusion.

Notes

I am grateful to my colleague Paul Warren for his insightful comments on this chapter.

1. Friedrich A. Hayek, *The Constitution of Liberty* (Chicago: University of Chicago Press, 1978), 85.

2. Ibid., 35, 139–42, and *Law, Legislation and Liberty*, vol. 1, *Rules and Order* (Chicago: University of Chicago Press, 1973), 106–9.

3. Hayek, *The Constitution of Liberty*, 148–59.

4. For an account of the "concentration effects" of poverty in racially identifiable groups, see William Julius Wilson, *The Truly Disadvantaged: The Inner City, the Underclass, and Public Policy* (Chicago: University of Chicago Press, 1987).

5. For some of the evidence, see Jeffrey H. Reiman, *The Rich Get Richer and the Poor Get Prison*, 2d ed. (New York: Macmillan, 1984), 77–110.

6. John Rawls, *A Theory of Justice* (Cambridge: Harvard University Press, 1971), 204.

7. See, for instance, Hayek, *The Constitution of Liberty*, 235.

8. See Reiman, *The Rich Get Richer and the Poor Get Prison*, 77–110.

9. For a detailed narrative account of how severely one local legal system penalizes those who cannot afford their own lawyers, see John Dorschner, "Rush to Judgment: In Dade County's Criminal Justice System, There Just Isn't Any Time for Frills and Extras. Like Trials," *Miami Herald, Tropic* (Sunday magazine), November 25, 1990, 8–16.

10. See Bernard Saffran, "Markets and Justice: An Economist's Perspective," in *Markets and Justice: Nomos XXXI*, ed. John W. Chapman and J. Roland Pennock (New York: New York University Press, 1989), 313–18, and work therein cited.

11. Robert Nozick, *Anarchy, State, and Utopia* (New York: Basic Books, 1974), 169.

12. Hayek, *The Constitution of Liberty*, 142–43.

13. Friedrich A. Hayek, *Law, Legislation and Liberty*, vol. 3, *The Political Order of a Free People* (Chicago: University of Chicago Press, 1981), 41.

14. Hayek, *The Constitution of Liberty*, 144–45.

15. Hayek, *The Political Order of a Free People*, 42–43, 147.

16. Hayek, *The Constitution of Liberty*, 307.

17. Ibid., 306–23, and *The Political Order of a Free People*, 127.

18. Hayek, *The Constitution of Liberty*, 153.

19. Richard A. Epstein, *Takings: Private Property and the Power of Eminent Domain* (Cambridge: Harvard University Press, 1985), 315, 316.

20. Hayek, *The Constitution of Liberty*, 321.

Part III

Equality and the Clash of Cultures

In a pluralistic, multicultural society, it often turns out that one group's exercise of liberty constitutes a potential infringement of the equality of another group or individual. It is also increasingly true in Western societies that the pursuit of equality of treatment for some groups can be achieved only if the liberties of some individuals are curtailed. This part will examine conflicts of liberty and equality in pluralistic settings. The two main cases considered are these. First, we consider campus hate speech in which individuals are said to harm members of minority groups when their speech belittles or ridicules these minority students. Hate-speech codes, designed to curtail such discriminatory and unequal treatment, so it is claimed, interfere with the free speech rights of members of the dominant group. Second, we consider the refusal by Christian Scientists to seek medical care for their children. In such cases, the goal of equality of health care for all children can be achieved, so it is claimed, only by infringing the right to freedom of religion of the Christian Science parents. Both of these cases arise from a clash of cultures having very different views about what is most valuable in the society.

Before discussing these cases, we will pursue a general discussion of liberty and equality in a multicultural setting. After the case analyses, we will consider how two seemingly different societies, Japan and the United States, have addressed issues of economic equality. An argument is advanced for thinking that Japanese society has achieved greater economic equality than United States society, but not at the cost of curtailing individual liberty.

The chief problem facing pluralistic societies is one of attaining agreement about the common good, a set of goals for which individual members of the society are willing to make sacrifices. And within this larger problem area lies the special problem of how to weigh the competing goals that constitute the common good. There are two approaches to these problems, liberal and communitarian. Liberal legal and moral theorists have focused on the principles of individual autonomy, self-respect, and tolerance as the key components of a liberal solution to the problems of pluralistic societies. Communitarian legal and moral theorists have focused on the values of diversity and group autonomy, as well as on the importance of sustaining communities.

Consider one of the Christian Science refusal cases. Colin Newmark was diagnosed as having non-Hodgkin's lymphoma, a potentially fatal disease. His physician recommended extensive radiation and chemotherapy, which would have given Colin a 40 percent chance of recovery, but with a high risk of serious side effects. His parents decided that the side effects of the treatment and the intrusiveness of the treatment regimen were beyond what they could accept, given their Christian Science background. The medical staff tried to get a court order to take Colin out of his home and place him into a foster care family that would conform to the treatment regimen. One way to approach this problem is to see it as a conflict between the right to equality of health care of the child versus the right to religious freedom of the parents. Another way to approach the problem is to see it as a conflict between the medical community and the Christian Science community. Focusing on individual autonomy and tolerance will often yield a different result than focusing on group autonomy because the individual's religious freedom pales when contrasted with the religious freedom of an entire religious group.

Emily Gill confronts some of the leading communitarians and argues that respect for individual autonomy can provide a resolution to the conflict between equality and liberty in pluralistic societies. She is especially interested in the possibility of a liberal consensus struck between greatly divergent communities within a larger society, an "overlapping consensus" as Rawls calls it. If a minority community—the community of gays and lesbians for instance—is regarded with abhorrence by the dominant community, can an appeal to the principles of moral autonomy and tolerance rationally convince the majority to show respect for the minority?

Gill contends that the promotion of autonomy is itself a source of intrinsic value or social importance. Toleration of one another's views is mandated by any serious attempt to promote autonomy. She argues that liberal toleration is a better principle to appeal to than is communitarian shared understanding. In the case of gays and lesbians, too great a deference to entrenched viewpoints and traditions will make it hard for despised minorities to gain respect. Because liberal toleration and autonomy are not tied to specific traditions or communities, they can support "thoughtful questioning" that challenges dominant viewpoints and creates a space even for many individuals whom the majority abhors. Her piece contrasts well with Patricia Werhane's defense of communitarianism and also with Diana Meyer's critique of liberal tolerance.

Diana Meyers provides an example that is designed to challenge the traditional liberal idea of tolerance. The case she addresses, hate speech directed at minority members on campuses, concerns the kind of conduct that liberals would say should be tolerated. The harm done is of a nonphysical type, and we risk the "chilling" of political debate if we attempt to thwart the speeches of the bigot. Meyers contends that this argument makes sense only when the speech is directed at members of a majority group, as opposed to previously disadvantaged minority groups. Indeed, she thinks that empathy can lead us to see that it matters whether the speech is aimed at an already disadvantaged person or not.

Meyers argues in support of a "right not to be subjected to discriminatory verbal or pictorial abuse," and she contrasts this right with the right to free speech. She contends that the borders of the right to free speech, like the right to property, are contested. Where the use of speech or property causes harm, then that right should be curtailed. Meyers contrasts this restricted view of free speech liberties with what she calls the bratty-kid view: "It's a free country; I have a right to say whatever I want." On her view, only the speech that is necessary for one's autonomy may be made even in the face of possible harm to others. Hate speech is not necessary for one's autonomy and hence can be restricted. But Meyers stops short of suggesting that hate speech be banned or criminalized. Instead, she argues for a moderate plan in which universities would compensate those who had been assaulted by hate speakers.

Joan McGregor picks up on just this point. In her view, hate speech is a serious harm, one that perpetuates divisions in the society and unfairly denigrates historically discriminated against minorities. Because hate speech is harmful, McGregor urges that it be treated as are other forms of harmful behavior, that is, that the perpetrators be punished. McGregor focuses on the analogy with fighting words, words that are used to insult the listener, to slap the listener in the face. Hate speech is very much like fighting words, she argues, because it is on the periphery of what the First Amendment to the U.S. Constitution was meant to protect. Neither hate speech nor fighting words contribute to political dialogue or the exploration of the boundaries of the arts and sciences.

Unlike Meyers, McGregor thinks that a liberal conception of liberties and rights can accommodate the prohibition of hate speech. Hate speech does not need to be tolerated merely because it is the expression of someone's rights, even if those rights in general are seen as fundamental to a liberal democracy, for within each category of rights there is a core and there is also a periphery. Liberal theory cannot sanction the deprivation of core liberties, but it can sanction the deprivation of peripheral liberties. It is in this way that liberalism is able to accommodate problems of pluralism that call for some members of society to rein themselves in so that the goal of equality can be achieved.

Our second main example in this section is the Christian Scientist's refusal of treatment for his or her child. Richard De George argues that religious liberty should be abridged in such cases only if it is clear that the rights of the child not to be abused or neglected are at stake. Because Christian Science parents are willing to deprive themselves of medical treatment, then when they decide the same for their children they cannot be understood to be abusing or neglecting their children. Competent adults are not legally bound to seek medical care for themselves, and the same should be true for decisions concerning the medical care of their children.

Indeed, De George thinks that there is no clash of rights here at all because both "the parents and the medical practitioners wish for the good of the child. The question is which of the two has the right to decide what care the child is to receive." Here De George contends that the "right of each person to practice his or her religion and to follow those beliefs is stronger than the state's interest in preserving life." No matter how implausible the beliefs of the Christian Scientist might appear to those of us who are not Christian Scientists, we have no basis on which to limit their freedom unless there is demonstrable harm being done, which, argues De George, there is not.

Kenneth Kipnis takes a position on the Christian Science refusal case opposed to that of De George. Kipnis contends that it is a case of child neglect for parents to fail to provide that child with necessary medical services. Children are at the margins of their communities and are quite vulnerable in many cases. If a medical treatment is likely to be effective, and if the burdens of the treatment are not very high, then a doctor has the responsibility to do what is necessary to protect the child by securing medical treatment for that child. Kipnis admits that if Christian Science prayer could be proven also to be effective, he would have a more positive view of the actions of Chrisian Science parents. But the anecdotal evidence offered by the Christian Science community simply does not establish that prayer is as effective as standard medical treatment, or effective at all.

Kipnis argues that it would be unfair to Christian Science children to treat them differently than non–Christian Science children. When exemptions are allowed to the child abuse and neglect laws for Christian Scientists who refuse treatment for their children, these children fail to get the kind of equal medical protection that a society owes to all of its children. Parents have a duty to provide appropriate care for their children. When this care is not provided, then the larger community has a duty to step in and make sure that the care is provided. Like McGregor, Kipnis opposes the communitarian attempts at reconciling competing claims of various communities. When there is likely to be harm, then all should be treated alike. Religious freedom should not blind us to this result.

Here we are faced with an interesting twist in the debates between liberals and communitarians on the conflict between liberty and equality. Kipnis believes that liberals should embrace equality of treatment and not be tempted by the appeals of some based on their freedom of religion. In this he is very close to the view that is expressed by Diana Meyers, who does not consider herself to be a liberal. Meyers argues that equality of treatment, specifically ending discriminatory treatment, is of such importance that it should not be overridden by the rights of free speech of bigots. In play here are two somewhat different conceptions of equality. Both are based on equality of rights. But Kipnis is interested in individual rights, whereas Meyers is interested in group rights. Meyers favors equality of groups over the claims of individuals; Kipnis favors equality of individuals over group-oriented claims by certain community members to deprive their members of these rights.

Our final chapter sheds light on this issue by describing the different construals of economic equality in the United States and Japan. According to Richard Parker, one of the main differences between the two countries is that Japan is tribal and group-oriented, whereas the United States is still highly individualistic. Economic equality in America is measured in terms of the equality of wealth of individual men and women, whereas in Japan equality is measured in terms of satisfaction of one's wants. Parker argues that the Japanese actually enjoy greater economic equality than the Americans, despite the fact that the Japanese do not measure up to their American counterparts in terms of salary and wealth.

Central to Parker's argument is his claim that Japanese society does not subscribe to the view, found in the United States's Declaration of Independence, that all people are created equal. Underlying this view is the doctrine of "metaphysical equality," that is, that regardless of actual differences between people, "in some important respect, all human beings are exactly the same." The Japanese subscribe to the view that there are fundamental differences between people. "The Japanese feel no moral requirement to offer individuals (or groups) a fair competition under conditions of equal opportunity for life's prizes." Yet, Parker argues, "they feel free to refuse to let economic inequality develop in the first place."

In Japanese society the pursuit of equality is not seen as conflicting with individual liberty. Indeed, this is true of many non-Western societies. This is at least partially due to the way that people see themselves vis-à-vis the rest of society. If one finds one's identity by standing apart and distinguishing oneself from the rest of society, then one's claims of liberty are a protective shield against the attempt by society to include everyone as equal even when we are not. If one finds one's identity by being a part of a society, then one's claims of liberty are not necessarily at odds with equality, for it is in equal treatment that one attains the inclusion in society that allows one to exercise one's liberties. James Sterba's chapter also focuses on this issue.

In a pluralistic, multicultural setting, the conflict between liberty and equality takes on added significance, and finding a resolution of this conflict takes on added urgency. When there are multiple communities within a larger society, there is an increased likelihood of entrenched struggles because the members of society often have divided loyalties. Japan has managed to avoid much of the social conflict nearly endemic to the United States because of the homogeneity of cultures within Japan. If everyone sees oneself as belonging to the same group, then a group member is less likely to feel the need for protection against a wider hostile society. The ability to forge a consensus is enhanced the more homogenous is the society. But in a multicultural society, decisions about common goals are hard to reach, especially if they concern equality of treatment. We hope that the following chapters will shed considerable light on the difficulties as well as the prospects of reaching compromise, if not consensus, among competing claims in pluralistic, multicultural societies.

—Larry May

Chapter 12

Liberty, Equality, and Liberal Toleration

Emily R. Gill

As is well known, theorists such as John Rawls attempt to be neutral among particularistic conceptions of the good. Although they accept at the private level constitutive commitments to substantive or comprehensive conceptions of the good, they maintain in the public sphere a political conception of justice grounded in an overlapping consensus on minimal principles of right. "This means that to serve as a public basis of justification for a constitutional regime a political conception of justice must be one that can be endorsed by widely different and overlapping though reasonable comprehensive doctrines."[1] This notion of an overlapping consensus ostensibly promotes pluralism and encourages equal concern and respect for a wide variety of beliefs and practices. And since the Protestant Reformation, conventional wisdom has suggested that policies of toleration enable potential enemies to live together in peace. Disagreement often emerges, however, as to what a policy of toleration requires.

Some communities, for example, have passed ordinances that would prohibit the inclusion of gays and lesbians as protected groups in antidiscrimination legislation. Supporters of these ordinances have argued that such inclusion amounts to granting gays and lesbians special rights not enjoyed by others. Opponents insist, on the other hand, that this sort of protection is necessary if civil rights are to have the same worth for gays and lesbians as for the rest of us. That is, opponents believe that because these ordinances implicitly permit discrimination on the basis of sexual orientation, they deny to certain groups an effective equality in toleration, which in turn diminishes the worth of liberty. Proponents of these ordinances believe, however, that granting protected status to these groups constitutes positive approval of their practices. This exceeds the requirements of traditional liberal policies of toleration, and it grants a preference to some over others that diminishes the equal footing of formal equality that should undergird the liberal polity. I wish to consider the case for equal concern and respect for those whose beliefs and practices appear abhorrent to many, focusing upon gays and lesbians in the liberal polity. I shall argue that the liberal focus on moral autonomy requires that we accord equal respect to all whose beliefs and practices are deemed acceptable on any level. In the process I shall attempt to probe the limits of Rawls's overlapping consensus as it functions to ground a political conception of justice.

In a recent account of the role of toleration in the liberal polity, Steven Kautz suggests that liberals too often conflate toleration with approval. Uneasy about making moral judgments, they tend to request not only permission but also esteem for various beliefs and practices, and on these they feel compelled to bestow not only toleration but also respect and praise. For Kautz, the dissenter who seeks praise as well as permission in effect denies that private pursuits and choices are indeed private. "Once the 'right to equal concern and respect' becomes a political 'entitlement,' the vindication of that right requires . . . that the community undertake to teach each citizen . . . what to think: 'sensitivity' is the new liberal cousin to republican 'virtue.'"[2] One of liberal politics' "most splendid achievements" is its protection of liberal individualists who are "moral strangers to the community," even when these strangers are neither understood nor admired. These individuals should reciprocate by refraining from demanding more than tolerance "from their more conventional fellow citizens. They thus honor those ordinary citizens who leave them alone, by refusing to repay this respectable generosity with contempt" (624). Because nonconformists always constitute a vulnerable minority, there must be "limits on what can be held respectable in a healthy liberal community. . . . It would follow that what may be privately tolerable and even admirable cannot be wholeheartedly praised by the community" (629).

Thus, Kautz relies on a type of overlapping consensus that assesses individual beliefs and practices, according to some only permission but to others both permission and praise. This consensus, he implies, benefits both individuals and the community, as individuals measure their beliefs and practices by comparing these with the standards of choiceworthiness accepted by the community. "Toleration understood as openness may become another easy excuse for thoughtless acceptance of one's own way of life, one of the many techniques now available to liberals who wish to evade self-criticism" (614). Yet, Kautz also criticizes advocates of community like Sandel for their emphasis on constitutive attachments in defining the individual, the roots of whose "self-esteem (as well as self-knowledge) are communal or social"

(621). Liberal individualists or "moral strangers" do not need praise but only permission, and a community that offers only grudging tolerance "is consistent with self-respect though not a right of equal respect" (628). The individualist, then, has recourse to an extracommunal standard of judgment outside the overlapping consensus, which underpins self-esteem and obviates the need for self-definition by a community standard.

This account of toleration raises issues central to liberal politics. But it is also, in my opinion, too narrow for a liberal polity. First, although any community judges its citizens to some extent by their contributions to the shared goods of that community, this judgment, as Kautz himself admits, is not and should not function as their only source of affirmation. Second, a liberal community in particular should be open to consideration of diverse beliefs and practices, some of which in time become part of the shared values or overlapping consensus of the community. Finally, an overlapping consensus is better achieved by forthright debate than by fine distinctions between permission and praise. Such distinctions impoverish the community both by foreclosing debate and possible revision of its shared conceptions of the good, and by foreclosing to individuals sources of self-criticism that may enlarge their own understandings. Enshrining a set of shared goods as uniquely worthy of praise in itself "may become another easy excuse for thoughtless acceptance of one's own way of life" (614).

I

Kautz suggests that liberals may now be "obliged to admit that certain ways of life and moral opinions that are in themselves unobjectionable or even admirable are more corrosive, politically and morally, than was once thought" (629). This bases the necessity for his distinction between permission and praise. Although Kautz is but one commentator, his arguments bear consideration because they address a common concern about the potential limits of the overlapping consensus that might ground a political conception of justice. William Galston, for example, writes that rational deliberation must be subordinate to rhetoric in the formation of future citizens. Philosophic education's focus on the pursuit of truth may have "corrosive consequences" for "structures of unexamined but socially central belief." Civic education, however, is "by definition education within, and on behalf of, a particular political order."[3] Therefore, "government may properly teach those beliefs and habits needed to bolster the institutions that secure liberal rights, and citizens of liberal polities who resist this civic education would be irrationally contradicting their own self-interest, rightly understood" (250).

The liberal understanding of toleration has been grounded on the desirability of public neutrality toward rival conceptions of the good. This claim has rested either upon moral skepticism, the idea that accounts of the good cannot be defended conclusively, or upon moral autonomy, the idea that each individual must define the good in his or her own manner. Kautz's understanding of toleration eschews public neutrality in that, as he straightforwardly declares, it allows for self-respect but not a right to equal respect. It is a theory of the good, however, guided by what he perceives to be required for the health of the liberal polity, one defined, in Galston's terms, within and on behalf of a particular political order.

Up to a point, any stable political community rests on some sort of consensus, either explicit or implicit. Michael Sandel has disseminated widely the idea that the individual is situated within the context of a community whose values define and constitute its members.[4] And Alasdair MacIntyre has emphasized that one cannot seek the good only as an individual. Notions of worth and merit vary from community to community, along with the practices, institutions, and traditions of these communities, and these notions become determinate for an individual only within the context of that individual's social identity.[5] Moreover, contingent attributes may become constitutive of individual identity insofar as their development and exercise are encouraged by the particular community within which an individual exists.

This account implies that all theories of the good are in some sense communitarian. The notion of a good human life is highly indeterminate apart from its interpretation within the context of a specific community and its practices, and it is this interpretation that assigns worth or merit to individual actions. The concept of desert, MacIntyre writes, requires both "some common enterprise to the achievement of whose goals those who are taken to be more deserving have contributed more than" others, and also "a shared view both of how such contributions are to be measured and of how rewards are to be ranked."[6] Such entitlements, then, are not preinstitutional claims of desert but, as Sandel suggests, instead "honor the legitimate expectations created by institutions designed to elicit my efforts."[7] Rewards accrue to individuals not by virtue of any sort of intrinsic worth but, rather, by virtue of what institutions attribute to them by the valuation these institutions place upon individual attributes. In sum, worth and merit are contingent attributes, not essential constituents of identity, because it is the community and its traditions that give substance and definition to the notions of worth and merit.

The liberal polity, like others, possesses shared conceptions of goods and virtues, as we shall see below. The difficulty lies in the fact that communally determined notions of worth and merit too easily allow the worth of the individual to be judged primarily in terms of how well he or she upholds these norms, which in turn are grounded "within the dominant understanding of a particular community's traditions." On this view, according to William Lund, "citizens need to discuss and decide on a substantive conception of the common good and then use it to measure the legitimacy of their private beliefs and desires."[8] This account does not suggest neutrality toward individual definitions of the good but, rather, suggests "that we treat people as equals when we hold their beliefs and conduct up to currently accepted understandings of our traditions and shared purposes." The practice, first, raises, "perhaps to prohibitive levels, the costs of citizens revising their conceptions of the good away from a recognized consensus." And second, it also makes it "difficult for the community as a whole to have enough experience with, or to hear arguments about, alternatives that might cause it to revise or even reject its current understandings" (588).

Rights claims by unpopular groups and their supporters pose a threat for those who would enshrine current norms: "Rights talk thus shakes citizens loose from the shared values and virtues which they need as criteria against which to measure their current projects, and allows them to sacrifice an essential interest in the good life to current needs and beliefs which may lead them away from publicly recognized modes of flourishing" (591). This point introduces a contradiction in views like Kautz's. His worry about a political entitlement to equal concern and respect is based on the fear that its vindication calls on the community to teach citizens what to think. That is, if public policies mandate equal treatment for those who adhere to unpopular beliefs and practices, the community is inculcating values that promote equal respect. Yet, is not the purpose of withholding praise but according grudging tolerance to inculcate and reinforce dominant understandings of our traditions? The distinction certainly functions to teach citizens what to think, even though this teaching is indirect. It inculcates values that can be used to measure the legitimacy of our private beliefs and desires against the communal consensus, eliciting and rewarding some beliefs and practices but discouraging and stigmatizing others. Thus, it conveys a message with consequences for both individual and collective understandings of the good.

Moreover, as we have seen, Kautz believes that self-esteem most properly springs from sources beyond the community. But in that case, how can either approbation or its absence function to shape beliefs and practices in the ways that he desires? Kautz cannot have it both ways. Either communal attitudes affect behavior in the ways he advocates, in which case he should admit that citizens are indirectly but properly being taught what to think, or else individuals look to transcendent sources of affirmation, in which case the distinction between permission and praise will mean little. As it is, he conveys the impression that teaching citizens what to think is abhorrent when it inculcates equal respect for beliefs and practices repugnant to the majority, but acceptable or desirable when it promotes beliefs and practices that reinforce the current consensus.

Kautz might well reply that prudential rather than moral reasons dictate this concern. If citizens feel thwarted in their private adherence to comprehensive doctrines of the good, seemingly forced to accord praise as well as permission to idiosyncratic ways of life, grudging tolerance as permission may be transmuted into public intolerance of those who appear to threaten the underpinnings of the liberal polity. Some "liberals thus altogether fail to respect either the sometimes honorable motives for popular intolerance or the often formidable power of that intolerance."[9] The liberal polity, however, possesses its own shared conceptions of goods and virtues. If political justice is to rest on an overlapping consensus, I believe that this cannot be simply whatever consensus a current majority happens to support. Next, I want to broaden this chapter beyond Kautz to examine some of the ways in which shared conceptions of the good may be framed. The context within which various beliefs and practices are examined carries significant implications for our judgments about them, and these judgments may in turn affect both the liberty and equality of members of the political community.

II

Liberals should experience concern, I believe, about the threat the above account of toleration presents to moral autonomy, or the ability to define the good in one's own manner, both for individuals who espouse unpopular beliefs and practices, and also for the majority who may pass up opportunities to reflect upon and possibly to revise its shared conceptions of the good. The liberal polity's openness to diversity and autonomy suggests that those who contribute to these qualities are entitled prima facie not only to self-respect but also to equal respect. In MacIntyre's terms, the liberal polity constitutes a common enterprise with shared views as to the value of inclusiveness, and these views in turn make determinate the concepts of worth and merit by suggesting that unpopular beliefs and practices do not void one's claim to equal respect. Although such views are not universally shared, citizens of a liberal polity have a particular responsibility to attempt to live up to the implications of their shared general conception of the good. This, in my opinion, means grounding toleration on an understanding of moral autonomy that promotes equal respect for individuals and encourages debate and deliberation about these shared conceptions by the community.

This deliberation may be framed, however, in a number of different ways. Sandel, for example, argues that specific practices are better defended for their "intrinsic value or social importance" than as instances of individual choice.[10] One might argue with respect to homosexual unions not only that intimate associations should be matters of individual choice but also "that much that is valuable in conventional marriage is also present in homosexual unions. In this view, the connection between heterosexual and homosexual relations is not that both result from individual choice but that both realize important human goods" (534). Both provide opportunities for mutual support and self-expression in ways that other relationships do not. Sandel concludes that the neutral or procedural case for toleration is inadequate. First, the voluntarist or choice-based justification of autonomy rights "is dependent—politically as well as philosophically—on some measure of agreement that the practices protected are morally permissible" (537). Second, precisely because they are not based on substance, voluntarist justifications of autonomy rights may secure merely "a thin and fragile toleration. A fuller respect would require, if not admiration, at least some appreciation of the lives homosexuals live" (537).

Sandel's case that basing rights on the value of autonomy alone may restrict the range of reasons for protecting them, however, does not always hold true. First, although it may expand the range of possible defenses if we can demonstrate the intrinsic value or social importance of tolerating a practice, we might then withdraw toleration from a practice with no perceived value or importance, which would then restrict the scope of toleration. If the definition of the common good—Sandel's intrinsic value or social importance—is rooted within the dominant understanding of a particular community's traditions, it will be used, as we have seen, to measure the legitimacy of individuals' private beliefs and desires. Thus, although privacy is currently a human good in the context of the dominant understanding of the goods of intimate association, if this changed, we might find little protection for privacy on grounds of autonomy or anything else.

Second, a community whose notions of the common good are circumscribed by the dominant understanding will have little incentive to transcend this understanding and to interpret accepted human goods in new ways. And those who lose out in the search for approval on substantive grounds will lose their claim to equal respect.

> Grounding coercive or even merely hortatory legislation on contested accounts of what is "intrinsically good" inevitably puts into play a publicly backed appraisal of citizens and their conceptions of the good. In the absence of various liberal constraints, those will be used to justify unequal distributions of the opportunities and costs of various lives, and they will be so used whether or not those who are penalized actually accept the worth of the "good" in question. . . . Even if their choices are "accommodated," the decision will be based on the assumption that they believe what they don't believe, and their freedom will be limited by their ability to act out others' conceptions of the good.[11]

According to Sandel's constitutive conception of community, "community would describe not just a *feeling* but a mode of self-understanding partly constitutive of the agent's identity," not a relationship chosen but an attachment discovered.[12] But we cannot as subjects of moral agency be completely constituted by today's community without losing the possibility of critical purchase, the ability to distance ourselves somewhat from today in order to contemplate what notions of right or intrinsic goodness we want the community to embody tomorrow. Moreover, if we are each constituted by our membership in terms of the current consensus on values, then it constitutes us with our differences as well as our similarities. How can the community make a distinction between what merits praise and what merits only grudging tolerance if the beliefs and practices considered are all alike products of our membership and constitutive of our personhood?

My wariness about requiring substantive justifications for specific practices does not mean, however, that we must retreat to a neutral or procedural case for toleration, as Sandel implies. As Philip Selznick observes, official neutrality need not preclude a recognition of "the moral worth of particularity and the limits of universalism."[13] Referring to practices such as incest, prostitution, and polygamy, Selznick concludes that "to say that there are many 'right' ways [of conducting intimate relationships] is not to say that *any* way is right. . . . Not every intimate association is defensible, nor is every one so fundamental as to merit constitutional protection" (511–12; emphasis in original). I believe that in a liberal community, the question is one of deciding what ways are "right" without our becoming completely submerged within, and therefore constituted by, the current consensus. Perhaps the fact that the toleration of certain practices protects autonomy functions in itself to impute intrinsic value or social importance to the practices so justified. I hope, therefore, that in a liberal polity, debate about the validity of beliefs or practices where this debate influences public policy or social attitudes would center upon the implications for individual autonomy of either their toleration or curtailment, and that participants in this debate would recognize both the intrinsic value and the social importance of this autonomy.

The variations that may exist in framing the debate about a community's shared conceptions of the good may be exemplified by an examination of *Bowers v. Hardwick* (478 U.S. 186 [1986]), wherein the Supreme Court upheld the constitutionality of a Georgia statute criminalizing sodomy in a case involving consensual homosexual sodomy in the home of the man convicted. Writing for the majority and relying on the shared goods of family relationships and of acquiescence in long-standing majority beliefs (478 U.S. 186, at 190–96), Justice Byron White framed the issue as that of whether the Constitution confers "a fundamental right to engage in homosexual sodomy" (478 U.S. 186, at 191). A practice that does not fall within these categories implicitly carries neither the intrinsic value nor social importance that would warrant its defense under the rubric of a fundamental right.

In his dissent, Justice Harry Blackmun suggested that we need to look not only at the types of rights that have been classified as fundamental but also at the reasons that these practices have been so designated. With regard to family relationships,

> we protect those rights not because they contribute, in some direct and material way, to the general public welfare, but because they form so central a part of an individual's life. . . . And we protect the family because it contributes so powerfully to the happiness of individuals, not because of a preference for stereotypical households. . . . The fact that individuals define themselves in a significant way through

> their intimate sexual relationships with others suggests, in a Nation as diverse as ours, that there may be many "right" ways of conducting those relationships, and that much of the richness of a relationship will come from the freedom an individual has to *choose* the form and nature of these intensely personal bonds. (478 U.S. 186, at 204–5; emphasis in original)

Courts should be able to make sound distinctions between private and consensual sexual conduct that injures no other parties and other sorts of sexual conduct such as adultery and incest (478 U.S. 186, at 209). Moreover, historical and traditional condemnations of sodomy do not justify using the law to endorse private biases (478 U.S. 186, at 210–12). "I cannot agree that either the length of time a majority has held its convictions or the passions with which it defends them can withdraw legislation from this Court's scrutiny" (478 U.S. 186, at 210). Overall, "depriving individuals of the right to choose for themselves how to conduct their intimate relationships poses a far greater threat to the values most deeply rooted in our Nation's history than tolerance of nonconformity could ever do" (478 U.S. 186, at 214).

Thus, Blackmun's dissent also singles out certain aspects of family relationships and of values deeply rooted in our history and traditions. But his view implies that when we look to history and tradition, we need to look not simply at what specific rights or practices have been protected but at the broader purposes that family relationships and traditional values might serve. Therefore, he does not defend family relationships for their own sakes, in which case he might confine himself to families as conventionally constituted. Instead, he looks to the purposes served by family relationships, finding them essential to and instrumental in individual self-development, which in turn requires choice: "A necessary corollary of giving individuals freedom to choose how to conduct their lives is acceptance of the fact that different individuals will make different choices" (478 U.S. 186, at 205–6).

In sketching the value of interpersonal relationships, Blackmun cited in passing *Roberts v. United States Jaycees* (468 U.S. 609 [1984]), in which the Court ruled that the Minnesota Jaycees must open its membership to women (478 U.S. 186, at 204). The Court stated that the Jaycees was not an intimate association, which would deserve greater protection than other organizations in its members' freedom of association. "The constitutional shelter afforded such relationships reflects the realization that individuals draw much of their emotional enrichment from close ties with others. Protecting these relationships from unwarranted state interference therefore safeguards the ability independently to define one's identity that is central to any concept of liberty" (468 U.S. 609, at 619). In her concurring opinion, Justice Sandra Day O'Connor stated that both intimate associations, which carry intrinsic value, and other associations that are instrumental in the effective exercise of First Amendment freedoms fall under the rubric of expressive associations, the formation of which "is the creation of a voice, and the selection of members is the definition of that voice" (468 U.S. 609, at 633). Any association not predominantly of these types is a commercial association, "and therefore subject to rationally related state regulation of its membership and other associational activities" (468 U.S. 609, at 635).

The language of *Roberts* illuminates issues discussed in *Bowers*, although Blackmun relied on Fourth Amendment guarantees of the privacy of the home (478 U.S. 186, at 207–8) rather than on the First Amendment. An intimate association is an expressive association. The sexual component that inheres in certain intimate associations, including but not limited to that of marriage, is a species of free expression that might be interpreted to fall under First Amendment protection. As a type of expressive association central to individual development, an intimate association between adults that includes sexual expression would not be subject to state regulation of its membership or of its other associational activities—that is, of the form that sexual expression might take. Engagement in homosexual sodomy is not itself a fundamental right. But engagement in an intimate association that may or may not include that practice *is* such a right, carrying both intrinsic value and social importance, and as such it and its components are constitutionally protected.

Both majority and minority justices in *Bowers*, then, are adducing arguments that consider the intrinsic value and social importance of particular practices. It is not that the majority is defending shared goods of a determinate sort, and that the minority is making a merely neutral or procedural case for toleration. Rather, each is adducing a different conception of what these shared goods are or what an overlapping consensus should embody. The majority defends a traditional definition of the good of intimate relationships and a historically sanctioned interpretation of our traditional values, whereas the minority adopts a broader definition of the goods served by intimate relationships and by our history and tradition. As Sandel suggests, practices may be best defended by looking to their intrinsic value or social importance, but we are often confronted with conflicting interpretations of what meets these tests. It is for this reason I have suggested that we look to the relationship between the toleration of particular practices and the promotion of autonomy as the ability to define the good in one's own manner, concluding that the protection or promotion of autonomy is itself a source of intrinsic value or social importance.

MacIntyre states that the concept of a coherent selfhood "resides in the unity of a narrative" that makes intelligible the disparate events of a life.[14] Our history and tradition possess the unity of a narrative. The catch is in the fact that different narrators will tell the story differently. The unifying thread in my own narrative is that of the protection and enhancement of a moral autonomy that promotes equal respect for individuals and encourages debate and deliberation about the community's shared conceptions of the good. Others will perceive different unifying threads in their own narratives. This is as it should be. As MacIntyre asserts, the common life of any institution "will be partly, but in a centrally important way, constituted by a continuous argument" about what that institution is and about what values it should embody. "Traditions, when vital, embody continuities of conflict" (206).

III

If political justice is to be grounded in an overlapping consensus endorsed by diverse and opposing "though reasonable" comprehensive doctrines of the good, as Rawls suggests, the central question, then, is that of how the content of this consensus is to be determined. Accounts of toleration that defer to the dominant understanding, I believe, appear to result from an overlapping consensus but constitute in reality a modus vivendi: we praise those who display worth and merit as defined by the current consensus whatever its content, and accord grudging permission to others, in order to preserve civil tranquility. The hegemony of some ways of life and the self-restraint of adherents of other beliefs and practices ostensibly form an overlapping consensus of reasonable comprehensive doctrines, and "the reasonable doctrines endorse the political conception, each from its own point of view."[15] At one extreme lies complete intolerance and at the other lies permission plus praise; the overlap appears at the point of consensus on toleration without approval. But tension persists because the community's shared general conception of the good is based on the dominance of some reasonable comprehensive doctrines and the resulting self-censorship of others rather than on a truly overlapping consensus to which all participants are equally welcome to contribute.

A modus vivendi model of the political order is not necessarily illegitimate. Patrick Neal, for example, proposes a resurrection of "vulgar" Hobbesian liberalism, noting that neutrality theorists tend to overestimate both the instability of the modus vivendi model and the stability of their own models. With regard to Rawls's overlapping consensus, "What is actually argued is the existence of a descriptive link or match between elements of an individual's conceptions of the good and elements of the public conception of justice. But what is not explained is why the existence of that analytical link provides the individual with a motivation (moral or otherwise, for that matter) to adhere to the public conception."[16] In essence, Neal argues that in the face of pluralistic conflict, neutrality theorists ignore the importance of a rough equality of power among competing groups to check both each other and the state. "Is it really the case that the continued stability of existing liberal regimes is in any way whatsoever dependent on a professor of political philosophy's ability to define the terms of an overlapping consensus among alternative conceptions of the good life?" (635).

Rawls does highlight a stability condition that he uses to differentiate an overlapping consensus from a modus vivendi. "This means that those who affirm the various views supporting the political conception will not withdraw their support of it should the relative strength of their view in society increase and eventually become dominant."[17] That is, changes in the distribution of power will not alter the consensus. Yet, if respect is a reward distributed in accordance with the individual's conformity to the dominant consensus, one of two conclusions follows. First, those who are unable to secure a commitment to equal respect for their own beliefs and practices will demand this if and when the strength of their view or the balance of power—that is, what appears to be the dominant understanding—makes this practicable. Second, if the balance moves in the opposite direction to weaken unpopular groups, the ostensibly overlapping consensus may be interpreted to require even less respect for them than before. And because the consensus is interpreted in terms of the current understanding, the likelihood is great that the dominant view will gain support over time. Thus, what seems an overlapping consensus turns out to operate as a modus vivendi, rooted in the actual convergence of interests at given points in time.

Moreover, even if citizens arrive at a consensus that they will continue to support regardless of the relative strengths of differing viewpoints, in a liberal polity this consensus is better developed by forthright debate among individuals who are accorded equal respect than by covert shaping of beliefs and practices by communal attitudes that both emanate from and reinforce the already-dominant consensus. In any case, we maintain the right and the desire to influence the terms of the way of life to which we subscribe. This, once again, implies debate and deliberation about our shared conceptions of the good. For some, our history and tradition point us in the direction not only of liberty but also of equal respect. Liberty may be exemplified by protecting intimate relationships from unwarranted state interference, and equality may be interpreted to require protection against discrimination on the basis of the sort of intimate relationships in which one engages. But these interpretations must be discussed. In sum, the construction of an overlapping consensus is an interactive process. As Brian Walker writes: "Fighting for toleration is not a matter of attempting to align other groups with a preexisting order, but a form of dialogue in the course of which the picture of what toleration is and requires gradually becomes clear. By attempting to build my ideal of toleration on the terrain of the other, I am myself affected by new and alien ideas, and perhaps my own view is changed."[18]

Government, as described by Galston above, may indeed need to encourage habits that secure liberal rights. But this need not mean subscribing to the dominant understanding or current orthodoxy as to what these habits might be. Although deliberation is necessary to decide which among many practices are by definition inimical to the liberal polity, even this goal is best achieved by forthright debate. Jeremy Waldron asserts that communitarians often defend communal particularity with regard to norms not because a norm seems right in a universalizable sense but because it is ipso facto a norm of that community in particular. But for Waldron, moral norms like that of fundamental human equality cannot for those who subscribe to them simply have the status of local customs. "To say that is to describe from the outside, rather than to participate in, the social understanding in question."[19] Although different communities do espouse a variety of shared understandings, "By asking what is really right and really wrong, the liberal is closer to participating in the spirit of our traditions than the communitarian who says that what matters to us is nothing more than that they happen to be *our* traditions" (581; emphasis in original).

Those who would defer to the dominant understanding often resemble Waldron's communitarian, defending this approach to toleration externally because of its contribution to stability rather than internally because there is something inherently right about it in terms of the demands of liberal principles. Sanford Levinson suggests that supporting the Constitution "commits me not to closure but only to a process of becoming and to taking responsibility for constructing the political vision toward which I strive, joined, I hope, with others. It is therefore less a series of propositional utterances than a commitment to taking political conversation seriously."[20] Similarly, toleration is less a matter of acceding to a given or current consensus than it is a commitment to deliberation among equals as to the meaning of our shared conceptions of the good. A community "is something that endures through and therefore changes over time. A community has a life that is longer than any of its members, but longer too than that of any of the circumstances and problems to which its particular mores are a response."[21] Members of vibrant communities recognize that their traditions do not stand still. These traditions may embody current belief and practice, but they are also "traditions of change, diversity, controversy, and reflection" (589).[22] I must therefore in the end conclude that the concept of toleration defined as according equal respect to all beliefs and tolerated practices is most likely to promote thoughtful questioning, both individually and collectively.

Notes

1. John Rawls, *Political Liberalism* (New York: Columbia University Press, 1993), 38.

2. Steven Kautz, "Liberalism and the Idea of Toleration," *American Journal of Political Science* 37 (1993): 620.

3. William Galston, *Liberal Purposes: Goods, Virtues, and Diversity in the Liberal State* (New York: Cambridge University Press, 1991), 242–43.

4. Michael J. Sandel, *Liberalism and the Limits of Justice* (New York: Cambridge University Press, 1982), and "The Procedural Republic and the Unencumbered Self," *Political Theory* 12 (1984): 81–95.

5. Alasdair MacIntyre, *After Virtue* (Notre Dame: University of Notre Dame Press, 1981), 204.

6. Alasdair MacIntyre, *Whose Justice? Which Rationality?* (Notre Dame: University of Notre Dame Press, 1988), 106–7. See also MacIntyre, *After Virtue*, 233.

7. Sandel, *Liberalism and the Limits of Justice*, 71.

8. William R. Lund, "Communitarian Politics and the Problem of Equality," *Political Research Quarterly* 46 (1993): 587.

9. Kautz, "Liberalism and the Idea of Toleration," 625; see also 620.

10. Michael J. Sandel, "Moral Argument and Liberal Toleration: Abortion and Homosexuality," *California Law Review* 77 (1989): 524.

11. Lund, "Communitarian Politics and the Problem of Equality," 595–96.

12. Sandel, *Liberalism and the Limits of Justice*, 150, emphasis in original; see also 148–50.

13. Philip Selznick, "Dworkin's Unfinished Task," *California Law Review* 77 (1989): 513.

14. MacIntyre, *After Virtue*, 191.

15. Rawls, *Political Liberalism*, 134.

16. Patrick Neal, "Vulgar Liberalism," *Political Theory* 21 (1993): 633.

17. Rawls, *Political Liberalism*, 148.

18. Brian Walker, "John Rawls, Mikhail Bakhtin, and the Praxis of Toleration," *Political Theory* 23 (1995): 121.

19. Jeremy Waldron, "Particular Values and Critical Morality," *California Law Review* 77 (1989): 579.

20. Sanford Levinson, *Constitutional Faith* (Princeton: Princeton University Press, 1988), 193.

21. Waldron, "Particular Values and Critical Morality," 584.

22. See also MacIntyre, *Whose Justice? Which Rationality?*

Chapter 13

A Nonpunitive, Compensatory Remedy for Discriminatory Abusive Speech

Diana Tietjens Meyers

Speech can inflict harm. No one denies this, and consequently laws forbidding libel and false advertising are not controversial. Yet, many people deny that racist, sexist, homophobic, ethnocentric, and similar forms of abusive speech are harmful enough to justify recognizing a right protecting people from this treatment. Discriminatory abusive speech is deplorable, they may say, but free speech takes precedence.

This chapter is premised on a claim that I defend at length elsewhere: Discriminatory verbal and pictorial abuse is harmful, and members of historically despised and currently subordinated social groups have a right not to be subjected to verbal or pictorial abuse based on their membership in one or more of these groups.[1] (Hereafter, I shall refer to this right as the right not to be subjected to discriminatory verbal or pictorial abuse.) Here I shall confine my defense of this right to countering some arguments advanced by a prominent opponent of this kind of right, Judith Jarvis Thomson. Still, my position differs significantly from those taken by other proponents of the right not to be subjected to discriminatory verbal or pictorial abuse, for I do not take a successful defense of this right to entail that discriminatory abusive speech ought to be prohibited. Rather, I believe that there are compelling reasons both to maintain a robust right to free speech and to implement the right not to be subjected to discriminatory verbal or pictorial abuse. Thus, most of this chapter is devoted to presenting and defending a proposal to respect the rights of members of subordinated social groups on U.S. college and university campuses without regulating anyone's freedom of expression. Briefly, I urge that colleges and universities should compensate victims of discriminatory verbal or pictorial abuse and that such compensation does not require punishing individuals who utter discriminatory verbal or pictorial abuse.

The Problematics of Regulating Harmful Speech

Challenges to the right not to be subjected to discriminatory verbal or pictorial abuse come from two main sources. The best-known objection is that this right would conflict with the right to free speech and that free speech is of paramount importance both from the standpoint of individual autonomy and also from that of the democratic political process. Because restricting speech could bring about disastrous consequences, the right not to be subjected to discriminatory verbal or pictorial abuse must be rejected. Another objection stems from Judith Jarvis Thomson's view that rights do not afford protection from "belief-mediated distress." Plainly, the point of the right not to be subjected to discriminatory verbal or pictorial abuse is to protect people from just this sort of suffering, for in the absence of beliefs about the pervasiveness of racism, sexism, homophobia, and ethnocentrism and beliefs about the social significance of certain symbols, no one would be the least bit upset by these utterances. I shall take up Thomson's position first.

Thomson acknowledges that belief-mediated distress can be more painful than non–belief-mediated distress.[2] Her reason for disallowing the right not to be subjected to discriminatory verbal or pictorial abuse is not that the suffering inflicted by this form of abuse is not sufficiently severe. Rather, her point is that one has more control over how much one suffers when one's distress is belief-mediated and therefore that one bears a share of responsibility for one's own suffering (253–54). Thus, she observes that people can "steel" themselves against the pain of belief-mediated distress (254). Yet, in view of the fact that people can take precautions to avoid or minimize the pain of many types of non–belief-mediated distress, as well, Thomson's position must ultimately rest on unstated assumptions about what precautions it is reasonable to expect people to take to secure their own well-being.[3] Evidently, in her judgment, steeling oneself against harmful speech is reasonable to expect. Steeling oneself against intense physical pain is not. But because many of our beliefs are not fungible and resist being changed, steeling oneself against belief-mediated distress may prove very difficult, if not impossible.

Apart from the feasibility of modifying those of one's beliefs that increase one's vulnerability to harm, there is the question of whether it is desirable to do so. Plainly, it is not always desirable to steel oneself against harmful speech. If one were to become inured to physical pain, one might fail to heed its warnings and fail to seek needed medical attention. Similarly, if one were to steel oneself against the fear and humiliation that discriminatory verbal or pictorial abuse precipitates, one might fail to recognize serious threats for what they are, and thus one might become excessively vulnerable to physical attack or unfair treatment.[4] In short, one might become complicit in one's own oppression.

In addition, steeling oneself against the effects of harmful speech may pave the way for morally objectionable conduct toward others. Patricia Williams's account of an incident that took place at Stanford University provides disturbing evidence for this claim. A student descended from German Jews, who is called Fred in the university's official report, became embroiled in an argument with an African-American student, who is called Q.C. in the report. Q.C. maintained and Fred disputed that Beethoven had black ancestors. The following night Fred and some friends drew stereotypical African-American features on a poster of Beethoven and tacked it outside Q.C.'s room. Williams cites further details from the report that reveal more about Fred's experience during his youth and about his interpretation of his conduct:

> [Fred] described incidents [at his school in England] that he called "teasing" . . . by his schoolmates about his being Jewish. They called him miserly, and his being a Jew was referred to as a weakness. Fred said that he learned not to mind it and indicated that the poster defacement at Ujaama House had been in the spirit of this teaching. He wondered why the black students could not respond to it in the spirit in which it was meant: "nothing serious," just "humor as a release."[5]

Surely, Fred's success in withstanding anti-Semitism contributed to his inability to empathize with Q.C. Moreover, his lack of empathy made him liable to engage in morally obtuse behavior—behavior that perpetuates the cycle of prejudice and persecution. In short, steeling oneself may lead one to join the ranks of the oppressors.

Of course, my point is not that vulnerable individuals should adopt no coping strategies to reduce the harm they suffer. Rather, my point is that it is important to recognize that there are dangers associated with steeling oneself against discriminatory verbal or pictorial abuse and that one must take care to avoid desensitizing oneself so completely that one loses one's sense of justice. Trading in one's attunement to injustice for a false sense of one's own security or for callousness toward others' suffering is a bad bargain.

I would stress, moreover, that the possibility of taking measures to protect oneself from certain harms and the reasonability of doing so does not entail that one has no right not to be harmed in these ways. When I learned of a rash of burglaries in my area, I had an alarm system installed in my house. My neighbors have chosen not to invest in similar equipment. Yet, if their house were burglarized, the police would accord their property rights the same respect that they would accord mine. And if my house were burglarized despite my alarm, the police would not ask me why I had neglected to run coils of razor wire around the perimeter of my property. The asymmetry in people's intuitions about rights is not governed by the availability of coping strategies—especially when the coping strategies are costly or interfere with one's enjoyment of one's rights.

Nor is this asymmetry governed by the distinction between belief-mediated distress and non–belief-mediated distress. Until recently, rape trials often turned on whether the victim had "asked for it"—that is, had forfeited her rights—by dressing seductively, by consuming alcoholic beverages, or by walking alone at night. If the victim had not taken all possible precautions to prevent a crime from taking place, including maintaining an unblemished reputation for chastity, the jury was likely to acquit the assailant. It seems there is no temptation to say that people who fail to adopt coping strategies have no rights except when the injured parties are typically members of marginalized social groups. But, plainly, whether people have a certain right does not depend on the social status of their group—it depends on the nature of the harm the right forbids.[6]

It seems to me, then, that the link between the right not to be subjected to discriminatory verbal or pictorial abuse and belief-mediated distress is no reason to reject it. On the contrary, since steeling oneself against this form of distress can be the height of irresponsibility, but since the harm inflicted by hate speech is often grievous, there is good reason to recognize this right. Still, the clash between free speech and the right not to be subjected to discriminatory verbal or pictorial abuse remains.

One way to resolve this conflict would be to tailor the right of free speech so as to cordon off racist, sexist, homophobic, and similar forms of abuse from the class of protected speech. This is the solution that Mari Matsuda, Charles Lawrence, and Richard Delgado advocate.[7] I am agnostic with regard to the feasibility of drawing this distinction in a way that prohibits the speech that seems to me to violate the rights of members of socially subordinated groups but that allows the speech that seems to me important to protect. In this regard, I was surprised and intrigued to learn that although Ronald Dworkin opposes regulating harmful speech, he denies that regulating harmful speech is likely to lead to tyranny.[8] But even supposing that the slippery slope argument is unconvincing, there are two further lines of argument in support of unrestrained speech that I find worthy of serious consideration.

I think of the first of these arguments as the "Sigmund Freud argument." This argument points out that people have a dark side and that hiding or denying what is seen as shameful or sinister in the human psyche is bad faith and potentially dangerous. Repressed material always returns in some form or other, and the menace of the repressed is redoubled because it is forbidden and because the forbidden is alluring. Thus, the effect of censorship might be to attract new converts to racist, sexist, homophobic, and ethnocentric doctrines and thereby defeat the interests of the very groups it aims to help. I call the second argument the "Lenny Bruce argument." This argument reminds us that racial and other epithets are just words and urges that the best antidote for harmful, emotionally charged language is to repeat it and broadcast it to the point where it becomes banal. This is the strategy behind naming a gay and lesbian political organization "Queer Nation" and chanting, "We're here; we're queer; we won't go away!" at demonstrations. All in all, then, it may not be such a bad thing that hateful thoughts and vicious language be aired.

Whatever the merits of these admittedly speculative worries about restricting speech, there remain two formidable practical obstacles. Here in the United States, many people are passionately attached to free speech as it is now delimited and are not at all likely to accept a narrower reading of their rights. Opponents of restricting speech doubt that speech is really all that harmful. They ask for proof that a particular incident of hate speech caused this individual's debilitating depression, and the proof is not forthcoming. Indeed, if it weren't for the climate of racism, sexism, homophobia, and ethnocentrism in the United States, discriminatory verbal or pictorial abuse would not be seriously harmful.[9] In addition, people are fearful that government officials will exploit new legal restraints on speech to persecute political dissent or personal nonconformism. *Butler v. Her Majesty the Queen* (1992) permits the Canadian government to suppress highly explicit sexual materials that harm women. It remains to be seen whether this bold social experiment will jeopardize artistic and political expression.[10] Whatever the outcome, at present there is no popular sentiment in the United States in favor of government intervention to restrain discriminatory verbal or pictorial abuse.[11]

This antipathy is reinforced by a venerable tradition of First Amendment jurisprudence that vigorously protects free speech from encroachments. Thus, a further concern is that any redefinition of the bounds of permissible speech that would pass constitutional muster would define verbal and pictorial abuse so narrowly that the change would not do much good. As Henry Louis Gates points out, angrily shouting a well-known racial epithet at an African-American student might be prohibited, but racist views cloaked in civil language or delivered in the guise of theory, however hurtful their expression may be, could not be prohibited.[12] Indeed, its speech code notwithstanding, Stanford University concluded that the students who defaced the picture of Beethoven and posted it in a predominantly black dormitory were acting within their constitutional rights.[13] If verbal and pictorial abuse is to be defined broadly enough both to recognize all the harm it causes and also to serve an educative function, it may well be advisable to uncouple the right not to be subjected to discriminatory verbal or pictorial abuse from censorship and punitive sanctions.[14]

Still, I strongly agree with Charles Lawrence when he admonishes partisans of unfettered speech rights that it is important to be mindful of how one participates in the hate speech debate. Too often free speech is defended, and the harm of discriminatory verbal or pictorial abuse is shrugged off—"It's a pity," civil libertarians sometimes say, "but it's the price we pay for freedom." Once harmful speech has been pronounced despicable, the discussion is summarily closed. Lawrence points out that taking positions like this does nothing to dispel the appearance of condoning bigotry.[15] It is unconscionable to betray the moral data gained through broad empathy with the victims of discriminatory verbal and pictorial abuse.[16] But how is it possible to keep faith with the moral data and also to endorse free speech as it is presently defined in United States law?

An Unorthodox Proposal

In what follows, I shall confine my comments to the proliferation of discriminatory verbal and pictorial abuse on United States college and university campuses. One reason for narrowing my focus is that concentrating on a single institutional setting makes the problem more tractable. The other is that it is especially important that the problem be solved in this particular setting. The obligation of the university to provide equality of opportunity to all of its students requires that it take measures to create a sanctuary for those students who are vulnerable to discriminatory verbal or pictorial abuse in order to ensure that their ability to learn is not impaired by others' stupidity or malice. Here the right not to be subjected to discriminatory verbal or pictorial abuse is salient. Yet, the mission of the university as a site of inquiry and open dialogue requires that all students and faculty feel free to express their views. Here the right to free speech must be robust. Thus, universities seem to be torn between a pair of equally compelling yet incompatible moral claims.

By framing these two rights using Hohfeld's technical rights taxonomy, it is possible to dissolve this paradox. It has often been noted that the U.S. Constitution construes free speech not as a claim right correlated with a duty of forbearance but, rather, as an immunity correlated with a legislative disability.[17] Censorship is not a crime. But, since government bodies lack the power to prohibit free expression, the courts will nullify legislative attempts to restrict speech unduly. Likewise, the right not to be subjected to discriminatory verbal or pictorial abuse need not be construed as a claim right entitling students who are members of socially subordinated groups not to hear hate speech and imposing a duty of forbearance specified in a restrictive speech code. Instead, this right could be construed as a power correlated with the university's liability to that power. Members of historically despised and currently subordinated social groups could be empowered to exact compensation from the university upon demonstrating that a fellow member of the university community subjected them to discriminatory verbal or pictorial abuse.[18] On this interpretation, there would be no new restrictions on speech, and yet the right not to be subjected to discriminatory verbal or pictorial abuse would be recognized and respected.

The funds that some states have set up to compensate victims of violent crime provide a precedent for this proposal. However, these funds differ in two major respects from my hate-speech compensation scheme. In the case of crime compensation funds, the state prohibits and punishes the conduct for which it compensates victims. Thus, it is in a position to minimize its liability. Likewise, in sexual harassment law, which holds employers responsible for compensating employees who are harassed by supervisory or peer employees, employers are permitted to institute and enforce policies prohibiting harassing behavior. Thus, it may seem unfair to hold universities responsible for compensating victims of discriminatory verbal or pictorial abuse and yet to deny them the right to deter these utterances by establishing and enforcing speech codes.

Of course, it is not true that rejecting speech codes renders universities helpless with respect to discriminatory verbal and pictorial abuse. Universities can establish orientation programs, courses, and workshops that educate students, faculty, and staff about the nature and the harm of discriminatory verbal or pictorial abuse; they can diversify their faculties and student bodies; they can enlist prominent conservative and civil libertarian faculty members and student leaders who claim to abhor hate speech to decry campus incidents publicly; university presidents and deans can vocally condemn hate speech whenever and wherever it occurs. Moreover, unlike crime compensation funds, which are statutorily mandated, compensating student victims for violations of the right not to be subjected to discriminatory verbal or pictorial abuse is a moral imperative. I shall leave aside the more complicated but undeniably important question of under what circumstances the legislatures or courts should impose this liability on universities. I shall urge only that these educational institutions should assume this responsibility voluntarily.

There are a number of reasons for thinking it proper for universities to accept liability for compensating students whose right not to be subjected to discriminatory verbal or pictorial abuse is violated on campus. Charles Lawrence and Frederick Schauer both question the legitimacy of leaving the victims of harmful speech to shoulder the costs of keeping the marketplace of ideas open.[19] If free speech is a social good, as well as an individual good, it is unfair that members of certain groups are required to bear a disproportionate share of the burdens of free speech by being barred from obtaining compensation for speech that harms them. Yet, requiring those who verbally assault others to pay for the harms they inflict would inhibit and thus constrain free speech. It seems, then, that we must turn to social institutions to defray these costs. Since universities benefit enormously from free speech, it seems especially appropriate that they should do so.

Also, discriminatory verbal or pictorial abuse is not a purely individual wrongdoing. It is substantially aided and abetted by the dominant culture. In the United States, this culture couples official condemnation of racism, sexism, and ethnocentrism (but, notice, not homophobia) with underhanded symbolic inculcation and reinforcement of these very attitudes and the behavior that goes with them.[20] In view of the pervasiveness of these prejudices, and in view of the fact that universities play a vital role in transmitting the dominant culture in which they are encoded, it is fitting that these institutions assume the costs of compensating the victims of discriminatory verbal or pictorial abuse on their own campuses.

Finally, although the fundamental reason for colleges and universities to undertake to compensate students who are victimized by discriminatory verbal or pictorial abuse is that justice demands that they do so, I would point out that it is also in their interest to respect these students' rights. Both because it is desirable to distribute the good of education as widely as possible and also because lively and fruitful intellectual debate requires assembling representatives of as many viewpoints as possible, these institutions seek to recruit a diverse student body. Presumably, students from historically despised and currently subordinated social groups would find colleges and universities that were committed to respecting their right not to be subjected to discriminatory verbal or pictorial abuse more attractive. If this is so, these institutions would gain a significant advantage in enrolling and retaining students from these groups and thus a significant advantage in achieving one of their principal goals.

Implementing the Right Not to Be Subjected to Discriminatory Verbal or Pictorial Abuse

Turning now to the mechanics of implementing the right not to be subjected to discriminatory verbal or pictorial abuse, I believe that this right calls for innovative methods. The forms of harmful speech and the nature of the harms that speech can cause need to be investigated. Also, compensation scales need to be set. It strikes me that universities are unusually well situated to conduct these inquiries and to implement the power and the liability I have proposed.

One objection that might be lodged against the right not to be subjected to discriminatory verbal or pictorial abuse is that we do not know enough about how speech harms people to identify violations of the right. To some, this may seem like a good reason to confine rights to physical or non–belief-mediated harms—harms that medical science can confidently document and trace to their causes. Compared to our knowledge of physical diseases and injuries, our knowledge of psychological maladies is undeniably in its infancy. But there is a revealing analogy between speech-inflicted harm and environmentally caused harm.[21] Scientists are far from clear about which pesticides and other pollutants endanger human health, and their estimates of what quantities of these chemicals cause serious ailments are very rough.

Still, few regard the trial-and-error approach of environmental medicine as a reason to abandon the inquiry or to forgo taking steps to protect public health. There seems to be a consensus (outside agribusiness and the chemical industry, that is) that it is best to prohibit substances and practices that appear to pose a danger, while continuing to do research and revising policy in accordance with the preponderance of the data. University committees charged with implementing the right not to be subjected to discriminatory verbal or pictorial abuse would be in a similar position—examining cases as they arise and doing their best to assess the harm and to devise appropriate remedies. The likelihood that they will occasionally make mistakes does not mean that they should not get to work and start developing a body of findings. Eventually, it may be possible to distill these findings into a cogent system of principles and policies.

Meanwhile, it is necessary to be mindful of the complexities and uncertainties surrounding the right not to be subjected to discriminatory verbal or pictorial abuse in planning for its implementation. Although university committees can undertake preliminary studies to determine what sorts of speech trouble members of socially subordinated groups and how these individuals are affected by these utterances, it seems clear that any definition of verbal and pictorial abuse that they formulate is best regarded as provisional. Because these committees will be exploring uncharted territory, it seems unlikely that any committee will be able to anticipate all possible forms of discriminatory verbal or pictorial abuse. Thus, committees created to administer this right will be learning as they go. The experimental nature of the undertaking argues against a punitive interpretation of the right and in favor of my compensatory interpretation, and it also argues against adversarial enforcement procedures and in favor of arbitration procedures.

Interpreting the right not to be subjected to discriminatory verbal or pictorial abuse as mandating a punitive speech code would establish two insuperable presumptions, one in favor of a sharp and narrow definition of harmful speech and the other in favor of adversarial enforcement procedures. Both the unfairness of meting out punishment when the offense is vaguely defined and the instrumental value of free discussion on campus necessitate minimizing restrictions on speech and maximizing the prerogatives of accused individuals to defend themselves. Yet, establishing such a definition would choke off inquiry into the various forms of harmful speech and would almost certainly prove underinclusive. Moreover, the virtue of adversarial proceedings is that they protect the accused, not that they foster inquiry and deepen understanding of vexing social problems.

In contrast, a social compensation scheme of the kind I am proposing does not require a neat and fixed definition of discriminatory verbal or pictorial abuse, nor does it oblige universities strictly to observe disciplinary procedures comparable to those of a fair trial, for no one would be accused of a punishable infraction. Although punishing an innocent individual is a grave injustice, benefiting a person who does not deserve it is a minor mishap as long as no one else is seriously harmed. No terrible moral wrong would be committed if occasionally a student were overcompensated.

The point of the right not to be subjected to discriminatory verbal or pictorial abuse is to protect vulnerable people from a particularly invidious form of harmful speech. Thus, a tenable interpretation of this right will advance three key aims: it will educate people about how speech causes harm; it will make up for harm that is caused by discriminatory verbal or pictorial abuse; and it will deter this harmful speech.

I believe that much harmful speech on campuses stems from ignorance—lack of information about different cultures and distorted beliefs transmitted through derogatory stereotypes that are in wide circulation. To reduce the isolation of different social groups and to counteract misinformation about these groups, Lawrence suggests that student victims be compensated by creating minority scholarships or minority faculty lines or by suspending classes and holding teach-ins on racism.[22] I certainly have no objection to the aims underlying Lawrence's proposals, and I would be happy if universities took such measures. However, I think that whenever possible, the individuals whose rights are violated should be recompensed personally. Thus, I shall offer a compensation scheme that preserves the educational potential of Lawrence's proposal but that gives due recognition to the harm individuals suffer.

A fair compensation scheme will take into account the gravity of the harm and the intent of the speaker. When a speaker unwittingly causes harm and the harm is slight, an apology and a promise to desist seems sufficient as compensation. However, when a speaker deliberately causes harm or when the harm is severe, material compensation seems necessary, for the sincerity of an apology would be doubtful, and severe injury calls for substantial recompense. In such cases, universities could award victims credit toward the next semester's tuition (or in the case of second-semester seniors, a refund on the current tuition bill), and they could tie the amount of credit to the egregiousness of the incident. This remedy seems fitting since it links the compensation to the victim's educational aspirations and contributes to those goals.

This method of compensation can be administered using an arbitration model rather than a legalistic adversarial model. If the right not to be subjected to discriminatory verbal or pictorial abuse is to serve an educational function, it is important to avoid exacerbating hostility and putting the parties on the defensive. When guilt and punishment, on the one hand, and exoneration, on the other, exhaust the possible outcomes for the accused individual, one cannot expect that person to be candid and forthcoming.[23] A compensation scheme that does not penalize the accused individual and that is implemented through arbitration provides a setting for mediation and an opportunity to reach mutual understanding and reconciliation. Student complainants must see these proceedings as an opportunity to learn, as well. As a result of the dialogue such proceedings initiate, a student whom an utterance offended and upset might come to understand the reasonableness and the justifiability of the speech and to regard his or her reaction as excessive. In that case or in cases in which the administrative committee determines that a student should accept this view of the matter, no compensation would be awarded.

In advocating arbitration proceedings, I am not suggesting that universities should accept all claims at face value or that the only issue is how much compensation the alleged victim should receive. On the contrary, to make sure that incidents are not being staged, these claims must be thoroughly investigated, and the testimony of witnesses must be sought. Moreover, I would advise universities to impose fairly onerous penalties when students are found to have lodged fabricated or frivolous complaints. Still, I expect that some cases will fall in a gray area, and it seems to me that it is better for universities to respond to such cases in a spirit of openness and compromise rather than in a harsh, incredulous spirit that requires students who claim to have been victimized by discriminatory verbal or pictorial abuse to produce incontrovertible proof to support their charges. I think that flexibility in enforcement, as long as it does not devolve into capriciousnes, is dictated by the typical university's administrative capabilities and also befits the unpredictable variety of the forms that abusive speech may take. On my compensatory interpretation of the right not to be subjected to discriminatory verbal or pictorial abuse, a somewhat elastic definition of abusive speech that allows for sensitivity to social context and variations in individual temperament is tenable. Since the alternative is to preempt inquiry and to deny justice to many victims of abusive speech, this flexibility constitutes a strong reason to adopt my interpretation.

I suspect that punitive sanctions would martyr many people who violate the right not to be subjected to discriminatory verbal or pictorial abuse, and that this veneration of abusive speakers as heroes of civil liberties would stigmatize their victims. Yet, by itself, answering abusive speech with more speech seems a toothless alternative. If education were as effective as educators would like to believe it is, the incidence of discriminatory verbal and pictorial abuse on campuses should be waning, but it is not. Although my compensation scheme imposes no punishments, it would nevertheless deter discriminatory verbal and pictorial abuse. It would defeat the purposes of malicious speakers, for voicing prejudice would ultimately benefit the very people the bigot wants to hurt. With respect to well-meaning but misguided speakers, using arbitration to implement the right not to be subjected to discriminatory verbal or pictorial abuse incorporates the advantages of the educational approach and strengthens the educational impact by personalizing the process. Tutorials work better than large lecture courses. Finally and most importantly, this interpretation of the right would not leave victims in the lurch. Whether in the form of an apology and an assurance that the harmful speech will not be repeated or in the form of tuition remission, the victim receives a significant, individuated benefit.

Now, it might be granted that my proposal provides a way for universities to discourage violations of the right not to be subjected to discriminatory verbal or pictorial abuse and to respect victims' rights without encroaching on free inquiry. Still, a critic might regard my proposal as unrealistic and possibly dangerous. First, it might be objected that universities will seek to minimize their liability by accepting only ideologically compatible students. But it seems doubtful that a university that would voluntarily institute the compensation scheme I envisage would secretly reverse its principles and undermine diversity by homogenizing admissions. Moreover, federal law provides further protection for diversity. Discrimination on grounds of race, religion, or sex is illegal at schools that receive public funding. I would add that conservatives who fear that like-minded applicants will be targeted and discriminated against should not concede that bigots can be weeded out by identifying prospective students' conservative political leanings. This stereotype, like all stereotypes, should be resisted.

Second, it might be urged that compensating all the victims whose claims were vindicated would bankrupt universities. If that is true, I would reply that it is all the more urgent for universities to take aggressive measures to implement the right not to be subjected to discriminatory verbal or pictorial abuse. Still, I would also stress that universities need not create lavish funds to compensate victims. Even if budgetary constraints render their compensation awards essentially symbolic, these awards will represent a colossal improvement over the institutional indifference that now prevails on United States campuses.

Contestable Claims and Respect for Rights

At this point, someone might object that my construal of the right not to be subjected to discriminatory verbal or pictorial abuse is an evasion and a pernicious one at that. This Hohfeldian sleight of hand, it could be argued, is mere trickery that makes the conflict between free speech and this novel right seem to disappear but that in reality aggravates the conflict. A policy of compensating victims of discriminatory verbal or pictorial abuse would provide a powerful disincentive to abusive speech. In litigation involving journalism, there is a presumption against similar disincentives for fear of the chilling effect they might have on vigorous investigation and uninhibited reportage of the news. Mightn't my compensation program also chill free debate on campus?

Let me bring this objection into focus by reformulating it. Insofar as the right to free speech and the right not to be subjected to discriminatory verbal or pictorial abuse are institutionalized and respected by universities, I think there is nothing wrong with conceptualizing this pair of rights as an immunity and a power, respectively. But I agree that we have to face the fact that conceived as moral or customary rights—that is, as rights that private individuals regard as action-guiding—these two rights conflict.[24] The reason for this is that our informal conventions regarding free speech oblige us to tolerate expression of ideas that we oppose and thus impose a duty on each member of an audience to allow the others to speak in accordance with certain rules of order. Hecklers come in for criticism because the right to free speech is commonly viewed as a claim right. Axiomatically, if someone has a claim right to forbearance, everyone else has a duty to forbear and therefore no one has a right not to forbear. But notice that conceived as a customary right, the right not to be subjected to discriminatory verbal or pictorial abuse would also be regarded as a claim right. As an individual seeking to respect this right, one would refrain from uttering abusive speech. Thus, we are back to the paradox with which we began. Everyone has a minimally fettered right to free speech, and everyone is at liberty to utter abusive speech. Yet, the members of historically despised and currently subordinated social groups have a right not to be subjected to discriminatory verbal or pictorial abuse, and no one is at liberty to utter abusive speech.

On some rights theories, this conflict would suffice to disqualify at least one of these rights or to require that exceptions be built into one or both of them. John Rawls, for example, maintains that each person has an "equal claim to a fully adequate scheme of equal basic rights and liberties, which scheme is compatible with the same scheme for all" and that these rights and liberties take precedence over economic welfare rights.[25] Likewise, Rex Martin argues that "careful drafting and redrafting" can (in principle) and should (wherever possible) eliminate conflicts between rights.[26] Others, notably Judith Thomson and George Sher, deny that rights conflicts can be avoided. Thomson denies that rights are absolute and examines the distinction between justified abridgments of rights and wrongful violations of rights.[27] Sher holds that incorrigible ignorance about the legitimacy of some people's claims and the fact that injustices will inevitably be committed entails that rights conflicts are inescapable.[28] I shall argue that it is feasible for individuals to respect both the right to free speech and the right not to be subjected to discriminatory verbal or pictorial abuse without universities' stipulating a resolution of the conflict between them in advance.

To frame this issue, I find it helpful to note some continuities between free speech and property rights. Some people regard possessions as extensions of persons and the unlimited right to acquire property as a basic moral right.[29] I myself doubt that any fundamental human interest entails that the right to property must authorize people to become billionaires if they can do so without resorting to force or fraud. There is a fundamental human interest in the satisfaction of subsistence needs, and there is a fundamental human interest in leading a fulfilling life. One way to secure these interests is to institute a scheme of property rights that sets out permissive rules for acquisition and that endows individuals with broad powers to dispose of their holdings. Although capitalism is by no means the only conceivable way of organizing commerce so as to safeguard these fundamental interests, it is defensible as a means to this end, for it has proven to be a relatively efficient way to generate goods and services and to conserve wealth.[30]

Still, capitalism introduces a paradox analogous to the paradox of free speech. On the one hand, all persons are permitted to acquire extensive holdings and to use their possessions however they please. Yet, those who fail to prosper under this system have fundamental human interests in subsistence and fulfillment, too. Thus, on the other hand, empathy with people who are disadvantaged by capitalism argues for a right to an economic share adequate to secure these interests—a right that obligates the well-off to aid the poor.[31]

There may be some people who believe that helping strangers is always supererogatory. But for the most part, debate centers on the questions of how much assistance to provide and to what extent the obligation to aid the poor should be discharged through mandatory redistributive taxation as opposed to voluntary philanthropy. At the border where the right to property intersects with and competes with the right to a minimally adequate economic share, the scope of each of these rights is contested. Because the right to property has a moral core, it resists outright expropriation; however, because the open-ended prerogatives this right confers are justified largely by instrumental considerations, it is not immune to moral trimming.[32] In sum, the libertarian right to property that undergirds capitalism is a right that permits conduct that is morally objectionable, but the extent to which the right to a minimally adequate economic share requires that the consequences of recognizing this property right be mitigated is a matter of ongoing dispute and changing public policy.

The right to free speech is similar. People's fundamental interests in their autonomy and integrity provide a moral anchor for this right. People need the liberty to express themselves, and this right guarantees it. Yet, these interests cannot account for the virtually unrestricted permissions this right is widely thought to confer. In interpersonal relations, people generally recognize moral constraints on what they may say and how they may express what they have to say. Autonomy and integrity are not equated with thoughtless spontaneity and tactless candor; these values are assumed to be reconcilable with consideration for other people's feelings and needs. The expansive constitutional interpretation of free speech gains its support from the role this right plays in fostering the spirited debate that democratic institutions thrive on. Arguably, the dangers of regulation and the potential damage to the democratic process outweigh most of the harms that unfettered speech inflicts. As with property, instrumental considerations enlarge the scope of the right.

Another way in which the right to free speech parallels the right to property is that both of these rights are associated with countervailing rights. Members of historically despised and currently subordinated social groups have a right not to be subjected to discriminatory verbal or pictorial abuse, and this right impinges upon the right to free speech. Thus, the borders of the right to free speech are contested, just as the borders of the right to property are contested. But whereas the right to a minimally adequate economic share is respected primarily through compulsory redistribution and secondarily through voluntary assistance, my account would leave respect for the claim right not to be subjected to discriminatory verbal or pictorial abuse largely to the conscience and judgment of individuals.[33] Not only is it more difficult to demarcate harmful speech that could never be necessary to autonomy and integrity than it is to identify levels of wealth that exceed what is needed to survive and find fulfillment, but also the threat to democracy that restricting harmful speech poses is more difficult to gauge than the threat to capitalist markets that taxation poses.

Many moral claim rights are not legally codified or enforced but are nonetheless vital to everyday social relations. People create claim rights by making promises and small loans and by joining improvised cooperative arrangements. Although respecting these rights is very important since many desirable, informal types of relationship would collapse if they were generally ignored, fulfilling these obligations and deciding when they are overridden is left to individual probity and discretion. Likewise, it is up to individuals to define the contours of the obligation to refrain from uttering abusive speech.

The tension between the right to free speech and the right not to be subjected to discriminatory verbal or pictorial abuse prompts people to pause and reflect on what they want to say, on whether there is good reason to say it, and on why they need to say it in this particular forum and in this particular way. Are one's autonomy and integrity really at stake? Is public debate really advanced? And so forth. To forget that members of historically despised and currently subordinated social groups have a right not to be subjected to discriminatory verbal or pictorial abuse is to embrace what might be dubbed the "bratty-kid" view of free speech—"It's a free country; I have a right to say whatever I want!" This juvenile conception of free speech is morally defective, for some things that one might be inclined to say are not necessary to one's autonomy and integrity, and saying them would violate others' rights. Still, self-betraying, albeit self-imposed, censorship is morally defective, too. If one automatically defers to others' complaints about one's utterances, if one silences oneself against one's better judgment, one surrenders one's own right to free speech and abrogates the values of autonomy and integrity. Exercising one's right to free speech is no less important than respecting the right not to be subjected to discriminatory verbal or pictorial abuse, and it is sometimes deeply perplexing which should take precedence.

A virtue of construing the institutional right not to be subjected to discriminatory verbal or pictorial abuse as a power to exact compensation from one's university rather than as a claim right that obliges universities to enforce speech codes is that this arrangement acknowledges these rival considerations. The fact that an utterance may result in someone's being compensated provides an incentive to reflect before one speaks.[34] Yet, since the costs of compensating victims of hate speech do not fall on the speaker alone, and since these costs are distributed so widely that no one will bear a great burden, this disincentive is not strong enough to foreclose controversial speech that someone sincerely judges to be worthwhile.[35] This scheme frees people to err without encouraging them to speak recklessly. The rights of the vulnerable are respected along with the rights of the advantaged.

Notes

I am indebted to Susan Brison, Judith Wagner DeCew, and Frederick Schauer for valuable comments on this project. Also, I presented this chapter at the University of North Carolina at Greensboro, the Graduate School of the City University of New York, the State University of New York at Albany, and a meeting of AMINTAPHIL at Charleston, S.C., and I am grateful to the members of those audiences for their many helpful suggestions.

This chapter is an excerpt from "Rights in Collision: A Non-Punitive, Compensatory Remedy for Abusive Speech," *Law and Philosophy* 14 (1995): 1–41.

1. Diana Tietjens Meyers, "Rights in Collision: A Non-Punitive, Compensatory Remedy for Abusive Speech," *Law and Philosophy* 14 (1995): 2–13.
2. Judith Jarvis Thomson, *The Realm of Rights* (Cambridge: Harvard University Press, 1990), 253.
3. Frederick Schauer, "The Phenomenology of Speech and Harm," *Ethics* 103 (1993): 650–52.
4. I do not mean to suggest that it is always inadvisable to steel oneself against the oppressive speech of others. Faced with massive propaganda glorifying large breasts and

promoting surgical breast enlargement, the best thing a woman can do is ignore it and accept her natural endowment. But this case differs from hate speech. First, because women are being induced to submit to elective surgery and to incur the risks associated with breast implants, failing to withstand these recommendations itself endangers women's health. Second, despite this propaganda, a wide range of female body types are in fact attractive, and ideals of beauty change periodically. Thus, women who undergo this surgery may not achieve the glamour they had hoped for. Since indifference to this oppressive speech poses no threat to women and is in many respects advantageous to them, Thomson's advice to steel oneself against belief-mediated distress is well taken in this case.

5. Patricia Williams, *The Alchemy of Race and Rights* (Cambridge: Harvard University Press, 1991), 111.

6. For discussion of the nature of and the seriousness of this harm, see Richard Delgado, "Words That Wound: A Tort Action for Racial Insults, Epithets, and Name Calling"; Charles R. Lawrence III, "If He Hollers Let Him Go: Regulating Hate Speech on Campus"; and Mari Matsuda, "Public Response to Racist Speech: Considering the Victim's Story"—all in *Words That Wound*, ed. Mari J. Matsuda et al. (Boulder: Westview Press, 1993). An intriguing dimension of Mari Matsuda's discussion of hate speech that I do not have space to take up in detail is her claim that censorship of the most egregious forms of racist speech is justified because the wrongness of the doctrine of racial superiority is universally accepted (37). Obviously, her position cannot be that each and every person rejects the doctrine of racial superiority, since this is patently, though sadly, false. Rather, she speaks of the public positions that governments have enunciated on behalf of their nations, that is, of the moral identities and values of societies. Interestingly, John Rawls's current account of the grounding of his principles of justice bears a striking resemblance to Matsuda's line of thought. For Rawls, the rights guaranteed by justice as fairness constitute the "kernel of an overlapping consensus" that articulates the "basic intuitive ideas found in the public culture of a constitutional democracy" ("Justice as Fairness: Political Not Metaphysical," *Philosophy and Public Affairs* 14 [1985]: 246; *Political Liberalism* [New York: Columbia University Press, 1993], 13–15, 175). Though I would argue that Rawls's interpretation of this public culture is much too legalistic and tradition-bound, I think that the idea of invoking the collective moral identity of one's society for purposes of defending novel moral claims is a promising strategy (Diana Tietjens Meyers, *Subjection and Subjectivity: Psychoanalytic Feminism and Moral Philosophy* [New York: Routledge, 1994], 157–62). On this view, inflicting certain harms and withholding certain benefits are serious injustices, for mistreating individuals in this way betrays the moral identity of a society.

7. Delgado, "Words That Wound"; Lawrence, "If He Hollers Let Him Go"; and Matsuda, "Public Response to Racist Speech."

8. Ronald Dworkin, "The Coming Battle over Free Speech." *New York Review of Books* 39 (1992): 58, 62.

9. Lawrence, "If He Hollers Let Him Go," 68–69, 74.

10. For evidence that it has already led to repressive measures, see Henry Louis Gates, Jr., "Let Them Talk," *New Republic*, September 20 and 27, 1993, 37–49, 44.

11. Indeed, there may be growing resistance to campus speech codes. According to Ann Cudd, the state of California has passed legislation affirming that people on college and university campuses have the same speech rights as people in any public place ("When Sexual Harassment Is Protected Speech," paper presented at the Conference on Feminist Ethics and Social Policy, University of Pittsburgh, November 1993).

12. Gates, "Let Them Talk," 45.

13. Williams, *The Alchemy of Race and Rights*, 112; Lawrence, "If He Hollers Let Him Go," 55.

14. It could be argued that prohibiting the most blatant forms of hate speech is worthwhile because doing so may sensitize people to the evils of hate speech in general and thus help to eradicate more subtle, nonprohibitable forms of hate speech. Perhaps, constitutionally defensible speech codes would have this desirable spillover effect, but my experience suggests that they might provoke a backlash that would renew some people's determination to exercise their remaining speech rights in harmful but permissible ways. It is hard to anticipate whether the overall consequences of narrowly drawn speech codes will be felicific.

15. Lawrence, "If He Hollers Let Him Go," 82–87.

16. For an account of broad empathy, see Meyers, *Subjection and Subjectivity*, 34–38; for the role of broad empathy in justifying the right not to be subjected to discriminatory verbal or pictorial abuse, see Meyers, "Rights in Collision," 5–14.

17. David Lyons, "The Correlativity of Rights and Duties," *Nous* 4 (1970): 50–51; Frederick Schauer, *Free Speech: A Philosophical Enquiry* (Cambridge: Cambridge University Press, 1982), 116; Rex Martin, *A System of Rights* (Oxford: Clarendon Press, 1993), 30.

18. This right should not be assimilated to the hostile-environment theory of discriminatory harassment. Charging an employer or educational institution with maintaining a hostile environment requires demonstrating that a pattern or practice of harassment exists. In contrast, the power I am proposing could be activated by a single incident of discriminatory verbal or pictorial abuse. Often the experience of being a target of hate speech on campus compounds the effects of similar experiences in childhood and off campus, and is compounded by widespread social tolerance of racism, sexism, homophobia, and ethnocentrism. No pattern of abuse need exist on campus for a hate speech incident to be harmful.

Also, one of the reasons for my proposal is that legal remedies are slow in coming and expensive to pursue. Thus, many victims who have a sexual harassment case under the hostile-environment theory mandated by the Civil Rights Act do not sue and never obtain any form of relief.

19. Frederick Schauer, "Uncoupling Free Speech," *Columbia Law Review* 92 (1992): 1321–57; Lawrence, "If He Hollers Let Him Go," 80.

20. Lawrence, "If He Hollers Let Him Go," 68. For an account of culturally normative prejudice, see Meyers, *Subjection and Subjectivity*, 51–56.

21. I want to call attention to the limits of my analogy. The analogy is confined to the state of our knowledge of speech-inflicted and pollutant-caused harms. It does not extend to advocating that speech, like pollution, be regulated. In fact, my proposal with respect to discriminatory verbal and pictorial abuse specifically rejects punitive speech codes (see "Contestable Claims and Respect for Rights" section, below).

22. Lawrence, "If He Hollers Let Him Go," 85–86.

23. Some faculty unions, for example, the PSC/CUNY, have protested university procedures for addressing sexual harassment complaints on the grounds that these procedures violate due process. Since a finding that someone has committed sexual harassment is grounds for punitive sanctions, it is crucial that universities enforce their sexual harassment regulations in a manner that respects due process. Still, it is clear that these procedural restrictions interfere with the educational function of sexual harassment proceedings since they provide a strong incentive for the accused individual to refuse to cooperate and to deny the charges regardless of the truth. I do not advocate stripping penalties from sexual harassment codes. Nevertheless, I want to point out that the absence of penalties in my interpretation of the right not to be subjected to discriminatory verbal or pictorial abuse eliminates the threat to the accused individual, defuses the conflict between this individual and the complainant, and thus maximizes the chances of fruitful dialogue leading to a mutually satisfactory resolution.

24. This line of thought is important since these moral rights are in a sense more fundamental than the institutional variants I discussed in the "Unorthodox Proposal" section. The moral backing for the power and liability I propose stems from the thought that people are entitled not to be subjected to discriminatory verbal or pictorial abuse. Thus, my compensatory, institutional interpretation represents a nonideal compromise designed to skirt the dangers of authorizing institutions to monitor speech and punish some utterances.

25. Rawls, *Political Liberalism*, 5–6; also see John Rawls, *A Theory of Justice* (Cambridge: Harvard University Press, 1971), 250.

26. Martin, *A System of Rights*, 110–15.

27. Thomson, *The Realm of Rights*, 120–22.

28. George Sher, "Rights Violations and Injustices: Can We Always Avoid Trade-offs?" *Ethics* 94 (1984): 212–24. For a helpful discussion of different approaches to weighting rights, see Judith Wagner DeCew, "Moral Rights: Conflicts and Valid Claims," *Philosophical Studies* 54 (1988): 63–86.

29. Robert Nozick, *Anarchy, State, and Utopia* (New York: Basic Books, 1974).

30. Diana Tietjens Meyers, *Inalienable Rights: A Defense* (New York: Columbia University Press, 1985), 68–71.

31. For discussion of the role of empathy in defending redistributive taxation, see Diana Tietjens Meyers, "Moral Reflection: Beyond Impartial Reason," *Hypatia* 8, no. 3 (1993): 27–31.

32. Diana Tietjens Meyers, "A Sketch of a Rights Taxonomy," in *Economic Justice: Private Rights and Public Responsibilities*, ed. Kenneth Kipnis and Diana T. Meyers (Totowa, N.J.: Rowman & Allanheld, 1985), 92–93.

33. An important exception is speech that creates a "hostile environment" in the workplace and thus constitutes sexual harassment under the U.S. Supreme Court's interpretation of Title VII of the Civil Rights Act of 1964 (see *Harris v. Forklift Systems, Inc.* [1993]). For interesting discussion of the possibility of adapting hostile-environment theory to the issue of hate speech in academic settings, see Timothy Shiell, "Hate Speech Codes and Hostile Environment Law," *APA Newsletter on Philosophy and Law* 92 (1993): 64–66.

34. For discussion of the abuse of rights, see Frederick Schauer, "Can Rights Be Abused?" *Philosophical Quarterly* 31 (1981): 225–30, and Schauer, *Free Speech*, 145–48.

35. It might be objected that I am overlooking the potential for social ostracism that my scheme creates. Students who resent contributing anything to compensating hate speech victims might put pressure on other students to desist from uttering abusive speech by shunning them socially. Although I grant that some students might try to strengthen the disincentive in this way, I think this would be good insofar as speakers are not deeply committed to the ideas and attitudes they express, and I do not think that such tactics will silence speakers who believe that they have something important to say. I doubt that students will be socially ostracized when the legitimacy of their utterances is genuinely debatable. Moreover, it is clear that student populations are diverse enough to ensure that virtually any strand of student opinion will find an enclave of friendly support.

Chapter 14

All Words Are Not Created Equal

Joan McGregor

How should liberal democracies handle racial hate speech? Speech that conveys messages of hate on the basis of individuals' racial group membership takes us directly to a tension that exists in a liberal democratic society between protecting the liberty of the individual to speak what he or she chooses and the equally important value of prohibiting harm to others. Many, possibly most, liberal theorists have tended to suppose that hate speech, though offensive, does not constitute a serious harm. Consequently, liberals have not seen the problem. Moreover, because the value of free speech is thought to be so great that even if hate speech does cause some harm to others, that harm is not great enough to override the value of free expression of opinion. Is it true that hate speech, particularly when directed against members of historically discriminated groups, does not cause a serious harm, a harm that warrants the coercive arm of the law? Critical race theorists argue that indeed the harm inflicted on members of historically discriminated groups by hate speech is serious.[1] We will look at Diana Meyers's arguments in "A Nonpunitive, Compensatory Remedy for Discriminatory Abusive Speech" wherein she agrees with the critical race theorists' conclusion that hate speech causes serious harm but disagrees with their calls for legal prohibition of hate speech.[2] Meyers's position leaves us in a paradoxical situation, attempting to have it both ways: recognizing that there is a serious harm but failing to prohibit it. This chapter will argue that if indeed we establish that hate speech causes serious harm and that the regulation of hate speech will not compromise important aspects of the right to free speech, then we ought to prohibit those harmful forms of hate speech.

Many liberal theorists, prominent among them John Stuart Mill and the contemporary philosopher Joel Feinberg, have held that harm to others is a good and important (possibly the only) reason for criminalizing behavior.[3] Opening discussions of criminalizing conduct is always easiest by identifying harm in the conduct. Thereby, prohibiting racial hate speech is made simpler with a determination that it is seriously harmful to its victims. Many have thought that racial hate speech, though unpleasant and offensive, does not go over the line and constitute a harm to its victim. (Remember the childhood chant "Sticks and stones can break my bones but words will never hurt me.") The question of what are harms and what are mere offenses is a complex and tricky one, and hence, one that is beyond the limited scope of this paper.[4] What is within the purview of this discussion is whether racial hate speech is a harm, and more important, how we would go about answering that question. Traditionally in establishing what is harmful, theorists have determined what rights we have based on an introspection of their own compelling needs. One determines how serious one would find certain kinds of offenses and then generalizes. Liberal analysis assumes all rights-holders are the same qua rights-holders. What, then, is discovered through the introspective process is an exhaustive account of all the needs and interests of all rights-holders.

Given this process and the assumption that all rights-holders are the same, the experiences of members of socially excluded groups when those experiences are not shared by the majority of citizens have been discounted. Critical race theorists and others have argued that if one decides what rights there are on the basis of an introspection of the compelling needs of only the dominant members of society, then one runs the risk of overlooking the compelling needs of others, particularly members of historically discriminated groups, who find themselves with very different histories and present circumstances. Mari Matsuda, recounting her experience in advocating legal restriction of hate speech, says, "I have found my most sympathetic audiences in people who identify with the target groups, whereas I have often encountered incredulity, skepticism, and even hostility from others."[5] Members of socially excluded groups claim that they are seriously harmed when subjected to discriminatory verbal and pictorial abuse. Again, Matsuda claims that there is a split in reaction to the presentation of case studies of hate speech. "The typical reaction of target-group members to an incident of racist propaganda is alarm and immediate calls for redress. The typical reaction of non-members is to consider the incidents isolated pranks, the product of sick but harmless minds" (20). The introspection on the part of the dominant members of society finds that no compelling needs of theirs are seriously affected by hate speech. Yet, minority group members find the opposite. If we are not to deny members of racial minority groups justice (by failing to prohibit harms perpetrated against them), we must recognize for members of those groups a basic right not to be subjected to discriminatory verbal or pictorial abuse. To admit this is, according to Meyers and others, to recognize a nonuniversal right.[6] The liberal analysis of rights cannot account for the nonuniversal quality of these rights. Meyers says: so much the worse for the liberal theory of rights because, she claims, members of different groups have different rights because of the different needs of the members of those groups.

Is rejection of the liberal commitment to universal rights in order? It is not so clear that it is the needs of members of historically discriminated against groups that differ as, rather, that it is what counts as harm or injury to one of our fundamental needs or interests that differs. The universal quality of rights arises in our commonality regarding some basic needs and interests, for example, the need for security and an environment conducive to self-respect. What counts as harm to these needs and interests can differ in different groups of people, given different historical, social, and political contexts. Because the introspection of their basic needs and interests has been done by members of the dominant group, mainly, white men, the standard for what counts as a harm or injury has been what affects white men. Hence, harms or injuries experienced by members of racial minority groups or women have gone largely unnoticed, legally. Empathy can be quite fruitful in showing the harm that is experienced by, for example, an African-American family having someone burn a cross on their lawn. Empathy illustrates which of their needs and interests are affected and to what extent.

Like critical race theory, feminist jurisprudence has helped us recognize a number of arenas in the law where we do not treat people equally by treating everyone the same. Feminist theorists argue, for example, that certain kinds of sexual behavior found in the workplace involved a significant amount of harm to women, harm that had not been legally noticed. We do not specify that only women can be victims of sexual harassment—although we recognize that the vast majority of those who are harmed are women.[7] Rape is overwhelmingly a crime that happens to women, yet men can and do become victims of rape. All persons have an interest in the integrity and control over their own bodies and their sexual lives. It happens that women are more vulnerable to sexual assaults than men are, but it does not follow that only women have those needs and interests. Analogously, the serious harm of racial hate speech is most cogently made out in the cases of attacks against members of historically discriminated groups.

So, for example, as Matsuda and Lawrence argue about cross burning: "There is no Black person in America who has not learned the significance of this instrument [the burning cross] of persecution and intimidation, who has not had emblazoned on his or her mind the image of Black men's scorched bodies hanging from trees. . . . Attackers use this symbol precisely because of the extreme and concrete distress it causes. Their aim is to cause harm."[8] The reasons for the significant reaction to hate speech has to do with this history of discrimination, intimidation, harassment, and violence experienced by members of these groups. The words get their force and significance because of the historical and social context. Whites have not had a similar history of experiencing hatred, terror, exclusion, discrimination, and violence because of their race. Racial hate speech, therefore, does not carry the same significance and harm when directed to white persons (at least in this country).

The law is supposed to protect against serious harm by prohibiting serious harm to others. It is to do this in an impartial and neutral manner—picking out serious harms regardless of who is significantly affected by them. What feminists and critical race theorists have been suggesting is that the law has not done a very good job of this. The law has taken as its standard, men, particularly white men, whose interests and experiences are understood to be representative of all persons. What is harmful to them is harmful. If something is not experienced as a harm by white men, then it is not sufficiently harmful to warrant the coercive arm of the law. Experiences vary quite radically, as the arguments of the critical race theorists show, hence the law can miss serious harms by not considering what harms the compelling interests of members of historically excluded groups. Racial hate speech is a harm to members of historically discriminated groups, but hate speech directed to whites is not so clearly a harm. Or if it is a harm to whites, it is not experienced by them as a very serious harm. We criminalize a particular form of behavior because it involves harm to others; nevertheless, that does not mean that all persons victimized experience the same level of harm by that behavior.

Critical race theorists use empathy to establish the difference in the level of harm experienced by historically excluded groups by racial hate speech. Critical race theorists Charles Lawrence, Mari Matsuda, and Kimberlè Williams Crenshaw use empathy to

> undertake to acquaint their readers not only with the immediate experience of being subjected to hate speech, but also with the social and psychological context

> that makes such attacks so disturbing. In other words, they seek to elicit *broad empathy* with the victims of hate speech. Posing the question "What is it like to be you?" broad empathy engages complex intellectual and affective capacities in order to gain insight into the other's subjectivity as a whole (or at least a good-sized stretch of it taking various aspects of it into account).[9]

Rather than merely trying to imagine what another person is experiencing, by constructing what you would feel like in the situation, they try to build up a fuller and more coherent picture in which to imagine the experience: "Broad empathy requires emotional atunement to the other, it also requires that the empathizer's affective understanding be situated in an understanding of the social conditions of the other's life, as well as an understanding of the other's distinctive constellation of beliefs, desires, abilities, limitations, vulnerabilities, and traits of character."[10] Broad empathy is contextualized: What is it like to experience this, given the history and contemporary events, given the hopes and desires of the person? Because of the contextualized nature of empathy it is necessarily evaluative; it is to understand the experience as valuable or not.

If empathy confirms or supports the claim of a serious harm to members of historically discriminated against groups, then why not prohibit such speech? Theorists, such as Meyers, argue that hate speech can inflict severe harm; it "undermines people's agentic capacities . . . agentic capacities are the very capacities that basic rights secure."[11] She apparently agrees that significant interests are harmed as a result of hate speech. Meyers argues that the main objection to regulating hate speech is that it conflicts with the right to free speech, and that free speech is "of paramount importance both from the standpoint of individual autonomy and also from that of the democratic political process."[12] When discussing speech, many theorists, including Meyers, are enamored by an absolutist approach to the First Amendment. Any distinctions such as cordoning off racial hate speech from the class of protected speech and regulating it is rejected. But why? The Court has never thought the First Amendment's free speech right is absolute.[13] Once it is established that a severe harm results from certain forms of speech, for example, libel, threats, conspiracy, fighting words, then that is grounds for prohibiting those forms of speech. It might be that even though harmful, if the form of speech in question contributed to the political process or somehow was essential for persons to live a meaningful autonomous life, then there would again be a strong argument against the prohibition. Because hate speech is neither essential for democratic processes (in fact it maybe antithetical to them, see, for example, the Canadian Supreme Court's decision that hate propaganda represents a pressing and substantial concern in a free and democratic society)[14] nor essential for a person's living a meaningful life, those are not arguments in this instance.

The Court has also argued that if a form of speech is on the periphery of the justification for the right, then there is little ground for granting wide protection. For example, commercial speech and obscenity can be regulated for that reason. Racial hate speech, arguably, lies far from the center of the justification for the First Amendment protection of speech. Other forms of speech that are in the periphery include commercial speech, libel of private persons, conspiracies, bribes, perjury, obscenity, and threats. As Cass Sunstein has noted: "Under current doctrine and under any sensible system of free expression, speech that lies at the periphery of constitutional concern may be regulated on the basis of a lesser showing of government interest than is required for speech that lies at the core."[15] If we can establish that hate speech lies in the periphery, which I think we can, then we should need only to show an important governmental interest in its regulation and how the legal prohibition is tailored to reach that outcome.

Another form of unprotected speech is "fighting words": "There are certain well-defined and narrowly limited classes of speech, the prevention and punishment of which have never been thought to raise any Constitutional problem. . . . It has been well observed that such utterances are no essential part of any exposition of ideas, and are of such slight social value as a step to truth that any benefit that may be derived from them is clearly outweighed by the social interest in order and morality."[16] Hate speech has often been discussed as a form of fighting words. The Court said of fighting words that "by their very utterance [they] inflict injury or tend to incite an immediate breach of the peace."[17] The experience of a racial insult, according to Charles Lawrence, is "like receiving a slap in the face."[18]

What I think the discussion thus far has shown is that all words are not equal. We make distinctions. A major reason for having wide free expression of ideas is to permit many perspectives on matters of public affairs. We do not want the government regulating ideas, particularly as they pertain to political discourse. Additionally, free expression of opinion allows a range of ideas exploring the boundaries of the arts and sciences. Racial hate speech contributes to none of these domains.

We need to make a distinction to clarify the appropriate target of legal regulation: on the one hand, racial hate speech presented in a noncognitive manner, directed to a specific person or persons to inflict injury (assaultive speech); on the other hand, speech that has racial content, even though the content is based upon hatred, yet leaves the audience room to respond, consider the claims put forth, and counter or avoid it altogether. The racial verbal assault gives the victim neither an opportunity to avoid the harm nor an opportunity to respond cognitively. By making such a distinction, individuals are left free to express their own viewpoints, and the state may not proscribe particular ideas or viewpoints. But what individuals may not do is use words as a substitute for blows or other physical assaults. Proscribing racial hate speech and permitting speech about race will not encumber the "marketplace of ideas" or other goals that the First Amendment is meant to protect.

One area of concern today is the problem of racial hate speech on university campuses. Meyers argues that universities ought to allow extensive speech rights on their campuses, including racial hate speech. Yet, because she thinks that there is serious harm that the speech causes, she argues that the university ought to be compelled to pay compensation to the victims of the hate speech. The solution that Meyers works out, allowing the speech but having the university pay compensation, is paradoxical. We admit that there is serious harm, but the university is not allowed to prohibit it, and the university must pay for the harms caused when someone over whom it has no control causes it. The university is caught in an odd situation; even the "best" schools, the ones that have worked hard to educate students and faculty about racial issues, can get stuck paying compensation. And what of the wrongdoer? The retributivists among us wouldn't be happy; the wrongdoer wouldn't be punished in any form for the serious harm that she or he intentionally caused. What message does this system send to wrongdoers and the victims of these assaults?

Universities must provide settings in which each student has equal access to educational opportunities. Individual opportunities are narrowed or undercut by environments where one is fearful about being attacked and humiliated on grounds of one's race. *Brown v. Board of Education* established that certain institutional arrangements, namely segregated schools, send the message of inferiority, thereby undermining children of color's educational opportunities. Certain institutional arrangements can cause psychic harm and also political harm by undermining a group's chance of being equal participants in our democratic process. Permitting the hurling of threats and insults against members of historically discriminated groups surely has a similar effect. Additionally, in permitting racial hate speech, as Meyers proposes, the university is sending the message that those harms experienced by members of historically discriminated against groups aren't as important as the harms experienced by others, that members of historically discriminated against groups are not as worthy of protection from the state. Couldn't this be just another case of the state's permitting the signs, symbols, and expressions of racial inferiority to go unencumbered? After all, segregationists argued their position with constitutional arguments as well—the right of association.[19]

Another common argument against the regulation of hate speech is the "but it is the price we pay for freedom" argument. The claim is that we should all accept the little "rough and tumble" that comes with free speech in order that we can all share in the fruits of maximal freedom of speech. The argument might be plausible if there were something like a rough equality in the distribution of the costs of extensive freedom of speech. If the empathy argument tells us anything, it is not only that some people are going to be more likely to be on the receiving end of hate speech but also that the effect of such speech is much more serious to members of historically discriminated against groups. The distribution of the cost is totally unequal; members of historically discriminated against groups are paying the price while others reap the benefits. We either cause an injustice to members of historically discriminated against groups by undervaluing the harm inflicted upon them when we claim that they should just put up with the assaults or we commit a gross distributive injustice by forcing them to shoulder a much larger share of the burdens of free speech while we reap the benefits.

If there is found to be significant harm to members of historically discriminated against groups from racial hate speech, it is consistent with a liberal conception of the First Amendment to prohibit those forms of speech. It is not that the state is proscribing or imposing an orthodoxy of belief about race. The state is not prohibiting the beliefs nor many forms of speech about those beliefs. The argument is that there are significant harms from racial hate speech and it is the job of the state to proscribe serious harms—the state, particularly in a liberal democracy, has a "compelling state interest" in preventing significant harms. The courts have focused on the "content-based" tests used by these laws and argued that they are impermissible because they involve the state in legislating a certain viewpoint. It is obviously beyond the scope of this brief discussion to detail the

Supreme Court's arguments on the First Amendment, but I would like to note that the Court does use content tests already to determine obscenity and commercial speech, among other kinds. The argument suggested here only delineates content because certain verbal insults, particularly directed against members of historically despised or discriminated against racial and religious groups, cause serious harm whereas others do not.[20] Burning a cross on an African-American family's lawn just is much more harmful than other nonracial insults.

One issue that I have not discussed, raised by Lawrence[21] and others such as Catherine MacKinnon,[22] is that the constitutional doctrine of free speech has developed without taking equality seriously. Both freedom of speech and equality are central values set out in the Constitution. MacKinnon contends that protecting some free speech rights can undermine the equality of subordinate groups. She argues that rather than viewing hate crimes, campus harassment codes, and antipornography legislation as equality-promoting provisions, they tend to be attacked solely in terms of the damage they do to speech. MacKinnon's arguments are quite compelling, but regrettably I do not have sufficient space to explore them here.

The issue of racial hate speech pulls at a number of threads in the fabric of liberal democracies. Meyers's arguments against regulating hate speech rest upon her uncomfort with drawing lines between permissible and impermissible speech. Although I too worry about the line drawing, I worry more about the harm being done. If a serious harm is occurring in a peripheral zone of the First Amendment right to free speech, then we need some stronger argument about why we should not make strides to protect people from that harm.

Notes

1. See Mari Matsuda, Charles Lawrence III, Richard Delgado, and Kimberlè Williams Crenshaw, eds., *Words That Wound* (Boulder: Westview Press, 1993).

2. Diana Tietjens Meyers, "A Nonpunitive, Compensatory Remedy for Discriminatory Abusive Speech," this volume.

3. See John Stuart Mill, *On Liberty*, ed. Alburey Castell (Arlington Heights, Ill.: AHM, 1947); Joel Feinberg, *Harm to Others* (New York: Oxford University Press, 1984).

4. See Feinberg, *Harm to Others*.

5. Mari Matsuda, "Public Response to Racist Speech," in *Words That Wound*, ed. Mari Matsuda, Charles Lawrence III, Richard Delgado, and Kimberlè Williams Crenshaw (Boulder: Westview Press, 1993), 20.

6. See Meyers, "A Nonpunitive, Compensatory Remedy for Discriminatory Abusive Speech."

7. The reasons for the majority of the victims of sexual harassment being women are social and cultural, and dependent on the difference in power possessed by men and women.

8. Mari J. Matsuda and Charles R. Lawrence III, "Epilogue: Burning Crosses and the R.A.V. Case," in *Words That Wound*, ed. Mari Matsuda, Charles Lawrence III, Richard Delgado, and Kimberlè Williams Crenshaw (Boulder: Westview Press, 1993), 133, 134.

9. See Meyers, "A Nonpunitive, Compensatory Remedy for Discriminatory Abusive Speech."

10. Ibid.

11. Ibid.

12. Ibid.

13. The Court said in *Roth*, "In light of this history [ratification of the Constitution], it is apparent that the unconditional phrasing of the First Amendment was not intended to protect every utterance" (345 U.S. 476 [1957], at 482–83).

14. See Kent Greenawalt's discussion of the differences of the two countries' Supreme Courts' treatment of free expression in *Fighting Words* (Princeton: Princeton University Press, 1995).

15. Cass Sunstein, *The Partial Constitution* (Cambridge: Harvard University Press, 1993), 264.

16. *Chaplinsky v. New Hampshire*, 315 U.S. 568 (1942), at 571–72.

17. Ibid.

18. Charles Lawrence III, "If He Hollers Let Him Go: Regulating Racist Speech on Campus," in *Words That Wound*, ed. Mari Matsuda, Charles Lawrence III, Richard Delgado, and Kimberlè Williams Crenshaw (Boulder: Westview Press, 1993), 68.

19. Why were segregationists' "Whites Only" signs not seen as protected under First Amendment expression?

20. Note, we have specifically recognized certain groups, based on race, ethnicity, or gender, as warranting heightened constitutional protection. The rationale for the special treatment is that some groups are more liable to be unjustifiably discriminated against than others. An analogous argument might be used as the justification for treating hate speech against historically discriminated groups different from whites.

21. Lawrence, "If He Hollers Let Him Go."

22. Catherine MacKinnon, *Only Words* (Cambridge: Harvard University Press, 1993).

Chapter 15

Religious Freedom and Medical Refusal

Richard T. De George

The U.S. Constitution's right to freedom of religion protects individual religious beliefs and freedom of conscience in religious matters, but that right is limited by the right of others. Some religious sects are fanatical and dangerous. Their claimed religious status gives them no license to murder, maim, injure, or threaten others.

Christian Science is in the United States a recognized religion that is neither fanatical nor dangerous to others, but its position on illness and its rejection of generally accepted medical practices and procedures have led to confrontations between Christian Scientists and the medical establishment. Two well-known cases are those of Robyn Twitchell and Colin Newmark.[1] Robyn was a two-year-old who died from an easily operable bowel obstruction because his Christian Science parents turned to a Christian Science practitioner rather than a medical doctor for help. Although the parents were initially convicted of involuntary manslaughter, the Massachusetts Supreme Judicial Court overturned the conviction.[2] Colin was a three-year-old whose Christian Science parents rejected chemotherapy for his non-Hodgkins lymphoma. The Delaware Supreme Court rejected an attempt by the hospital to obtain custody so it could administer chemotherapy.[3]

At issue is both the right of adults to refuse treatment for themselves and the right of adults to refuse treatment for their children. The medical profession has argued for the right—often by being appointed a legal guardian—to intervene, especially in life-threatening situations, and especially with respect to children. In this clash of rights, which should override, and is the case similar whether Christian Science adults or children are involved?

I shall first present a brief defense of refusal of medical treatment for children; and then I shall suggest a social policy consistent with that defense.

We can start from certain assumptions that seem widely held and securely established in our society. One is that informed consent on the part of a competent adult patient is a normal and legitimate requirement before any member of the medical profession proceeds with surgery or other intrusive procedures. There is no legal requirement that ordinary people (as opposed, e.g., to members of the military) go to a doctor, that they follow a doctor's prescription or orders, or that they submit to any treatment to which they do not wish to submit. This follows from respect for the dignity and autonomy of individuals. It also follows from a second assumption, namely, that normal individuals value their own interests and lives, have the most at stake in these, and are in the best position to decide for themselves what to do with their lives, providing they have full information concerning the various alternatives open to them and the consequences of each. If someone chooses to die rather than undergo chemotherapy, that is a choice most people believe they are permitted to make. If in a living will they ask not to be resuscitated, that desire should be respected.

Medical doctors are people with specialized knowledge who can often provide help to the sick and injured and who can promote healing. They are available (most of us hope) when people get sick, and they can check people for early signs of illness. They provide enormous benefits, and they appropriately charge for their services. Their mission is not to cure everyone of every illness. That is a mission they could not possibly fulfill and it is one that no society can impose on its medical practitioners. Because of the great service doctors contribute to a society and because they have specialized knowledge, our society has given them special privileges, including the right to control access to the profession and to set standards for practitioners. But our society has not given them the right to command people to visit them or to coerce patients into following a doctor's orders, taking the medicines the doctor prescribes, or submitting to operations or therapies the doctor deems appropriate. There is no overriding state interest in legislating any of this, and there is the strong argument from respect for persons that militates against it. The doctor's authority is based on knowledge, and we can and should resist the temptation to move from acknowledging the medical knowledge of doctors to giving them the authority to command their patients or to coerce the patient's obedience to the doctor's commands.[4]

It is within this framework that Christian Scientists hold their views. Despite what anyone may think of the wisdom of their views, there is no sound argument to the effect that Christian Scientists (or anyone else) can be forced to visit a doctor when they have physical problems, that they must listen to doctors, follow their prescriptions, take the medicine they prescribe or allow them to operate. Any person may refuse, and the Christian Scientist is in no special position in this regard.

Most doctors realize and acknowledge that they cannot force adults to have physical exams or to get consultations when they have physical pain or problems. Yet, when people do go to a doctor, some physicians feel they have an obligation to do what they can to help, especially those suffering from life-threatening ailments that the physicians believe can be cured. It is not uncommon to hear of doctors ordering their patients to enter the hospital immediately. There have been some attempts to pass legislation giving them such authority, but these have been, rightly I believe, resisted. It is because of such attempts and because of the aggressive approach some doctors take toward their patients with life-threatening ailments that some people—including many Christian Scientists—choose not to visit doctors, even for a diagnosis. The not-unfounded fear is that once one submits to a medical examination, one opens oneself up to pressures to pursue the prescribed treatment.

If the position I have described above is accepted with respect to adults, why is it not with respect to children? The obvious answer is that children are not considered competent to make informed decisions on medical issues. This is clearly the case with infants, and almost as clearly the case with respect to two- and three-year-old children. The question, then, is whether parents should be allowed to decide for their children, just as the parents decide for themselves, or whether that right should be taken from some parents by a court and given instead to doctors or hospitals or other members or representatives of the medical profession. In the overwhelming majority of cases the answer is that the right to decide rests with the parents of the child. The exception is where there is evidence of child abuse or incompetence on the part of the parents.

The same general doctrine applies to Christian Science parents as well as to any other parents. Hence they have the right to make medical decisions for their children, just as other parents do, unless there is evidence of child abuse or of incompetence. Does the fact that they are Christian Scientists provide adequate grounds for charging either incompetence or that they are guilty of child abuse?

Christian Science views may be considered strange and mistaken by many non–Christian Scientists, just as the beliefs of many other widely held religions may seem strange and mistaken by those who do not belong to the religions in question. So the strangeness or nonscientific or even antiscientific beliefs of a religion are no grounds for declaring those who follow that religion mentally or otherwise incompetent and ipso facto unfit to raise their children or to make decisions for them.

So the only plausible remaining grounds is that at least some Christian Science doctrine at least some of the time leads to child abuse. Following Christian Science doctrine when that leads to refusing to seek medical attention for a child with serious symptoms is to act in such a way that if similar action were taken by other parents it would be considered child abuse. Can such action be justified and should it be permitted because of the beliefs of the parents? Do not the rights of the child to life and to care take precedence over the religious beliefs of the parents? Are not the interests of the state in the life of the child more important than the religious beliefs of the parents?

Consider the first question. Some Christian Scientists may be child abusers, just as the members of any other group of believers or nonbelievers may be. But the issue is whether Christian Science doctrine leads to child abuse. Let us assume, which seems entirely plausible, that Christian Science parents love their children no less than other parents do, and that on the whole they are more concerned about and have a greater interest in promoting the welfare of their children than the doctor they visit does. They no more wish their children to die than do other parents. They do not beat, neglect, or maltreat them. So the ordinary forms of child abuse are not part of Christian Science doctrine or practice. The only issue is whether Christian Science parental refusal of medical treatment constitutes child abuse.

We have already seen that competent adults are not legally bound to seek or submit to medical examinations or treatment. Nor is it the case that if a wife or husband of a Christian Science couple does not seek conventional medical treatment for his or her spouse that person is guilty of abuse, nor if the spouse dies, is the wife or husband guilty of murder or involuntary manslaughter. Our attitude, and I believe a proper attitude, is that although that person might have been saved by using conventional medical practices and procedures, people have the right to follow their religious beliefs, even if in extreme circumstances the exercise of that right leads to what many will consider a preventable death. The justification is that the right of each person to practice his or her religion and to follow those beliefs is stronger than the state's interest in preserving that life.

Let us pursue the right to practice one's religion a step further. In the United States the Constitution guarantees the right of adults to practice the religion of their choice, providing that it does not endanger others. Part of the right to practice one's religion is the right to raise one's children in accordance with that religion and to teach the children the beliefs of that religion. It would be a truncated right to religion that did not allow parents to raise their children in their religion. It would similarly be a truncated right to religion that allowed adults to follow their religious beliefs but precluded their children from doing so or precluded the parents from acting for their children in accordance with those beliefs.

If we accept this and if we allow Christian Science parents to choose whether to visit a doctor for their own treatment and whether to submit to an operation, it seems to follow that Christian Science parents ought to be allowed the same right with respect to their children. The proper test with respect to parental decisions for their children should be: If the parents act the same way with respect to the symptoms or illnesses of their child as they do with respect to their own illnesses, and if they would take the same action themselves for themselves if they had the same symptoms their child has, then neither the state nor the medical profession has any right to take action against them or force them to act differently. To argue that either the state or doctors have a greater interest in the welfare of the child than the parents do is as gratuitous as to argue that the state or doctors have a greater interest in the welfare of the ordinary adult than those individuals themselves do.

But, the objection to this principle goes, this allows child abuse and if not outright murder, then at least gross negligence resulting in death or involuntary manslaughter.

The first reply is that such action is by no stretch of the imagination murder. To label it such is to attribute to the parents the wish to kill their child. There is no evidence of that in the vast number of cases, anymore than there is evidence of the desire to commit suicide on the part of Christian Science adults who refuse treatment.

The second reply it that there is a price that freedom, respect for freedom of conscience, and respect for people carry with them, both for the individual and for the state. The price for Christian Scientists may be a higher mortality rate; but that has not to my knowledge been shown to be the case. If it were, that is a cost they bear. They do not impose costs on society by following their beliefs and practices. To argue otherwise is to give the state the authority to legislate a certain view of life and death assumed by modern medicine—an authority that arguably infringes upon every citizen's right to religious freedom.

A second less radical objection is that Christian Science parents, by refusing medical treatment for their sick child, violate the rights of their child. It is one thing to refuse medical treatment for oneself, but children have the right to medical treatment, and unless they refuse to exercise that right themselves, their parents have no right to refuse for them. If the children are too young to refuse to exercise the right, then their parents cannot refuse for them. If the children are old enough to refuse but are not yet adults, and they do refuse, we can assume they have been unduly influenced by their parents and deny that such refusals are truly informed. In either case the parents cannot legitimately refuse to exercise the children's right to medical care.

We have already given one answer to this objection. To hold that adults may be Christian Scientists but that if they are parents they may not raise their children according to Christian Science principles is to deny Christian Scientists the full right to the practice of their religion that the state allows other religions. If there is no overriding harm to the state from Christian Science adults refusing treatment for themselves—and there seems to be none—then there is by like reason no overriding harm to the state for Christian Science children to refuse treatment or for parents to refuse for them on the same principled grounds on which they would refuse treatment for themselves.

The second answer to this objection is that any assumption that the rights of the child are violated by the religiously predicated actions of the parents is simply an assumption that the Christian Science view of the relation of faith and healing is so obviously mistaken as to grant it no weight. The constitutional guarantee of religious freedom aims to prevent the state from making and acting on such assumptions.

To equate Christian Science beliefs with child abuse is gratuitous. Refusing medical treatment for one's children when one would refuse like treatment for like symptoms for oneself is not child abuse. That some people who abuse their children may try to escape punishment by claiming to be Christian Scientists may be true, but this simply shows that there can be abuses of any principle. It is poor policy to legislate on the basis of exceptions rather on the basis of the rule. Child abuse can and should be distinguished from principled refusal of medical treatment.

The clash is not between the right to religious freedom on the one hand and the child's right to care on the other. Both the parents and the medical practitioners wish the good of the child. The question is which of the two has the right to decide what care the child is to receive. The supposed right to medical treatment is derived from the right to care on the assumption that medical treatment is the proper and only treatment that amounts to care. This view is at least implicit in Kenneth Kipnis's article in this volume in which he discusses the limits to parental authority. It is precisely that claim that the Christian Scientists challenge.

The case of Robyn Twitchell shows that sometimes refusing treatment results in death. After his death his parents left the Christian Science Church. It is not clear whether they then believed they had earlier been guilty of child abuse or neglect. From the account we have, they were interested in the welfare of their son, and they took what they believed to be the proper means to restore him to health. That the consequences destroyed their faith in Christian Science beliefs does not show they were guilty of child abuse or neglect. Suppose that instead of Robyn his father had suffered the same bowel obstruction. Suppose that the family took exactly the same action that it took with respect to Robyn. Suppose the comparable result occurred—namely, the father died. His wife may well have left the Christian Science Church after his death just as she did after Robyn's death, and for the same kind of reason. But in neither case would she have been negligent or abusive. If after the fact she holds that Christian Science beliefs are false, and then claims that Christian Scientists should not be allowed to act on *their* beliefs because *she* holds them to be false, she flies in the face of the constitutional right of everyone to their religious beliefs, regardless of whether others think those beliefs are false. The death of her son was sufficient ground to change her beliefs; such a death is not sufficient grounds for the United States to change its Constitution.

If we take this approach to the issue, then a solution to the conflict between Christian Scientists and the medical establishment does not call for accommodating both the Christian Scientists and the medical profession by some sort of compromise.[5] Although Christian Science beliefs allow for purely mechanical procedures, such as surgery necessary to clear a blocked intestine, many Christian Scientists avoid seeking a medical evaluation for fear of being forced into treatment. If the aim of the medical profession and of interested members of society is to encourage Christian Scientists to seek medical evaluations so that they may take advantage of "mechanical" medical procedures to save their own lives and those of their children, then society should guarantee them the right to refuse treatment for themselves and for their children, even if the treatment is considered purely mechanical by the medical profession.

The right to refuse treatment and the right to follow one's religious beliefs take precedence over the interest of the state or the desires of medical practitioners. In the confrontation of Christian Science and the medical establishment we have a confrontation between the right of one group, guaranteed by the Constitution, to practice its religion and live by its religious beliefs, and the interest of some medical practitioners or subgroup thereof, such as the American Academy of Pediatrics (AAP). The two parties do not have comparable status. Freedom of religion is a constitutionally guaranteed right and religious communities have an acknowledged standing. The AAP is not a religion and has no constitutionally protected standing. It is a group of physicians that may be given special privileges by the state under certain justifiable conditions. It has interests that it seeks to promote. It has no special rights, even though it seeks to extend its power by claiming to protect the rights of children. Neither the AAP nor any other physician or medical group should be given paternalistic powers that violate the constitutional or human rights of people.

What many non–Christian Scientists, as well as many Christian Scientists, correctly want is for Christian Scientists who wish to do so to be able to avail themselves of a medical diagnosis for their children without fear that they will be forced to follow a doctor's prescription or to submit to surgery or other procedures they do not want. I argued earlier that this is a right that all adults should have, and that, unless there is reason to think that parents do not have the welfare of children at heart, it is a right that parents retain with respect to their children. All that is required to achieve this desired result is that this right be recognized in law, and that any laws to the contrary by repealed. If what prevents Christian Scientists from seeking medical diagnoses for their children is fear that they will be forced to submit to whatever the diagnosing doctor prescribes, then the grounds for that fear can and should be eliminated by law. No compromise is needed. What is needed is that the rights of Christian Scientists be respected, that the authority of the medical profession—and in this case of the American Academy of Pediatrics—be appropriately checked, and that legislatures be convinced of the soundness of the arguments in favor of the proposed legislation.

The decisions, both in the Twitchell case, in which the parents' conviction for involuntary manslaughter was overturned, and in the Colin Newmark Supreme Court decision, which upheld the right of the Newmarks to refuse chemotherapy for their child, were favorable to the parents. The salient aspect of these cases is that they are cases at all. The fact that they are cases is an indication that many people, perhaps many doctors, some legislatures, and some courts do not understand what freedom of religion means if we take it seriously.

There remains one further and crucial concern. The right to medical refusal is derived from the right to informed consent. And here the Twitchell and the Newmark cases differ, even though the children died in both cases. In the Newmark case the parents refused chemotherapy for their child. The success rate for chemotherapy in similar cases is about 40 percent, and it involves a good deal of pain and suffering. Armed with that information, any adult might refuse treatment. There seems to have been informed consent on the part of all affected. But in the Twitchell case whether the parents made an informed decision is not clear. The parents turned to a Christian Science nurse. Did the nurse inform the parents that the condition was a blockage and that it could be surgically (and hence mechanically) removed? Did she and should she have known?

Christian Science parents, I assume, can be expected to desire the health and recovery of their children. Under normal circumstances there is no conflict of interest in their making decisions for their children. But if they turn to Christian Science nurses or practitioners, then the nurses or practitioners may well have a conflict of interest. Namely, it is in their financial interest that the parents engage their services rather than the services of medical doctors. The same may be said of medical practitioners. Hence, public policy here should be so structured that it ensures to the extent possible that all health care providers, including Christian Science nurses and other practitioners, provide full information to their patients or to the parents of children brought to them for help.

The court correctly decided that the Twitchell parents were not guilty of child abuse or neglect. They did what they thought appropriate and what they would have done if either of them suffered from similar symptoms. But freedom of religious choice does not prevent parents from holding those to whom they turn for alternate treatment accountable for being competent and for providing full information so the parents can make an informed choice of treatment. If there was neglect or child abuse in the Twitchell case, it is arguably attributable not to the parents but to those faith healers on whom they relied.

The public policy to which this leads us is that legislation should capture what most courts have practiced. Informed refusal on principled religious grounds is permitted. When such refusal is made by a parent for a child it does not constitute child abuse or incompetence any more than a similar decision made with respect to himself or herself constitutes legal incompetence. Nonetheless, legislation can and should hold those who practice alternative approaches to medicine accountable and liable to both civil and criminal suits, especially in cases in which the person dies, if incompetence or malpractice can be shown.

There is a difference between recognizing an individual's right to practice his or her religion and the state's certification or recognition of alternative medical practitioners. Freedom of religion protects the right of one to pray for oneself or another. It does not protect payment of any sort. Nor does it automatically sanction payment by Medicare or health insurers. The argument for such payment cannot be religious. It must be made on other grounds, namely, on some evidence that the alternative treatment by prayer satisfies whatever criteria Medicare or the insurance companies specify. Nor does the claim of Christian Science practitioners to be practicing alternative health care treatment carry immunity from malpractice or negligence or other suits. The choice of an individual to refuse medical treatment does not render immune those who provide alternative treatment, no matter what they do or do not do.

The public policy approach I am suggesting respects an individual's right to refuse treatment, and it respects parental rights to refuse treatment for their children on principled religious grounds, when the decision they make is the same as the one they would make for themselves if experiencing similar symptoms. But this assumes that the adults are making an informed choice. Public policy should be so arranged that Christian Scientists feel they can consult a medical doctor to hear a medical diagnosis for themselves or their children without fear that the doctor or hospital will take from them their right to decide whether to proceed with treatment for themselves or for their children. Public policy should hold both the medical practitioner and the Christian Science practitioner accountable for accurately presenting the facts of the case and the alternatives to the parents. If a surgical procedure that can be considered "mechanical," and so allowable according to Christian Science doctrine, is not recommended by a Christian Science practitioner, if the patient dies, that practitioner should be held accountable for satisfactorily explaining why he or she did not recommend the procedure.

Some of the public concern with Christian Science and parental medical refusal for children is not that Christian Science parents are child abusers but that they are sometimes led to make bad decisions based on misinformation. Legislatures should do what they can to keep Christian Science parents from fearing to seek medical diagnosis on the one hand and from receiving less than full disclosure from Christian Science practitioners on the other hand. Doing so should adequately address public concern.

Notes

1. See Larry May, "Challenging Medical Authority: The Refusal of Treatment by Christian Scientists," *Hastings Center Report*, January-February 1995, 15–21; *New England Journal of Medicine* 309, no. 26 (December 29, 1983), "Sounding Boards" section, 1639–44, which contains an article attacking and an article defending Christian Science practice; Shelli Dawn Robinson, "*Commonwealth v. Twitchell*: Who Owns the Child?" *Journal of Contemporary Health Law and Policy* 7 (1991): 413–31; Paul A. Monopoli, "Allocating the Costs of Parental Free Exercise: Striking a New Balance Between Sincere Religious Belief and a Child's Right to Medical Treatment," *Pepperdine Law Review* 18 (1991): 319–52; and *Commonwealth v. Twitchell*, No. 89-210 (Mass. Super. Ct., May 23, 1989).

2. *Commonwealth v. Twitchell*, S–6115 Supreme Judicial Court of Massachusetts, 617 N.E. 2d 609 (decided August 11, 1993).

3. *Newmark v. Williams/DCPS*, 588 A. 2d 1108 (Del. 1991).

4. See Richard T. De George, *The Nature and Limits of Authority* (Lawrence: University Press of Kansas, 1985), chap. 3.

5. Larry May, for one, suggests one kind of compromise in "Challenging Medical Authority."

Chapter 16

Parental Refusals of Medical Treatment on Religious Grounds: Pediatric Ethics and the Children of Christian Scientists

Kenneth Kipnis

Much recent work in ethical theory explores the tensions between liberalism and what has come to be called communitarianism. It is useful to see the interplay between these two views as, in part, a dispute about what communities should be allowed to do both to their own members and to members of other communities. The debate asks whether we, as a society constituted by multiple communities, want to (1) adopt a thoroughgoing hands-off attitude, that is, let each group do what it wants; (2) take up supportive postures regarding multicultural efflorescences; or (3), as liberals, strive collectively toward a consensus regarding basic rights that, when secured, will clearly limit what some in those communities are permitted to do, notwithstanding the impact of those rules upon the communities.[1]

Recollect the professional deprogrammers who, acting on behalf of family members from a "mainstream" community, were participants in the "kidnapping" of adult sons or daughters who had entered "cults." Some might say that these abductions were justified, given the illicit psychological manipulations used to ensnare potential devotees. If so, then there should be public, enforceable standards prohibiting all communities from engaging in certain types of recruitment practices.[2] But others might say that these kidnappings should be treated as serious criminal offenses even when the perpetrators are loving family members and the crimes are motivated by a communitarian desire to bring dear ones back into the fold. If so, there should be public, enforceable standards limiting what communities can do to retain or retrieve their members.[3] And while we are pondering these questions, of which community is the deprogrammer's "client" a member? It seems the liberal project is forced upon us.

Like the deprogrammer's client, children are at the margins of their communities. Although they are in the custody of their parents, and although their parents may belong to communities with unusual health-related practices—Christian Scientists, Jehovah's Witnesses, Vegans, Samoans, African Muslims, Orthodox Jews, and Pentecostalists are a few—it has been an ongoing question for liberals how best to reconcile everyday concerns about child abuse and neglect with a commitment to religious and cultural tolerance.[4] The reconciliation of these competing social values is not a problem for everyone: communities can thrive without both of these commitments.

Parental refusals of indicated medical care on religious grounds are a striking example of this conflict. The issues can arise dramatically in law and pediatric ethics when the patient is the child of Christian Scientist parents. Two well-known cases will illustrate how this can occur.

In *Commonwealth v. Twitchell*,[5] Christian Science parents were convicted of manslaughter following the death of their two-year-old son, Robyn, from a surgically correctable bowel obstruction. The parents had relied on a Christian Scientist practitioner at home; medical professionals were not involved until after the child's death. The Massachusetts Supreme Court overturned the Twitchell's conviction in 1993 but warned that parents relying on spiritual healing could be convicted if they wantonly or recklessly violated their duty to seek medical attention for their child.

In *Newmark v. Williams*,[6] the Christian Science parents of three-year-old Colin Newmark refused chemotherapy promising a 40 percent chance of recovery from cancer. Fearing criminal liability, Colin's parents had brought the child to a hospital for examination. But after learning about the illness and the significant risks and burdens associated with the recommended treatment, the Newmarks decided instead to place the child in the care of a Christian Science practitioner. The Division of Child Protective Services was notified and petitioned the family court for temporary custody for the purpose of authorizing chemotherapy. Though the court found Colin to be a neglected child and awarded custody to the state, the case was appealed. The Delaware Supreme Court held that parents could not be charged with child neglect under Delaware law where the treatment was highly invasive and the prospect of success unlikely.

Three Perspectives

There are several levels at which religiously based refusals of treatment create problems. Because the intellectual strategies for analysis differ depending on the level, the context of discussion must be clear if ambiguity and confusion are to be avoided.

Criminal Law

At the first level, we can talk about the substantive criminal law, specifically, the elements and defenses regarding the offenses of involuntary manslaughter (or negligence manslaughter) and child neglect. The critical issue here is whether the legal definitions of manslaughter and child neglect should treat as an excusing condition membership in one or another of these communities. Ordinarily, if a parent fails to provide appropriate medical care for a child who is obviously and seriously ill, and the child dies, there can be a charge of involuntary manslaughter. Parents do go to jail for this. In determining whether the failure of the parents to obtain medical care caused the death of the child, it is essential to know whether there was an available and demonstrably effective medical treatment that could have prevented the death. The teachings of the Church of Christ, Scientist encourage members to avoid medical interventions for disease and, instead, to summon Christian Scientist practitioners and pray.[7] Christian Scientists have appealed to freedom of religion in defending themselves against charges of involuntary or negligence manslaughter where they have, for religious reasons, rejected medical care as a response to their children's illnesses.[8]

As interesting as these issues are, the criminal law is not the focus of this chapter. For now, it is allowed that the threat of imprisonment is too blunt an instrument to apply in these cases and that out of a respect for religious differences, we should hesitate before officially labeling conscientious Christian Science practices as criminal. Accordingly, the conviction of the Twitchells was an error.[9]

Family Law

A second level of analysis involves family law, specifically, the grounds for the appointment of a guardian. Having set aside the criminal process, one can still ask whether and on what basis the courts should suspend or terminate some or all parental rights where parents are unwilling or unable to provide appropriately for children. If, in our social order, we are to have any common standards specifying what parents owe to children, and it becomes clear that some parents are neither meeting those obligations nor delegating the appropriate authority to others who will, then it can fall to a court, acting as *parens patriae*, to relieve parents of responsibility and delegate it to another. There is not necessarily blame in these cases. Where a mentally retarded couple lacking sufficient understanding or capacity to make or communicate decisions is unable to manage responsibilities associated with their child, a court may appoint a guardian for the child or even for all three. The parents retain custody but their abilities are appropriately supplemented.[10] Guardians are sometimes appointed in divorces when rancorous conflict renders parents incapable of reaching agreement on simple matters. Legally, the focus should be here: the standards that courts should use in deciding whether to suspend elements of the parents' authority and appoint a substitute medical decision maker, a guardian, for the child of Christian Scientists. We will return to this issue.

Clinical Ethics

A third level of analysis, and the central focus of discussion here, involves clinical ethics, specifically, the circumstances under which a physician should act to override a parental decision for nontreatment. Apart from the legal questions, there is a separate question about what physicians and hospitals should do when confronted with refusals of medically indicated treatment by the children themselves or by their parents or guardians. Under what circumstances should physicians operating within a liberal society (a society committed to respecting substantial differences in orientation and values) either disregard such refusals directly or seek to have them overturned in court? Although the criteria the courts use in deciding to appoint guardians will be relevant to a medical decision to seek a court order, the medical profession, arguably, has an ethical duty to try to get the courts or the legislature to adopt criteria that are consistent with medical ethics.

Notwithstanding the central involvement of doctors, it is not the case that physicians have the legal authority to impose treatment against the will of the minor's parents. Except under rare, emergent circumstances (and even there, only when the law is unclear), this is not so. At the hospitals at which I work, the standard procedure is to ask the administration to direct the hospital attorney to petition the family court for a hearing to appoint a guardian. In Honolulu, a family court judge carries a beeper for this purpose at all times. Emergency hearings can be convened in hours. If the motion is granted, the parents' authority over the child will be partially suspended and delegated to another individual, the guardian, who will then have the authority to give or withhold consent to medical treatment in the interest of the child. Conceived as a problem in medical ethics, the bottom-line issue is when to seek in this way to suspend or terminate a parent's legal authority to give or withhold consent to a minor's treatment. Such a decision faced the health care professionals who were caring for Colin Newmark.

It is true that many physicians leap galvanically from the premise "Here is a parent who is refusing medical treatment for a child on religious grounds" to the conclusion "Go for a court order" (if there is time) or "Do the procedure anyway" (if there is not). But medical ethics is more concerned about what the standards should be than it is with how physicians behave. It is important to distinguish between what medical ethics has to say about this issue and what many physicians are prone to say.

The Ethics of Honoring Parental Refusals of Treatment

There is now a rather useful literature on the topic of medical decision making for minors.[11] At least three factors should carry weight in honoring a refusal of medical treatment on behalf of a minor.

Decisional Capacity of the Minor

The emerging trend, both in law and medical ethics, is to distinguish between mature (i.e., decisionally capacitated) minors and other minors. Minors often have the abilities to understand their diagnosis, the treatment options, and the risks and benefits attaching to each. Their personal values may be stable and well reflected upon, and not the manifestations of either a developmental phase or a transient or treatable psychiatric condition. There may be grounded confidence that the child will still own the decision later on in life. It is now common for medical ethicists to maintain that a refusal to assent to treatment from such a "mature minor" should be given great weight in medical decision making,[12] and several court cases support the right of Jehovah's Witness minors to refuse blood.[13]

For this reason, a Christian Scientist minor, perhaps even as young as seven,[14] could have a refusal of treatment honored, especially if that refusal made sense against a background of what appeared to be reasonably stable personal values. The case would be stronger if either or both of the next two conditions obtained.

Burden and Risk of the Treatment

Though medical treatments can be risky and burdensome, many doctors tend to focus on the best outcomes and not on the human costs of getting there. Where treatments carry high prices in this way, that factor can call into question whether the treatment is on balance a clear benefit. The greater the burden and risk, the less clear it is that the physician is doing a favor for the child in treating and that the treatment is "medically indicated." The fact that a parent is withholding consent on religious grounds should carry no weight if the treatment being rejected is "elective" on the basis that it is burdensome or risky to the point that it could be plausibly refused on those grounds alone. It is worth noting that there are a number of effective and standard life-prolonging treatments—chemotherapy for cancer, dialysis for end-stage renal disease, and immunosuppressive therapies following transplants—that adults commonly reject as too burdensome or risky to endure.

Effectiveness of the Treatment

There is also a need to consider whether the treatment is likely to be effective in securing some significant and subjectively valuable benefit for the child. The strongest case for overriding parental authority involves treatments that are demonstrably effective—not experimental or investigational—in securing or recovering some very significant benefit that is subjectively valuable to the child (e.g., saving the child's life with good function).[15] But where a treatment has less than a 50 percent chance of realizing such a benefit, and where it is burdensome and/or risky, then these two conditions can entail that it is more likely that the child will be harmed by the treatment instead of being helped by it. If, let us say, a certain drug has a side effect harmful to everyone who takes it but provides significant compensating benefits to 30 percent, then a patient has a 70 percent chance of ending up harmed by the treatment without any compensating benefit. It would be difficult to argue that parents should have a legal obligation to authorize treatments that were reasonably expected to harm the child without a compensating benefit. It should not be overlooked that the psychosocial stresses of official intervention in the family and litigation, and the imposition of treatment against the expressed wishes of the parents may themselves cause significant damage to the child and his or her social support system, and all of these at a time when, because of the illness, the integrity of the family is likely to be critically important to the child.[16]

But where the intervention is virtually without risk or burden, then even a small chance of a significant subjectively valuable benefit might conceivably carry great weight. A treatment's effectiveness, burdens, and risks are relevant in applying the Hippocratic principles that whatever the physician does shall be for the benefit of the patient and that, above all, the physician is to do no harm.

In *Newmark*, the second and third conditions would have justified honoring the parental refusal of treatment notwithstanding the religious basis for the parents' decision. Medical ethics, as I understand it, would have supported honoring that parental decision.[17] Ethically, the Division of Child Protective Services should not have been brought in.

The Limits to Parental Authority

When, then, may a physician seek to override a parental refusal of treatment on religious grounds? Certain preconditions would have to be met for the issue to arise as a problem in clinical ethics. First, the child must somehow be delivered into the care of a physician. Many Christian Science children who are ill—like Robyn Twitchell—are never brought to the attention of physicians.[18] Second, there must be a recommendation of medical intervention. Education is essential at this stage. More than a duty of disclosure, there should be evidence that the decision maker(s) understand the nature of each course of action and the risks and benefits that attach to each. Third, there has to be a refusal of the recommended treatment. And fourth, it must be clear that the refusal of treatment is not accompanied by any of the conditions, listed above, that would support honoring such a refusal. Consider the following fictionalized case.

> Suzie Ray, age four, becomes ill at a preschool outing. A physician-parent-chaperone notices symptoms consistent with meningitis, a devastating and deadly disease if not treated promptly. The parents cannot be located and, at the doctor's urging, Suzie is brought to an emergency room. Meningitis is diagnosed by spinal tap just as the parents arrive. Antibiotics are the indicated medical treatment for this infection. The success rate is over 95 percent when the infection is treated promptly. Without treatment, the prognosis is extremely poor. If the child survives without antibiotic

> treatment (which is unlikely), severe central nervous system deficits can be expected: coma, seizures, paralysis, blindness, deafness, and so on. The parents refuse to allow the physicians to treat Suzie. They ask the doctor to return her at once and they telephone a Christian Science practitioner to join them immediately.

This case meets the standard for raising the medical ethics question. Meningitis is readily diagnosed and easily and effectively treated but is otherwise devastating. The medical risks of treatment are negligible in comparison to the risks of the untreated illness. At age four, Suzie is not yet decisionally capacitated. The conflict between Christian Science parents and the community standards for child rearing could hardly be more patent. The issue here is not whether Suzie's parents are good people, nor whether their faith is worthy of respect. Based on the standards set out above, the sole factual question is whether there is evidence that Suzie is likely to survive and recover if she is treated and unlikely to survive and recover if she is not, even if she receives proper Christian Science ministrations.[19]

What medicine can offer to the courts that Christian Science cannot is quantitative measurements of the effectiveness of the treatment. We do know what the recovery rates are following timely use of the proper antibiotics. We don't know what the recovery rates are following prayer. The literature of Christian Science is filled with testimonials, tens of thousands of examples where prayer was followed by healing. But equally meticulous records are not available for the cases where prayer was followed by deterioration or a failure to heal. The Christian Science response is to point out that medicine has its failures too, but the difference is that medicine is clear about its percentage of failures. It is well known in medicine that most episodes of illness are self-limiting and, for that reason, the sick will usually get better regardless of what anyone does. Except for some interventions that damage patients, virtually all "treatments" can be shown to have "successes." In that sense, almost everything "works." Accordingly, research on the effectiveness of therapeutic modalities must be done in controlled studies, preferably double blind.[20]

Being a physician is not like repairing appliances. The doctor has an independent responsibility for the well-being of the minor; he or she is not a mere functionary, beholden to the whims of the parents. There are some things a physician should not do to a minor patient even if the parents ask, and there are other things a physician should do for a minor patient even if the parents object (see note 4). Now, the healing practices of Christian Science could be tested in controlled studies. Indeed, it might be a useful form of cooperation between medicine and Christian Science to determine if the natural (or clinical) course of an illness could be changed by prayer. Certainly, a judge would be hard-pressed to justify appointing a guardian if presented with solid clinical evidence that prayer was as effective in treating meningitis as medical treatment. But in the absence of such evidence, and where there is an effective and reasonably nonburdensome treatment available, the doctor and the courts should opt to protect the child. If we are serious about preventing the unnecessary deaths and suffering of children as a consequence of medical neglect, it is unjust to carve out an exception to this policy for the sons and daughters of Christian Scientists.

Although things can go back to normal after an acute meningitis episode, chronic diseases can require continuous monitoring and medication. The problem is serious. How can the child's well-being be secured in a household that is unsympathetic to the only treatment modality that can promise a reasonable expectation of survival? Several years ago a Samoan girl was taken to a hospital with diabetic ketoacidosis, a life-threatening condition that was the effect of improperly managed diabetes. Her father was notable in his community for his mastery of traditional Samoan healing arts, and his sense of protocol made him unwilling to accept the recommendations of a much younger physician about his daughter's need for daily insulin and a controlled diet. It was a problem as well that Samoan "medicine" has no concept of chronic illness: either you recover or die. There was no notion that a disease might have to be managed over most of a patient's life. Although there had been a children's protective services intervention and a charge of child neglect following the hospitalization, within days there was a medical anthropologist practically living with the family and repeated visits by an older Samoan physician. The girl's siblings were taught to administer insulin and do tests. The physician helped the healer improve his knowledge and ability, describing in some detail the discovery of insulin and explaining the role of the pancreas. Meals became exercises in understanding the elements of nutrition. (The family was unaware, for example, that soft drinks contained sugar.)

There is a fourth perspective here: that of medical social work. There is sometimes a need to mobilize and enhance the resources of the immediate family and community in the interest of ensuring that the patient receives vital care. For diabetic minors whose parents are Christian Scientists, the question is whether the child's interest in avoiding an unnecessary death can be adequately addressed within that family. What social resources can be mobilized that would provide assurance that the child will be protected against serious physical harm? Can a guardian be appointed on a continuing basis to consent to treatment? Can mechanisms be set up to ensure that appropriate parties are notified in the event that the child needs medical attention? Can neighbors, teachers, home visits by social workers, be parts of the solution? Much can be gained, especially for the child, if a formula for cooperation can be found.

It was noted earlier that guardians are sometimes appointed—almost as a prosthesis—where mentally retarded parents are unable, by themselves, to manage the responsibilities associated with child rearing. In a comparable way, Christian Scientists sometimes cannot be counted upon to provide their children with medical interventions that are necessary in the senses defined above. There may be no blame in these cases, but it is unfair for the larger community to undertake to protect all children against unnecessary suffering and untimely death from medical neglect, except for the children of Christian Scientists. The special legal privileges that parents have over their children make sense only in relation to the reciprocal responsibilities parents have to provide appropriate care. Where it becomes evident that parents, for whatever reason, cannot be expected to meet the standard,[21] the larger community has a duty either to relieve the parents of responsibility—delegating all or part of it to another—or, as with the diabetic Samoan girl, to augment the family's resources to the point where the child's well-being is reasonably assured.

Notes

I am deeply grateful to Robert A. Herlinger, Ruth Guffee, Jennifer Schember-Lang, and Donald Ridley for suggestions and assistance in the preparation of this chapter.

1. There is a fourth option: Use the tools of government to impose one community's standards over all the others. The principle of separation of church and state was developed as a social prophylaxis against the intractable conflicts that are historically identified with this posture. Position three is sometimes taken as a variation on this one, but I trust that the differences will be clear to the reader.

2. The issues involving recruitment practices of religious organizations are reviewed in chapter 3 of Margaret Battin's *Ethics in the Sanctuary* (New Haven: Yale University Press, 1990).

3. This is one of the issues raised in *Wisconsin v. Yoder*, 406 U.S. 205 (1972), where an Amish community asserted a right to withdraw children from school after the age of

fourteen, notwithstanding a Wisconsin law mandating schooling to sixteen. The Amish were concerned that the added educational experiences would encourage their children to leave the community. I am reminded of a story—I think it is from H. L. Mencken—about a family that had worked as clowns for generations. In his adulthood, one of these entertainers expressed warm appreciation for his father, who had carefully broken his son's legs in infancy, causing him to walk thereafter with a peculiarly amusing gait. In both cases families severely constrained the life choices open to their children.

4. Refusals of treatment on behalf of minors typically raise issues of neglect. I shall set aside the issue of abuse, although that too can be present in the medical context. Physicians have been asked by African Muslim parents to do what has become known as "female genital mutilations." And in another case—not necessarily involving a Christian Science family—the parents of a young child refused on religious grounds to permit the use of pain medications during debridement (the removal of debris and dead tissue following severe burns). Even with medication, this is one of medicine's most painful procedures. Certainly, anyone inflicting a like amount of unnecessary suffering upon a child would be guilty of abuse.

5. No. 89-210 (Mass. Super. Ct., 1989). The Massachusetts Supreme Court overturned their conviction in *Commonwealth of Massachusetts v. Twitchell*, 617 N.E. 2d 609 (Mass. 1993).

6. 588 A. 2d 1108 (Del. 1991).

7. This may well have been very good advice in 1875, when the canonical text of Christian Science was written.

8. If a Christian Scientist fails to pray and the child subsequently dies, there is still a defense because, under negligence manslaughter, the jury would have to determine, beyond a reasonable doubt, that but for the failure to pray, the child would not have died. It is unlikely that this question would ever be put to a jury. The failure to pray could conceivably be introduced as evidence that the accused was not really a Christian Scientist, and the argument made that for that reason, the defense should not be available. But there are many who properly identify themselves as members of some community who do not always honor all of its practices. One could ask what the position of the Church of Christ, Scientist would be if a Christian Science practitioner negligently failed to attend properly (by the church's own standards) to a seriously ill client and the client subsequently died. Would the church or the practitioner accept blame or civil liability for the death?

9. This is not to say that a refusal by the Twitchells to consent to essential medical care should have been honored by the courts.

10. It should be noted that all parents are, from time to time, unable to manage certain of their child-rearing responsibilities entirely by themselves. Public schools, hospitals, day care centers and preschools, foster homes, juvenile detention facilities, pharmacies, family courts, and so on are all social mechanisms intended to augment the resources of parents in the interests of the community and its children.

11. A review of some of this literature is contained in Kenneth Kipnis and Gaillynn Williamson, "Nontreatment Decisions for Severely Compromised Newborns," *Ethics* 95 (October 1984): 90–111.

12. See, for example, Sanford L. Leikin, "Minors' Assent or Dissent to Medical Treatment," in President's Commission for the Study of Ethical Problems, *Making Health Care Decisions* (Washington, D.C.: Government Printing Office, 1983), 3:175–83. Leikin says most minors under the age of ten cannot competently consent, but most above fourteen can.

13. See, for example, *In re E.G.*, 549 N.D. 2d 322 (Ill. 1989) and *In re W.M.*, 823 S.W. 2d 128 (Mo. Ct. App. 1992). *Belcher v. Charleston Area Med. Ctr.*, 422 S.E. 2d 827 (W.Va. 1992), involved a non–Jehovah's Witness minor.

14. The standard has been characterized as the "rule of sevens" (see, e.g., *Cardwell v. Bechtol*, 724 S.W. 2d 739 (Tenn. 1987). Below age seven the child is unrebuttably decisionally incapacitated; from seven to fourteen there is a rebuttable presumption of incapacity; and for fourteen and above there is a rebuttable presumption of capacity.

15. My views on these issues have been informed by work as an expert witness in a court case involving a Jehovah's Witness couple whose infant had cancer. The parents had refused an experimental "rescue therapy" involving transfusion, requesting instead a standard treatment the physician thought of as less effective. I had agreed to testify on behalf of the parents. Notwithstanding their "medical authority," the physician and hospital backed down.

16. The analysis here closely follows Terrence F. Ackerman, "The Limits of Beneficence: Jehovah's Witnesses and Childhood Cancer," *Hastings Center Report* 10 (August 1980): 13–18.

17. In addition to the three considerations discussed here, there is a fourth, the absence of public health risks, that is not relevant in this context. The concerns here are with the well-being of others in contact with the child. Vaccinations and treatments for infectious diseases like TB and Hansen's disease are well-known examples, but medications for certain psychiatric conditions can also fall into this category. It is useful to ask whether there are other ways to reduce risks to others without imposing medical treatment that has been refused. In a short-term outbreak, quarantining an unvaccinated child can be an option. Where virtually every other child is vaccinated, "herd immunity" should be taken into account. Christian Scientists generally seek to comply with laws intended to prevent the spread of contagious diseases.

18. The pattern is different with Jehovah's Witness children, who are routinely entrusted to health care professionals but with clear instructions that they not receive blood.

19. *Walker v. Superior Court of Sacramento County* (47 Cal. 3d 112 [1988], at 253) deals with the prosecution of a Christian Science mother following the death of her child from meningitis. Having failed to seek medical attention for her child, she was eventually convicted of involuntary manslaughter.

20. Battin makes this point in *Ethics in the Sanctuary*; see chap. 2, "High-Risk Religion," 96–99. In "Christian Science, Rational Choice, and Alternative World Views," *Journal of Social Philosophy* 3 (winter 1995): 89–104, Peggy DesAutels, responding to Battin, downplays empirical claims of effectiveness and argues that Christian Science is more concerned with religious experience than with physical healing, a "side-effect of advanced spiritual consciousness." Although that posture must be respected in adults, the courts' concern is narrowly with the physical well-being of children. DesAutels faces a dilemma. She wants to say that physical healing has often been experienced as following the achievement of the deep understanding of one's spiritual being that Christian Science seeks. Now, either Christian Science is being held out as an effective means of healing disease, in which case it is appropriate to measure its effectiveness in controlled studies, or it is not being held out as an effective means of healing disease, in which case the courts need not consider it as an alternative to medical treatment. DesAutels seems to want it both ways: that it is effective (as medicine is) but that it is not appropriate to assess its effectiveness in standard ways.

21. Sometimes the community's interest in the standard's being met can be protected by the expedient of a court order explicitly requiring Christian Scientist parents to arrange regular checkups for their children and seek medical attention whenever one of their children becomes ill. Following conviction, the Twitchells were subject to such provisions as a part of their probation.

Chapter 17

Economic Equality in the United States and Japan

Richard B. Parker

Methodology

I discuss two abstract entities in this chapter: "the Japanese" and "the Americans." At this level of abstraction, truth can be no more than statistical. There are millions of actual Japanese and Americans who do not believe what I say they do about equality. The best arguments against my assertions will be alternative generalizations more plausible than mine, or examples of American and Japanese social institutions, or even legends or literary traditions that contradict what I say about "the Americans" and "the Japanese." My intellectual model is Alexis de Tocqueville, whose generalizations about Americans in *Democracy in America* are so apt that they ring true 150 years after they were written.[1]

Japanese and Americans share many values. Japan and the United States both have advanced economies. The two have a long history together of conflict and cooperation in which each country has heavily influenced the other. Although there are major differences in language, architecture, foods, and religion, Japanese and Americans resemble each another more than either resemble, for example, Malays.[2]

Japanese and Americans generally employ the same list of virtues and vices, and apply them in the same way in judging the character of individual men and women in everyday life. The same kind, warm, and generous person is recognized and esteemed as such by both Japanese and Americans. A cold, selfish, and mean person is also recognized and rejected by both. There are some interesting differences in the value placed on some minor virtues such as patience or self-assertiveness, but these are less important than the general agreement between Japanese and Americans on how actions and people should be judged.

Japanese and Americans also share the same notions of cause and effect. Both are at home in the world described by modern science. Ghosts or black magic are not recognized as causes of misfortune by the legal system in either society (although some members of both societies use religious amulets in their cars to protect themselves against automobile accidents).

Japanese and Americans both regard government, law, and politics as secular matters. Both societies run regular local and national elections and neither society elects church ministers or priests to public office.[3]

Japanese and Americans share so many values that a person of a given age, sex, and occupation will be able to understand more easily a person of the same age, sex, and occupation in the other society than they will most of their own countrymen. An American career military officer in his fifties is likely to share more in outlook and experience with his opposite number in the Japanese Self-Defense Forces than with a young American assistant professor of philosophy. Two young female stockbrokers, Japanese and American, living in Tokyo and New York, will have more in common with each other than either will with two old family matriarchs (much less two old patriarchs) living in small farming communities in Ehime Prefecture and Iowa. In sum, differences in age, gender, and occupation within Japan or the United States put more distance between individuals within each society than do general differences between all Japanese and all Americans.[4]

Despite the fact that most values are shared, some are not. One of the most striking differences is that the Japanese, together with a majority of people in the world, do not accept the notion of human equality found in the American Declaration of Independence that all human beings are "created equal." By the phrase "created equal," Americans mean that, in some important respect, all human beings are exactly the same. Because all persons are exactly the same, they are, in some important way, of exactly equal worth, despite their obvious differences in size, strength, appearance, gender, class, abilities, virtue, and character. This American notion that all human beings have, in some important way, exactly the same worth, I will call *metaphysical equality* because this sort of equality seems to fly in the face of all actual inequalities, and because the most powerful expression of this equality was the moral philosophy and metaphysical idealism of the German philosopher Immanuel Kant. Metaphysical equality is historically rooted in the Western religious notion of the equality of all human souls under the judgmental eye of an omniscient, omnipotent Creator God.[5]

Today virtually all Americans believe in the metaphysical equality of human beings even if they do not believe in any such God or in any particular metaphysics.[6] Modern Americans take metaphysical equality so much for granted that even those who argue that one race is inferior to another will concede the metaphysical equality of all human beings.

In cross-cultural discussions between Japanese and Americans, it is useful to distinguish between agreement on what sorts of social institutions and distributions of wealth or power or work are desirable on the one hand, and agreement on the philosophical justifications for those institutions and distributions on the other. From the point of view of the Japanese, Americans too often identify theory with practice. For example, Americans tend to regard a belief in the metaphysical equality of persons as a necessary foundation for any serious practical commitment to economic equality. The fact that the Japanese value economic equality without a commitment to metaphysical equality is an interesting counterexample to the American belief in the fundamental nature of metaphysical equality. But the challenge of the Japanese rejection of the importance of metaphysical equality is a challenge to American theory concerning equality, not a challenge to American practice. Americans are all too likely to confuse a rejection of their theory with a rejection of actual American institutions and practices. From the Japanese point of view, theory and practice are much more separable and theory much less important than Americans seem to think.

This separation of theory and practice, and the devaluation of theory, is especially evident in the case of law and politics in Japan. The Japanese have been greatly influenced by the Americans in these areas since World War II, but the influence has been in Japanese adoption of legal and political practices derived from American models, not in Japanese acceptance of American political morality. Their retention of the many American legal and political practices imposed upon them by the U.S. occupation, such as a free press, has not been because they have accepted American political morality; there was simply no good reason to change a political system that was part of Japan's participation in a prosperous Pax Americana. If that order collapses, American political practices may be abandoned by the Japanese.

Not only do the Japanese often have a different justification for economic equality, but they place less value on providing any theoretical justification at all for their beliefs concerning the value of equality. The Japanese see the American need for philosophical justifications to provide legitimacy for American political and social institutions as a peculiar feature of Western and especially American culture. They will concede that Americans are better at political philosophy than they are, just as they are better at making pottery than Americans are. They do not insist that Americans care about pottery, and think that Americans should not insist that they care about political philosophy.

More generally, the Japanese are averse to communicating their deepest thoughts and emotions, and are not driven to discover and describe the way things "really" are. Truth runs a poor third to beauty and goodness as a value for the Japanese.[7] They are highly visual and centered in the everyday world. Their sense of design and their craftsmanship is perhaps the best in the world. They are extraordinarily clear-eyed about cause and effect, and about human emotions, in part because they are not much interested in theology or philosophy. The Japanese see the world and the people in it with startling clarity because they are not distracted by theory. Their mottoes might be "The more naive the realism, the better" and "Avoid construction and you can avoid deconstruction."

What philosophizing there is in Japan is like a simple pen-and-ink drawing. Most of the surface is left blank. In contrast, the best Western philosophy is like a painting by the Dutch painter Jan Vermeer. It is done in painstaking detail. The total is presented to the viewer or reader as a highly finished product. No blank space is left on the canvas.

This difference between Japanese and Americans in the importance placed on theory suggests two strategies for fruitful discussion with the Japanese about equality. The first is that different sorts of equality (economic, gender, racial) should be discussed separately without much emphasis on how they all fit together in a grand theory that might, for example, make metaphysical equality basic. The second strategy is that the discussion should be carried on in terms of inequalities to be avoided rather than equalities to be attained. Most of the time when Americans or Japanese use conceptions of equality to criticize social institutions or distributions of wealth, power, or work, they use them to attack existing inequalities. It is much easier to agree on what existing inequalities both Japanese and Americans deplore than to agree on what a truly equal society would be like.

Both of these strategies are applications of the insights of American liberalism that it is best to agree to disagree on matters of philosophy and religion, and that agreement on what is evil is easier than agreement on what is good. (One of the reasons for the longevity and success of the U.S. Constitution is that church and state were kept separate and most of the important rights guaranteed by the Constitution are negative rights, rights to be free from circumstances that Americans agree are undesirable, rather than positive rights to some ideal state of affairs.)

Utilizing both of these strategies, I talk below about economic *inequality* without trying to set out some more general theory of equality on which Japanese and Americans might agree.

Japan's Success in Avoiding Economic Inequality

The achievement of the Japanese in avoiding economic inequality within their own society is extraordinary. Table 1 gives some comparative data.[8] Japan is not the richest of the G-7 (the seven major industrial nations—the United States, Japan, Germany, France, the United Kingdom, Italy, and Canada—whose presidents and prime ministers meet together each year to coordinate economic policy). Japan ranks behind the United States, Canada, and Germany in real gross domestic product (GDP) per capita as measured by the actual purchasing power (PPP$) of a nation's currency in its domestic markets (column 2). Yet there is less economic inequality in Japan than in any other of the G-7 or Nordic countries (column 5). As the figures on income share for Japan show, the ratio of the income of the 20 percent of the population with the highest income to the 20 percent of the population with the lowest income is 4.3 to 1; Sweden comes closest to Japan with a ratio of 4.6 to 1.

Japan achieves these low levels of economic inequality with the second-lowest taxation burden (only the United States has a lower total tax burden),[9] and the lowest government spending among the G-7 nations on education, health, and social security (columns 6, 7, and 8). In the United States, it is assumed by those on the left, the right, and the center of the political spectrum that redistribution of income by government through taxation and the governmental provision of education, health, and other social benefits is the only way to lower levels of the sort of economic inequality registered in columns 4 and 5. How has Japan achieved such low levels of economic inequality despite lower taxes and fewer government benefits?

The answer to the question is complex. Some social and historical causes must be mentioned. These causes are in a chicken-and-egg relation to Japanese beliefs about economic inequality. They are both cause and effect of those beliefs.

Table 1. Wealth, Poverty, and Social Investment in the Industrial Countries with the Highest Human Development Index Rankings

HDI Rank	Real GDP per capita (PPP$) 1990	Country share of industrial market economy (%) 1990	Lowest 40% of households (%) 1985–89	Ratio of highest 20% to lowest 20% 1985–89	Total education expense (as % of GDP) 1988	Total health expenditure (as % of GDP) 1990	Social security benefits expenditure (as % of GDP) 1985–89
Japan	17,616	19.8	21.9	4.3	5.0	6.7	6.0
Canada	19,232	3.4	17.5	7.1	7.2	9.3	17.3
Norway	16,028	0.6	19.0	5.9	6.6a	8.0	17.6
Switzerland	20,874	1.4	16.9	8.6	5.1a	7.8	13.3
Sweden	17,014	1.3	21.2	4.6	5.7	8.6	33.7
USA	21,449	34.4	15.7	8.9	5.7	12.2	12.6
Australia	16,051	1.9	15.5	9.6	4.8a	8.2	8.0
France	17,405	7.0	18.4		5.7	8.8	18.6
Netherlands	15,694	1.6	20.1	5.6	6.6	8.6	27.7
UK	15,804	5.9	17.3	6.8	4.7a	6.1	17.0
Iceland	16,496					8.7	
Germany	18,213	8.9	19.5	5.7	6.2	8.6	23.0
Denmark	16,781	0.7	17.4	7.1	6.9	6.6	27.8
Finland	16,446	0.8	18.4	6.0	6.8	7.8	20.6

Note: The Human Development Index (HDI) is a complex measure of fundamental goods necessary to most conceptions of the good life including income, education, and life expectancy. The United Nations now ranks all the nations of the world on their ability to provide these goods to their citizens.

First, what remained of the hereditary landed aristocracy in Japan was stripped of its power and wealth by the U.S. occupation (1945–1952). At the end of World War II, almost 50 percent of the farmland in Japan was being farmed by tenant farmers. Through forced sales and postwar inflation during the occupation, the land was confiscated from absentee landlords and turned over to those who were actually farming it.[10] (A professor of history at the University of the Philippines once remarked bitterly to me that the United States did more for the redistribution of wealth in five years in Japan than in fifty years in the Philippines.)

Second, there has never been in Japan a governing professional class of lawyers, academics, doctors, and ministers similar to that found in the United States. People in these occupations in Japan are all called *sensei*, a term of respect, but then so are artists and craftsmen in the traditional Japanese arts called *sensei*. To be well-educated in Japan is to be highly skilled in a specialized way, to be a craftsman. There is no tradition of a well-educated generalist. There is no ideal of a Renaissance Man and thus no rank of University Professor at Japanese universities.[11] Lawyers and academics do not move from law firms and universities into the highest reaches of government and back again.

There is also no tradition in Japan, as there is in Confucian China or in France and England, of a social class of well-educated generalists (gentlemen) who by virtue of their superior intellect, judgment, and character (or virtue) are best suited to run the society. The highest people in the permanent bureaucracy of the Japanese government are the administrative vice-ministers of the government ministries. These people and those who work for them are career civil servants who join their ministry when they graduate from university. They are too small a group, and too narrowly specialized, to constitute a governing social class that could appropriate any significant amount of the nation's wealth.[12]

Almost by default, it has been businessmen who have controlled Japan since World War II. The U.S. occupation did not destroy the *zaibatsu*, the large conglomerations of banks and manufacturing companies such as Mitsubishi and Mitsui. However, the occupation did remove from power the founding families and their heirs, who by and large lost their personal wealth. (A Japanese professor of corporate law once remarked to me that the greatest benefit bestowed upon Japan by the occupation besides land reform and votes for women was the professionalization of the management of Japanese industry.) To a remarkable degree, the share of the nation's income appropriated by business interests in Japan has been widely distributed among the millions of salarymen who toil for the large corporations or plowed back into further investment.

Britain has both the remnants of a landed aristocracy, who are still at the top of a social ladder that their presence helps to maintain, and a tradition of well-educated and bright Oxbridge generalists who run Britain. (Britain's business class is now, to Britain's detriment, underdeveloped.) The United States has a professional class that, along with its business class, runs the country. Japan has neither an aristocracy nor a professional class that feels entitled to a large share of Japanese income. Japan's business community, with the help of the small bureaucracy, has run Japan for its own benefit. Taxes are low. Consumer prices are high. The question remains: If business is in control, why is the distribution of income still so much more equal in Japan then elsewhere?

One of the major reasons is that economic equality is a condition more favorable to business interests than to an aristocracy or to a professional elite. As Henry Ford discovered, if his workers could afford his cars, his company was going to be more secure financially and politically than if a car was a luxury item for the professional and upper classes. One of the keys to the economic growth throughout the world in the twentieth century has been the more equal distribution of income throughout national populations. It took Britain, the first nation to industrialize, more than one hundred years of class warfare to understand this. In the United States it took fifty years. Japan, South Korea, Singapore, and the other developing nations of Asia that have taken the Western nations as a model have assumed that the faster income is widely distributed, the faster their economies grow, and the more stable their societies become.

The failure of communism has made clear that income distribution cannot take place by government fiat (although Asian governments, supported by business elites, have been much more paternalistic toward their citizens in, for example, forcing them to save for their old age and, as a by-product, making more capital available for business investment). Instead, Asian governments and business elites have made income distribution more equal by making the distribution of education and job skills more equal. This in turn is good for business, which is why business in Japan has generally supported the equality in education and employment that has been a major cause of the extraordinary economic equality in Japan.

Consider first equality in education. Although Japan spends less of its total GDP on education than does the United States (see table 1, column

6), Japan concentrates that spending at the primary and secondary levels. More than 90 percent of Japanese children graduate from high school as compared with 74 percent in the United States, and the Japanese high school diploma generally requires higher achievement in academic subjects. Although about the same percentage of students go on to higher education in Japan and the United States, the United States spends proportionally much more on higher education, thus exacerbating economic inequality in the United States.[13]

I am not arguing that Americans should spend less on their universities. One of the major advantages the United States enjoys in its competition with Japan and the rest of the world is its university system. That system makes American society more productive and thus wealthier. (Generally, the wealthier a country is, the less economic inequality there is. The poorer nations of the world have much more economic inequality than do the richer nations.)[14] Nevertheless, Americans should recognize that their relatively higher spending on universities compared with primary and secondary education is a major reason for their relatively greater inequality of income distribution compared with the other economically advanced nations.[15]

A second major cause of economic equality in Japan is the equal distribution of employment. One of the most striking features of Japan is the extraordinarily low unemployment rate. Even now, in one of the longest recessions Japan has suffered since World War II, the unemployment rate is under 4 percent. As many have correctly pointed out, the Japanese economy is structured to favor the small farms and firms that provide employment for all. Even large corporations go to extraordinary lengths to avoid firing employees. Social customs and government policies restrict competition from outside Japan and, much more importantly, among the Japanese, to prevent unemployment. Many of these economically inefficient customs and practices would not survive in a freer market. The Japanese often justify this inefficiency in terms of compassion for those who would otherwise be unemployed. As Japan slowly opens its economy to the world, many of these customs and practices will cease to exist. Fortunately, the supply of labor in Japan is in a long-term decline and, unlike the United States and Europe, Japan does not have millions of workers who are so uneducated as to be unemployable in a more efficient economy. Japan will be able to continue to provide employment for almost everyone and will not, in the next twenty years, suffer the high unemployment rates of the United States, much less of Europe. Were this not the case—if Japan's supply of unemployable labor were increasing—its commitment to its extraordinarily equal distribution of employment would be sorely tested.

Health care in Japan also follows the same pattern of directing resources at the entire population rather than mainly to the upper third. All residents are eligible for the national health system if they are not covered by their employer's health insurance. The national system pays from 70 percent to 80 percent of all medical expenses. The quality of health care is not as good as that available from an average American health maintenance organization.[16] With the Japanese patient paying from 20 percent to 30 percent of personal health costs, serious illness is still a financial setback for most families. The system is basically a fee-for-service system, with doctors selling their own prescriptions at their own proprietary hospitals. Corruption is rife. If adopted in the United States, the Japanese system, when combined with American middle-class standards of health care, would bankrupt the federal government even more quickly than present American arrangements. The system works in Japan only because the health care provided is comparatively meager and inexpensive. Yet, despite its deficiencies, Japan's system does provide universal coverage and does not exacerbate inequality. Virtually all Japanese receive a yearly medical examination from either their employer or their municipal government. Japanese enjoy the longest average life expectancy of the G-7 nations, not because their standard of health care is the highest but because what health care they have is so equally distributed.[17]

We have still not answered the basic question: Why is Japan so committed to economic equality? We can see that the control of Japan by business interests over the past fifty years has at least not worked against economic equality because business interests tend to flourish under conditions of economic equality and so have not opposed it. But business has been largely in control in the United States as well, and although the American professional class feels itself entitled to a big chunk of society's income and is able to appropriate that income, the existence of such a class in the United States, but not in Japan, is not the primary reason that Americans tolerate so much more economic inequality than do the Japanese.

Why are Americans of all social classes so much more tolerant of economic inequality than are Japanese? The heart of the matter is one of the most interesting differences in values between Americans and Japanese.

Americans see economic inequality as an unfortunate but unavoidable consequence of the fair competition between individuals or groups required by the American conception of equality of opportunity. This unfortunate but unavoidable consequence must then be corrected for by government transfer payments or by private charity, depending whether one is on the left or the right of the American political spectrum.

It may even be questionable whether most Americans see their relatively unequal distribution of economic wealth, compared with the rest of the G-7, as unfortunate at all. Even some liberal Democrats seem to favor only a minimum level of support under which no one should be permitted to fall. If this floor is maintained, then most Americans seem to believe that people should be able to keep the fruits of their labors regardless of the resulting unequal distribution of economic wealth.

The Japanese, on the other hand, see economic inequality as an unnecessary evil detrimental to the well-functioning of their society. It causes ill will and envy and has no redeeming social merit.[18] The Japanese feel no moral requirement to offer individuals (or groups) a fair competition under conditions of equal opportunity for life's prizes. They feel free to refuse to let economic inequality develop in the first place. Unencumbered by the quasi-religious American belief in equality of opportunity, the Japanese can nip economic inequality in the bud.

For example, imagine a man with a small gasoline station in a small village in Japan doing a moderately successful business because his station is the only one in the village. People living in the village are willing to pay a small premium for the convenience of not having to drive into town. Imagine a second man who wants to have his own small business and applies to local authorities to open another gas station in the same small village.[19] Unless the village can clearly support two gas stations, the Japanese have no trouble saying no to the second man. He should not cause trouble by opening a second station. A claim by the second man that he should have an opportunity equal to the first to open his own station will be met with puzzlement. It will be clear to the Japanese that the two men are not equal, if only because one of them was there first. Although being there first is not the basis of a right in an American sense, it does mean that the first man has expectations that he will be able to continue making his living from his station. Why should the second man be allowed to disappoint the expectations of the first man? The Japanese making the decision about the second station will consider relevant to their decision the strength of the desire of the second man to own his own business, and his prior residence and commitment to the village community. But a claim to equal opportunity to compete in business based on the equality of the first man and the second man as citizens will not be given any weight.

If the second man is not a local citizen but a large corporation, then the idea of the new competitor having the right to an equal opportunity to compete against the first man will seem bizarre to the Japanese. Why should the first man be ruined and lose his livelihood? From the Japanese point of view, however, the first man should go out of business if the entire village would benefit greatly from an open competition in which corporations competed to sell gas in the village. Ideally, the first man would put the interests of the village ahead of his own individual desires and voluntarily go out of business so no one would feel bad about buying gas from the new corporate stations. Rights of any sort would not come into it. If the first man voluntarily went out of business, others in the community would feel obligated to help him in the future.

The Japanese attach much importance to what people actually expect and want. Simply to want something or to expect something in Japan is to give other people a reason to give it to you. Americans on the other hand think that wants or expectations must be justified by some system of rights or entitlements before they need be given consideration.

Americans may ask how it is possible to adjust peacefully the wants and expectations of various people without some system of rights and entitlements to sort out competing claims. Indeed, Americans say, the American notion of metaphysical equality is simply the notion that everyone starts from the same baseline in the systems of rights and entitlements used to adjudicate conflicting claims.

The Japanese would respond that they are trained from birth to moderate their own desires in light of the desires of others. They constantly strive for a harmonious situation in which everyone feels comfortable. The sort of person who constantly expresses his own desires and forces others to take account of them without a reciprocal sensitivity to what others might want is shunned and ultimately unsuccessful. In Japan, guys who are not nice usually finish last. Without a belief in metaphysical equality, the Japanese feel no moral pressure to run their economy as a series of fair competitions in which everyone ideally has the same opportunities to win. For them, what is most important is people's actual wants and expectations and the welfare of the community.

The Japanese tend to see gross economic inequality as a major evil to be avoided because it is so obviously detrimental. Japan has a history of starving peasants and rich landlords. The U.S. occupation was like a divine intervention that, among other things, took the farmland of Japan out of the hands of its traditional owners and gave it to the people working that land. This was so clearly a desirable result from the point of view of the smooth functioning of Japanese society that once it was done, no one seriously tried to undo it. In the American tradition in which people have a strong sense of their right to keep what they (or their parents or grandparents) have gained in fair competition, a similar transfer of wealth by an outside conqueror would have produced generations of dispossessed landowners protesting their loss and using every available means to right the wrong done to them.

From the Japanese point of view, Americans are too tolerant of economic inequality, which the Japanese see as the root of most of the social ills of the United States. They do not understand why the Americans do not attack the problems of economic inequality by giving people on the bottom the minimal education and employment that would at least mitigate the most severe economic inequalities.

Justifying a Society's Commitment to the Ideal of Equality

The idea of people being metaphysically equal ends in themselves is not the way the Japanese support their commitment to equality. Instead, the Japanese believe that gross inequalities are such an obvious handicap to a well-functioning Japan that they should be avoided. This way of justifying equality will seem to Americans to shift the argument to the problem of defining what it is for Japan to be "well-functioning." It is crucial to an understanding of the Japanese point of view to see that this is not an obvious or pressing problem to the Japanese.

For Americans, social institutions are completely malleable. Americans see themselves as being able to choose how their society should be. A sense of the basic structure of society as something that can be chosen and must be justified is stronger in the United States than in any other major industrial society. In a tribal society such as Japan, any existing social structure seems "natural" and has a presumption in favor of continued existence.[20]

The lack of interest of the Japanese in providing a theoretical justification for their major social institutions seems a moral failing to Americans, especially to American philosophers, law professors, and political scientists, but it is useful to see the elaborate American theories of justification and legitimacy as no more than ornaments of American civilization, impressive intellectual and artistic achievements but not, as the example of Japan shows, a necessary condition for a relatively just and humane society.

Notes

I am indebted to Mary Becker, John Benson, Malcolm Benson, Steven Lee, Robyn Lim, Larry May, Tamayo Okamoto, Warren Redlich, Carol Rinnert, Bonnie Ryan, William Ryan, Hideyoshi Sakai, Kathleen Shinagawa, Kenneth Winston, Ulrike Wöhr, Alisa Woodring, and Hitomi Yoshida for their written comments on earlier versions of this chapter. Comments from the floor at the AMINTAPHIL Conference in Charleston, S.C., in November 1994, led to changes. Portions were given in a seminar at Harvard Law School, where comments by Dan Foote, Yumi Kakuta, Susan Weld, Takaaki Yamamoto, and several others forced revisions. A faculty seminar at Hiroshima Shudo University, in which some of the people listed above participated, led to still more changes. My thanks to all of these people. Not one of them agrees with everything I say here. Parts of this chapter appeared in *Shudo Hogaku* 17, no. 2 (October 1995).

1. Alexis de Tocqueville, *Democracy in America*, ed. Alan Ryan (New York: Knopf, 1994; originally published in French in Paris in 1835). Tocqueville's work is based largely on his travels around the United States in 1831–1832. His judgment in singling out from his own experience what is of most importance and generalizing accurately is astonishing. What he cannot do is refer to empirical studies to support the large-scale generalizations he makes about American attitudes and beliefs.

Even today, the state of the art of sociology or social psychology in empirically testing for social attitudes or general beliefs is not adequate to serve as a supporting foundation for, or even as a persuasive refutation of, the sort of sweeping generalizations that Tocqueville makes about the United States and I make about Japan. An example of a worthy attempt to empirically establish the existence of certain beliefs and attitudes among Japanese and Americans is V. Lee Hamilton and Joseph Sanders, *Everyday Justice: Responsibility and the Individual in Japan and the United States* (New Haven: Yale University Press, 1992). Testing a "microsociological model of responsibility" with surveys in Japan and the United States, they come up with unsurprising conclusions. If they had simply stated their conclusions in ordinary English without the survey evidence, readers familiar with the Japanese would have agreed. However, if they had come up with counterintuitive conclusions, one would have said so much the worse for the survey.

Such survey evidence of the attitudes of individuals is useful only as a corroboration of ethnographic research (including literature and legends), historical research, and "macrosociological research" (including demographic and economic statistics). And all of these methods taken together are more useful for *refuting* a view of social attitudes than for constructing one. See John Braithwaite, *Crime, Shante, and Reintegration* (Cambridge: Cambridge University Press, 1989), chap. 8, for a brilliant discussion of how to use all four of these methods to test a theory of crime that takes Japan as its inspiration. Even Braithwaite's theory of crime, ambitious as it is, is less general than many of the assertions made in this essay. My speculations and generalizations should be seen by social scientists as suggestions for empirical research rather than an attempt to get away with something.

2. I use Malays as an example of Asians whom Japanese resemble less than Japanese resemble Americans because the prime minister of Malaysia has recently been arguing that "Asians" should stick together against the West, but the unified notion of "Asians" he has in mind is a false creation of the European colonial mind. Malays are only one of many Asian peoples that share less with Japanese than Japanese share with Americans.

3. When this does happen in Japan or in the United States, it is regarded as anomalous. Examples are the Komeito (Clean Government Party), which was founded by Soka Gakkai, one of Japan's new religions, and the election of Father Robert F. Drinan, a Roman Catholic priest, as a congressman from Massachusetts. Komeito was required by public opinion to sever its connections with Soka Gakkai, and Father Drinan was required by his church to resign his seat in Congress. Jesse Jackson or Pat Robertson could never be elected president of the United States, in part because they are preachers.

4. Japan and the United States can be pictured as two tall trees of two different species located next to each other, with branches and roots intertwined. The roots of one resemble the roots of the other much more than either set of roots resembles any other part of either tree. The picture to be avoided is of two self-contained spheres with no interpenetration at all.

5. Buddhist tradition places a high value on living things, human beings among them. In some variations of Japanese Buddhism, there is a hell in which the wicked are punished; but there is nothing like the omnipotent, omniscient God of the Old Testament in any Japanese religion, and nothing like the extraordinary anthropomorphism of the Judeo-Christian tradition. For more on contemporary Japanese religion, see Ian Reader, *Religion in Contemporary Japan* (London: Macmillan, 1991). Without the equality of naked souls before a judgmental God, the Western notion of metaphysical equality could never have developed.

6. An example of metaphysical equality in contemporary American political philosophy is John Rawls's metaphor of an original position in which participants chose the principles of social justice without knowing what place they will occupy in society. Rawls's assumption that all participants are equal in this original position is a modem expression of metaphysical equality (although Rawls explicitly rejects the necessity of any metaphysical or religious foundation for such equality). John Rawls, *A Theory of Justice* (Cambridge: Harvard University Press, 1971). See also John Rawls, *Political Liberalism* (New York: Columbia University Press, 1993).

Another expression of metaphysical equality in modern American political philosophy is the notion that in any utilitarian calculus, each individual's desires should count equally in determining what policies would secure the greatest happiness for the greatest number. See, for example, Thomas Nagel, *Equality and Partiality* (Oxford: Oxford University Press, 1991), 78: "The utilitarian idea is that we all count equally at the primary level."

7. The Western ideal of truth presupposes the Western idea of an omniscient point of view, that is, God's point of view. Western science seeks to see the world from the point of view of God. Western morality seeks moral truth, that is, what is the correct thing to do judged from a point of view outside any particular society, that is, what is the correct thing to do judged from God's point of view. The Japanese do not share this notion of an omniscient point of view from which things are known or seen as they truly are. For more, see Richard B. Parker, "Law, Language, and the Individual in Japan and the United States," *Wisconsin International Law Journal* 7 (fall 1988): 179– 203.

8. *United Nations Human Development Report, 1993* (Oxford: Oxford University Press, 1993), 202.

9. *Japan Almanac, 1994* (Tokyo: Asahi Shimbun, 1994), 81.

10. For a general account, see "Land Reform of 1946," *Kodansha Encyclopedia of Japan* (Tokyo: Kodansha International, 1983), 4: 364–65.

11. The rank of University Professor at, for example, Harvard University, officially entitles that person to teach in any faculty in the university. The rank is given only to people of wisdom and broad learning. Brilliance in a single field is not enough. After he returned to Harvard from being the U.S. ambassador to Japan, Edwin Reischauer was given the rank of University Professor. My point here is that the Japanese model of the ideal scholar is one of narrow and deep learning. For more on this topic, see Shigcru Nakayama, *Academic and Scientific Traditions in China, Japan, and the West* (Tokyo: University of Tokyo Press, 1984).

12. Japan's top civil servants are more powerful than their American counterparts. That power is compatible with my assertion that Japanese bureaucrats are too small and specialized a group to constitute anything like a *social* class. For one thing, they cannot easily pass on to their children what few advantages they enjoy. They may not even be a *governing* class. For an interesting argument that the power of Japanese bureaucrats in policy formation is overestimated by outside observers, see J. Mark Ramseyer and Frances McCall Rosenbluth, *Japan's Political Marketplace* (Cambridge: Harvard University Press, 1993), chap. 6.

13. Table 1 does not include the enormous amount of money spent by Japanese parents on private for-profit cram schools to prepare their children for high school and college entrance examinations. In 1989, private cram schools were a 668-billion-yen industry, more than $6 billion U.S. dollars. *Japan Almanac, 1995* (Tokyo: Asahi Shimbun, 1995), 189.

14. *United Nations Human Development Report, 1993*, 170–71.

15. In addition to greater spending per student, the other major reason that Japanese secondary students are two or three years ahead of American students by the time they graduate from high school is that they spend more time studying academic subjects. Cultural differences in the ways Japanese and Americans run primary and secondary schools are of much less importance than the Japanese advantages of time and money. The United States would be well advised to lengthen its public school year to 220 days from 180 days, which in itself would require the investment of more money in public education. The resulting growth in productivity, increase in wealth, and lessening of economic inequality would do a lot to ameliorate many of the country's worst social ills.

16. A health maintenance organization, or HMO, in the United States is an organization that undertakes, for a set fee per month, to cover a person's medical needs. HMOs now cover more than 25 percent of Americans. Unlike traditional fee-for-service, in which a doctor or hospital collects for each service rendered, and often makes more money the sicker the patients are, an HMO does everything it can to keep its clients healthy because it is responsible for paying for whatever care they need. HMOs are often very large and render efficient but impersonal service more cheaply than fee-for-service providers.

17. The Japanese diet is often given credit for the long life expectancy of the Japanese. It is true that a remarkably low fat content makes the Japanese diet healthier than the American diet, but the Japanese diet is also high in salt and deficient in bulk when compared to the American diet; Japanese have more intestinal problems and a much higher rate of stomach cancer than do Americans.

18. The notion that economic growth may require relatively great disparities of wealth as a reward for entrepreneurial success is not deeply rooted in Japan. The Japanese tend to see the relatively greater economic inequality in the United States as more a cause of the country's social ills than as the basis for its economic success. A real resurgence of the U.S. economy combined with continued sluggishness of the Japanese economy might, however, convert many influential Japanese to the American faith in the necessity of economic inequality for robust economic growth.

19. Local government control over who can open a business in a community is taken for granted in Japan. Such control illustrates the paternalistic nature of all levels of government in Japan compared with the United States.

20. I do not mean to imply that the Japanese elite never consciously manipulate the notion of being Japanese. They do. See David L. Howell, "Ainu Ethnicity and the Boundaries of the Early Modern Japanese State," *Past and Present*, no. 142 (February 1994), 69–93, for an interesting example.

One of the attractions of Marxism or Christianity for a small number of Japanese intellectuals is that such a total worldview undermines the normal Japanese sense of the naturalness of existing social arrangements and institutions.

INDEX